INFORMATION AND COMMUNICATION TECHNOLOGIES AND REAL-LIFE LEARNING

IFIP – The International Federation for Information Processing

IFIP was founded in 1960 under the auspices of UNESCO, following the First World Computer Congress held in Paris the previous year. An umbrella organization for societies working in information processing, IFIP's aim is two-fold: to support information processing within its member countries and to encourage technology transfer to developing nations. As its mission statement clearly states,

> *IFIP's mission is to be the leading, truly international, apolitical organization which encourages and assists in the development, exploitation and application of information technology for the benefit of all people.*

IFIP is a non-profitmaking organization, run almost solely by 2500 volunteers. It operates through a number of technical committees, which organize events and publications. IFIP's events range from an international congress to local seminars, but the most important are:

• The IFIP World Computer Congress, held every second year;
• Open conferences;
• Working conferences.

The flagship event is the IFIP World Computer Congress, at which both invited and contributed papers are presented. Contributed papers are rigorously refereed and the rejection rate is high.

As with the Congress, participation in the open conferences is open to all and papers may be invited or submitted. Again, submitted papers are stringently refereed.

The working conferences are structured differently. They are usually run by a working group and attendance is small and by invitation only. Their purpose is to create an atmosphere conducive to innovation and development. Refereeing is less rigorous and papers are subjected to extensive group discussion.

Publications arising from IFIP events vary. The papers presented at the IFIP World Computer Congress and at open conferences are published as conference proceedings, while the results of the working conferences are often published as collections of selected and edited papers.

Any national society whose primary activity is in information may apply to become a full member of IFIP, although full membership is restricted to one society per country. Full members are entitled to vote at the annual General Assembly, National societies preferring a less committed involvement may apply for associate or corresponding membership. Associate members enjoy the same benefits as full members, but without voting rights. Corresponding members are not represented in IFIP bodies. Affiliated membership is open to non-national societies, and individual and honorary membership schemes are also offered.

INFORMATION AND COMMUNICATION TECHNOLOGIES AND REAL-LIFE LEARNING

New Education for the Knowledge Society

Edited by

Tom van Weert
Hogeschool van Ultrecht
The Netherlands

Arthur Tatnall
Victoria University
Australia

 Springer

Library of Congress Cataloging-in-Publication Data

A C.I.P. Catalogue record for this book is available from the Library of Congress.

Information and Communication Technologies and Real-Life Learning, Edited by Tom van Weert and Arthur Tatnall

p.cm. (The International Federation for Information Processing)

ISBN-10: (HB) 0-387-25996-1
ISBN-13: (HB) 978-0387-25996-3
ISBN-10: (eBook) 0-387-25997-X
ISBN-13: (eBook) 978-0387-25997-0
Printed on acid-free paper.

Printed in the United States of America.

9 8 7 6 5 4 3 2 1   SPIN 11426592 (HC) / 11428510 (eBook)
springeronline.com

TABLE OF CONTENTS

PREFACE

Information and Communication Technologies and Real-Life Learning – an IFIP Working Conference

This book presents the results of an International Federation for Information Processing (IFIP) working conference, held December 2004 in Melbourne, Australia. The working conference was organised by IFIP Working Group 3.2 (Informatics and ICT in Higher Education) and IFIP Working Group 3.4 (Professional and Vocational Education in Information Technology).

Challenges originating in large scale economic and social change, rapid transition to a knowledge-based society and shortage of knowledge workers demand new approaches in higher and professional education. International trends can be observed towards:
–   Learning in real-life situations;
–   Development of relationships with business and industry;
–   New forms of assessment.

The International Programme Committee of this event was formed by:
–   Bill Davey, Australia (IFIP Working Group 3.4, Professional and Vocational Education in IT)
–   Mike Kendall, United Kingdom (IFIP TC3 Special Interest Group on Lifelong Learning; IFIP Working Group 3.1 Secondary Education)
–   Mikko Ruohonen, Finland (IFIP Working Group 3.4, Professional and Vocational Education in IT)
–   Organising Committee Chair: Arthur Tatnall, Australia (IFIP Working Group 3.4, Professional and Vocational Education in IT)
–   Programme Committee Chair : Tom van Weert, Netherlands (IFIP Working Group 3.2 Higher Education; IFIP TC3 Special Interest Group on Lifelong Learning)

THE EDITORS

Tom J. van Weert holds the chair in ICT and Higher Education of the Hogeschool van Utrecht, University of Professional Education and Applied Science, Utrecht, The Netherlands. Earlier he was managing director of Cetis, centre of expertise for educational innovation and ICT, of the same university. Before that he was director of the School of Informatics (Computing Science) at the University of Nijmegen, The Netherlands. Tom has studied applied mathematics and computing science. He started his working career in teacher education and software engineering. He has been chair of the International Federation for Information Processing (IFIP) Working Groups on Secondary Education and Higher Education. He currently is vice-chair of IFIP Technical Committee 3 (TC3) on Education. He is also member of the TC3 Special Interest Group on Lifelong Learning.

Arthur Tatnall is an Associate Professor in the Graduate School of Business at Victoria University in Melbourne, Australia. He holds bachelors degrees in science and education, a Graduate Diploma in Computer Science, and a research Master of Arts in which he explored the origins of business computing education in Australian universities. His PhD involved a study in curriculum innovation in which he investigated the manner in which Visual Basic entered the curriculum of an Australian university. Arthur's research interests include technological innovation, information technology in educational management, information systems curriculum, project management and electronic commerce. He has written several books relating to information systems and has published widely. Arthur is currently vice-chair of IFIP working group 3.4 (Professional and Vocational Education).

THE PAPERS

This book has been produced from peer-refereed papers by invited authors from Australia, Austria, Belgium, Brazil, Estonia, Finland, Germany, The Netherlands and the United Kingdom. In addition the book contains Focus Group reports, produced during the working conference, on:

1. Experiences and challenges in fostering industry and university collaborations.
2. The developing importance of formal and informal professional communities of practice.
3. The challenge of creating and establishing the role of online and virtual learning environments for all.

The papers in this book present a cross-section of issues in real-life learning in which Information and Communication Technology plays an important role:
- Educational models for real-life learning enabled by Information and Communication Technology (ICT)
- How to effectively organise a real-life learning environment, including its ICT-components;
- Changing role of the student;
- Changing role of educational institutions and their relationship with business and industry;
- Changing role of teachers and their use of ICT;
- Management of ICT-rich educational change.

The papers will help educationalists, researchers, practitioners and educational designers to develop and implement real-life learning in diverse settings. But also technologists, policy makers, educational managers and community learning organisers will find approaches to deal with the issues of Real-life learning.

CONTRIBUTING AUTHORS

Till Becker (Germany)
John Bentley (Australia)
Erlaine Binotto (Brazil)
Stephen Burgess (Australia)
John Byrne (Australia)
France Cheong (Australia)
Antônio C. R. Costa (Brazil)
John Cripps Clark (Australia)
Bill Davey (Australia)
Paul Darbyshire (Australia)
Hannelore Dekeyser (Netherlands)
Graçaliz P. Dimuro (Brazil)
Helen Edwards (United Kingdom)
Julie Fisher (Australia)
Roger Gabb (Australia)
Eduardo Gomes (Brazil)
Colin Hardy (United Kingdom)
Daniel Garcia Haro (Brazil)
Marijke Hezemans (The Netherlands)
Darco Jansen (The Netherlands)

Rob Jovanovic (Australia)
Peter Juliff (Australia)
Alexander Karapidis (Germany)
Mike Kendall (United Kingdom)
Anton Knierzinger (Austria)
Marina Keiko Nakayama (Brazil)
David Kelly (Australia)
Timo Lainema (Finland)
Kevin Leung (Australia)
Glenn Lowry (UAE)
Joberto Martins (Brazil)
Anne McDougall (Australia)
Paul Nicholson (Australia)
Con Nikakis (Australia)
Peeter Normak (Estonia)
Sami Nurmi (Finland)
Luiz A. M. Palazzo (Brazil)
Bianca Smith Pilla (Brazil)
Patrick Poppins (Australia)
T. Quadros (Brazil)

Gina Reyes (Australia)
Magda Ritzen (The Netherlands)
Mikko Ruohonen (Finland)
Geoff Sandy (Australia)
Christine da Silva Schröeder (Brazil)
Carmine Sellitto (Australia)
Mohini Singh (Australia)
Fernando Schirmbeck (Brazil)
Stephan Schwan (Austria)
Ricardo Silveira (Brazil)
Andrew Stein (Australia)
Arthur Tatnall (Australia)
Barrie Thompson (United Kingdom)
Rod Turner (Australia)
Felix van Rijn (The Netherlands)
Tom van Weert (Netherlands)
Rosa Vicari (Brazil)
Julia Walsh (Australia)
Caroline Weigner (Austria)
Geoff White (Australia)

REAL-LIFE LEARNING: WHY, WHAT AND HOW?

Keynote address to IFIP ICT and RLL working conference

Peter Juliff

Emeritus Professor, School of Information Systems, Deakin University, Australia

Abstract: This paper presents a personal perspective on the evolution of ICT education at university level in Australia. It focuses on the development of IT courses in Institutes of Technology, which had a real-life orientation and recruited their academic staff with this in mind. Issues relating to real-life learning are discussed with a warning on the need for vigilance against over-stressing the benefits of 'real-world' as opposed to 'mere theory'. The paper approaches this discussion by considering issues under the headings: why, what and how.

Key words: Vocational/ professional education, real-life learning, Institutes of Technology.

1   INTRODUCTION

I was pleased to be asked to make the keynote presentation for this conference. Its theme of Real-life Learning has been one of the major concerns during my own academic career over a period of approximately forty years. I came to academia after ten years spent in public administration, by which time I had been appointed to a position of Public Service Inspector (EDP) in the state of Victoria. This was in the mid-60s when commercial computer-based systems were in their infancy and computing education was an emerging discipline. Like others of my kind, I had no academic computing qualifications and was recruited because of my "real-life" experience. From then it has been a continual scramble to keep up with advances in technology, advances in the nature of ICT education, advances in ICT practices and the growth of the ICT profession.

The progress of my working career reflects the progress of ICT education in this country:

- 1956-67: Employed by the Victorian Public Service, commencing in the Office of the Government Statist and Actuary using the electro-mechanical calculating devices of the time, ending in the EDP Inspectorate overseeing the introduction of the first administrative computing systems in the Public Service and completing an Associate Diploma in EDP (Accounting) at Caulfield Technical College – then part of the Technical Division of the Victorian Education Department.

- 1967 – 78: Appointed as a Teacher at Caulfield Technical College, re-classified as a Lecturer in the re-named Caulfield Institute of Technology on the formation of the Victoria Institute of Colleges in 1969. During this time I graduated in the first cohort of the Bachelor of Applied Science (Computing) awarded as a result of the general upgrading of Institutes' qualifications from Diplomas.

- 1978-79: Deputy Programming Manager, Health Computing Services of Victoria on the campus of Monash University – an escape from academia back to "real life".

- 1980-89: Head of EDP Department, Prahran College of Advanced Education, re-named Victoria College on amalgamation with two Teachers' Colleges in the first series of institutional amalgamations in 1982.

- 1990-92: Head of Department of Software Development, Chisholm Institute of Technology (the re-named Caulfield Institute of Technology) and amalgamated in 1990 with Monash University, becoming part of the Faculty of Computing and Information Technology in a second series of institutional amalgamations.

- 1993-98: Professor and Foundation Chair of the School of Management Information Systems, Deakin University, by then incorporating the former Victoria College as a result of the same amalgamations which saw the Chisholm/Monash merger.

So, as can be seen, most of my time in academia has been spent in Institutions of Technology where the commitment to real-life learning was an essential part of the culture. During that time, I have maintained an on-going association with the ICT industry and have been involved in the design and implementation of a wide variety of commercial computer-based systems. These started with applications written in assembler for a Burroughs B400 (because it had 400 memory locations) keying in the code via an accounting machine keyboard and processing data on punched paper tape, through numerous systems on Honeywell, ICL, Burroughs and Control Data hardware programmed in COBOL and updating magnetic tape master files with transactions recorded on punched cards to PC-based applications written in Visual Basic maintaining relational databases.

It is this experience I would like to draw upon in this address.

2   SOME GENERAL HISTORY

- Until around 15 years ago, Australia had a binary system of tertiary education. Go back another 15 years before that and there was also a binary system of secondary education. In both cases, the binary division was broadly on the basis of "vocational" vs. "academic" studies.

- At secondary level, students were often separated into a vocational or an academic stream after the second year of secondary education (Year 8, in current parlance), i.e. at about age thirteen. The vocational stream essentially meant training for a trade and often led to an apprenticeship. It was not impossible for a student in this stream to move across to the academic stream but it was not regarded as a common occurrence.

- Secondary students completing the academic stream after Year 12 then had a further choice if they wanted to pursue tertiary education. There were the Institutes of Technology, or Colleges of Advanced Education as some were named, and there were the Universities. Until the mid-1970s, the awards from the Institutes were designated as Diplomas and those from the Universities as Degrees. Institutes/Colleges offered courses mainly in Business Studies, Public Administration, Teaching and Engineering. Graduates were recognised as having practical skills and knowledge enabling them to fit into a working environment and become productive in a minimal time. Universities offered the traditional disciplines of Arts, Commerce, Law, Medicine, Science, Engineering, etc. Graduates were generally regarded as being well versed in the theory of their discipline and having acquired the ability to conduct research enabling them to extend that body of knowledge but not necessarily having much in the way of practical experience.

- Recruitment of staff by the various institutions reflected the differences in the perceived requirements of their students. Academic staff in the Institutes were often chosen on the basis of their practical knowledge and experience and were expected to have or to acquire teaching qualifications the better to be able to impart their skills to their students. University academics were usually chosen on the basis of their achievements as students and their ability to conduct research in their chosen discipline. They were not expected to have nor to pursue any particular skill in teaching, the implication presumably being that students would acquire the knowledge of their lecturers by an osmotic process.

- In the late 1980s, the then Labor government engineered the mergers of the Institutes and Colleges with existing Universities or, in very few cases, their conversion to university nomenclature. This was ostensibly in the interest of homogenising tertiary education and thus providing all students with the dual benefits of vocational/practical education and a scholarship/research culture. Thereby, in a single stroke, they extinguished the benefits of both branches of tertiary education. This was coupled with an exhortation from the Treasury for universities to go forth and multiply their enrolments of overseas, fee-paying students and the subsequent embarrassing touting for students which has seen universities indulging in a scramble for enrolments and, arguably, compromising their standards in terms of entry requirements and course criteria.
- The role of TAFE (Technical and Further Education) Colleges has expanded to absorb much of the vacuum left by the demise of the Institutes of Technology. Their Diploma courses have been standardised across the country to remove the idiosyncrasies of individual institutions' delivery and some courses now lead to Degree awards.
- It is interesting that, after 30 years, it was one of the planks in the Liberal Party's recent re-election platform to re-introduce vocational senior high schools for students not aspiring to the heights of the university system which has long since been tuned down to accommodate those entering from the single high school stream no longer given the choice of tertiary study at an Institute of Technology.

3   SOME HISTORY OF ICT EDUCATION, IN PARTICULAR

- Against the above background, we can trace the evolution of ICT education in Australia. In the late 1950s and early 60s, Australian universities began to acquire computing equipment. This was the province of Science departments and was available to a small number of science/mathematics students for whom the computer represented an advance on the electro-mechanical computation equipment then available. This expanded over the years to form the computer science curricula typical in most of the world's universities. The emphasis was on the electronics of the computer's operations and the production of software such as operating systems and compilers. Programming was typically done at an assembler or machine language level, or using a home-developed higher-level language or, in due course, proprietary languages such as Fortran, Algol, Pascal or C. There was little attempt made to orient course material towards the burgeoning commercial computing/data processing market or to use software common in that environment. Systems analysis and design, for example, was nowhere to be found among university curricula, the conventional wisdom of the time being that this was impossible to impart to undergraduate students.

- ICT education in the Institutes of Technology, on the other hand, was almost entirely commercially oriented. The early courses were a mixture of Diplomas in Electronic Data Processing (as it was then termed) for school leavers and the pre-cursors of today's Graduate Diplomas for professionals in the workplace wishing to understand, and take advantage of, the emerging technology. The interesting factor about the school leavers enrolling for Diploma courses was that many of them came not from the academic high school stream but from the technical/vocational stream. These were students who originally opted, or had their choice made for them by their parents or teachers, not to eventually pursue an academic tertiary education. Their technical high school education, however, had inspired them to aim beyond a manual trade and the newly emerging data processing technology appealed to them as a hands-on, rather than a book-learning, activity. In this state of Victoria, vocational ICT education stemmed entirely from the area of technical high school education. The curricula typically embraced the three areas of equipment, programming and systems analysis and design. The early equipment curricula used to embrace also the areas of accounting machines and punched card systems which existed in parallel with early computer systems.

- In the tradition of the Institutes of Technology, teaching staff were recruited on the basis of their knowledge and experience in the ICT marketplace. This became evident in curricula developed and nature of practical work undertaken by students. The aim of the courses was, as it had always been, to produce graduates with the skills and knowledge to be immediately productive in a working environment.

- By way of rounding off the picture, in the early 1980s computer science subjects began to be introduced into the final year of high school curricula in the teeth of opposition from the university Computer Science academics who initially refused to count marks obtained in this subject towards a student's university entrance criteria.

4   REAL-LIFE LEARNING

- We in this Working Group are proponents of vocational and professional education in information technology. It is therefore natural to expect us to raise the banner of Real-life Learning. It begs two questions, however: What is "real" about the Real-life; and, what is "learned" in the education process?
- Whose reality do we teach to our students? At first blush, it is attractive for a lecturer to be able to say to a group of students, "This is the way we did things where I worked". Even more attractive, of course, to say "This is the way we do things where I work." This is real-life experience. But, wait a moment: is the way they do, or did, things at the lecturer's workplace the correct or best way to do them? Is the lecturer merely delivering a history lesson? Is the lecturer reinforcing a less-than-perfect (this could be a euphemism for just-plain-wrong) set of practices? So, what do the students learn? Do they learn only one way to approach a particular problem because it is the only way the lecturer has ever known? I worked with an academic whose burning desire was to write the definitive work on the sorting of magnetic tape files. This was long after the world had moved on to disk storage. However, he would deliver his standard lecture on the intricacies of pre-stringing and multiple passes because he "knew" that this was the stuff of real-life systems.
- It is necessary to be eternally vigilant to avoid over-stressing the benefits of the "real world" as opposed to "mere theory". Indeed, in a nutshell, this had been a perennial bone of contention between Institute and University academics. Skills may be acquired more readily than knowledge, and practice based only on skill without an understanding of the underlying theory has a very limited usefulness.

5   WHY?

- The values of real-life learning are numerous:
  - It illustrates practical implementation of theory. The world of ICT is one of solving problems. A theory must be able to be implemented to be of use in the marketplace. A real-life example is an excellent way to demonstrate usefulness.
  - It provides motivation. Which of us has not had a student ask "Do we really need to know this stuff you're teaching us?" If we can lead the student to a working example of the application of "this stuff", the question is already answered.

- o It builds confidence in the student. Faced with a problem in a working situation, the graduate is better equipped to solve it if he or she has seen or, better still, done something similar before.
- There is a basic assumption here which comes from my own background of over 25 years in Institutes of Technology: that is, we are preparing students to become productive contributors to the ICT marketplace. For the vast majority of my own academic career, the main criterion on which I judged the success or otherwise of my courses and teaching efforts, and the efforts of my staff, was whether or not my graduates were able to gain employment as ICT practitioners. My last 10 years spent in the University system has, of course, required me to re-evaluate that criterion. University education has never been primarily about graduates being employable at its conclusion. Such an outcome might be considered by some to be a serendipitous by-product of graduation but surely not the guiding principle for academics and course developers. Given the propensity for universities to hire graduates as tutors while they pursue research for higher qualifications and then to appoint them as lecturers until they have served on enough committees to become heads of departments, what could be more "real-life" for an aspiring academic than sitting in a class room?

6   WHAT?

- The most obvious "what" is the work itself. ICT is essentially a practical profession. It is about getting things done and, usually, done in a hurry. Requirements of ICT systems are constantly evolving. The largest problem of the dinosaur systems in the past was not that they didn't do a job but that the job was outdated by the time they did it. The tools currently available for rapid system development enable and encourage evolutionary system design. Students often enter the workforce not merely without an understanding of the realities of ICT system development but without an understanding of the realities of the working environment both internal and external to their place of employment. A large slab of this "real-life" component is indeed – real LIFE. Students need to be aware of the realities and restrictions involved in systems interacting with others of their species.
- Why can we not achieve our goal by providing students with realistic assignment work during their course? Do we need to push them out of the nest to do this? The answer to that lies in the

difference between systems in the large and systems in the small. By necessity, student assignments must be devised so as to be realistically possible of solution within the duration of their parent academic subject; i.e. one semester of around 10 to 13 weeks. Some of even this short time must be devoted to the learning of whatever skill level is needed to commence the assignment. Academics are aware that their unit is only one of many being undertaken concurrently by their students and assignments from one unit must not monopolise the students' time. So, we devise systems in the small. The problem is hopefully representative of a working situation but of such a small scale as to remove many of the problems which size alone brings.

Size may be manifested in many ways:

o   Allowing concurrent access to system resources by N users;
o   Maintenance of fast access to N entities in a database;
o   Development of software by N parallel programmers;
o   Writing a program of N lines of code;
o   Satisfying the requirements of N users of a system;
o   Maintaining acceptable service levels over a network of N nodes.

All of the above are likely to increase by an exponential rather than a linear function of N.

Real-life exposure can give students a feeling for systems in the large. Only by seeing the difference which this makes to the process of system development and operation can the gulf between a student assignment and a working project be appreciated. I have often advocated the criterion of a professional programmer being able to produce 1,000 lines of debugged code per day. Many students would not produce 1,000 lines of debugged code in the entirety of their course.

•   Another "what" to be learned is the difficulty which most working professionals have in keeping up with their profession. Students come to the workforce after three or four years of having had the luxury of being able to increase their knowledge base. Indeed, they are rewarded for doing so; in addition, they are force-fed by their lecturers. It may come as a complete surprise to them that their newly-found workmates do not have the time or, in many cases, the funds to enrol in enrichment courses just for the sake of learning something new. It may also be a surprise to the graduates that their employer is not prepared to reward them for efforts expended in keeping abreast of technology which is not immediately relevant to their current work.

- I would like to think that a further benefit of exposing students to real-life learning would be the gaining of experience in professional ethics and codes of practice. It has been my experience that undergraduate students have polarised attitudes to the issue of ethical behaviour among practitioners of a profession. Some will learn the code promulgated by their local professional body and merely regurgitate the chapter and verse which they perceive applicable to a posed question. Others will cynically adopt an attitude that you do whatever you can get away with without being caught. Graduates working in ICT should be prepared to evaluate their chosen vocation to reach a conclusion as to whether it really is a profession. Students with a cavalier attitude to matters of ethics in an ICT context are often horrified when asked if they would be happy for their lawyer, tax accountant or doctor to adopt the same approach to the privacy of data.

  The lack of espousal of a truly professional code of ethics and public practice has been the largest factor in the reluctance of the community to accept ICT as a true profession.

7 HOW?

- The real-life component of learning may be imparted internally or externally. Internal embedding of such concepts may be reflected in the nature of the course material presented to students and the assignments required to be undertaken. The problems related particularly to assignments were discussed earlier. One means of injecting reality into course content is the use of real-life software and hardware in the students' education. The early days of ICT education often saw educational institutions using home-developed programming languages in lieu of those used at the time in industry. It is interesting to note that, in this category, a distinctly non-academic language – Basic – has survived to become one of today's cornerstones while a much more academic example – Pascal – was never accepted outside academia. A further example of this dichotomy was the widespread popularity of COBOL in the commercial marketplace because of its ability to get a job done. Given that getting a job done was never a criterion of the average academic, the language was generally regarded as beneath a computer science academic's dignity to include in course material. The principle of exposing students to real-life software applies also to the use of proprietary products such as Windows and its related companions for text processing, data storage and manipulation, spreadsheets and presentation media.

- An approach taken by some universities, not without its critics, is that of building a whole course, or a substantial part thereof, around a particular workplace product or qualification. Many courses are built around enterprise-wide products such as SAP. Technology courses often incorporate training to enable graduates to acquire an industry qualification such as Microsoft's MCSE or Novell's CNE. The benefits to graduates are obvious: a ready-made entry into a corner of the marketplace. The danger, of course, is the possibility that "education" is replaced by "training".

- The internal imparting of a real-life flavour to course material relies on the developers and presenters of the material having some real-life to impart. The binary system of Institutes of Technology and Universities, as already discussed, encouraged the employment of practitioners with real-life experience in the Institutes while not providing the same encouragement for University staff. However, the propensity for many of the Institute practitioners to become "snap-frozen" upon employment meant that both arms of the education process were faced with the same problem: how do you keep the experience of your staff current?

  One approach to solving this has been to release staff into the general workforce periodically: the concept of sabbatical or industrial leave. In a currently under-staffed environment such as tertiary education has become, the problem is: how to you manage to release staff for prolonged periods? And, in a traditionally highly-paid and manpower-hungry profession such as ICT has usually been, the problem is: can you be sure that they will return?

- External real-life learning for undergraduates has traditionally been accomplished by sandwich courses. Students are released into the workforce, usually with one further year of study still to complete, to work in a full-time industry environment for which they are paid a normal rate of salary. While this may seem ideal for the student, the realities for the educational institution are extremely demanding. The finding of industry sponsors, continued mentoring of students by liaison with nominated academics and the associated administration are a heavy burden on the university. It is not uncommon to find that this organisation requires the full-time attention of one member of academic staff. Students' experiences are also often mixed in terms of perceived benefits. Some employers are reluctant to commit the resources needed within their own organisation to make the students' work experience meaningful and professionally rewarding.

- One of the significant areas of distinction between Institutes and Universities was the Course Advisory Committee. Institutes of Technology would invariably have such a committee composed of representatives from industry, the relevant professional body and sister Institutes to review course structure and content. This was done with the express purpose of ensuring that courses had a real-life basis in terms of the need for graduates of the type intended to be produced and the knowledge and skills to be acquired in the course. With the abolition of this arm of education went the existence of the committee. Universities obviously have no need for such input. They are fiercely committed to self-governance. Yet another opportunity for some real-life to be injected into our learning is extinguished. To be fair, it must also be admitted that some industry-based members of such committees were equally inclined to dismiss as irrelevant any course material not seen as directly leading to a workplace skill.

- Some of the institutions at which I have worked have had active student associations which have organised guest speakers from industry to make periodic presentations on matters of real-life interest. This enables students to obtain a feel for the issues which are felt to be important in the marketplace and also, embarrassingly on occasions, to invite the speakers' comments on the material which the students are currently being taught. In the absence of this initiative on the part of the students themselves, the academic staff have sometimes attempted to organise this facility for the students. This has inevitably resulted in failure due to terminal apathy on the part of the students and embarrassingly low attendances at the speakers' presentations.

8   CONCLUSION

- There is enough of the educational dinosaur in me to make me feel that real-life learning is valuable.
- For students to see it as valuable, staff must be able to present such experience with confidence and conviction.
- For staff to be able to do that, they must be at least aware of what real-life entails even if they have had no such experience themselves.
- Professional bodies such as the Australian Computer Society devote considerable effort to organising activities aimed at maintaining the level of relevance of their members and members of the profession in general. University staff have

traditionally ignored both the professional bodies and their activities.

- Students of ICT disciplines have traditionally had little difficulty in obtaining well-paid employment upon graduation and have had an expectation of life-long employment without much more effort on their part in terms of continuing education. That is no longer the case.

- Academics in ICT disciplines have traditionally had little difficulty in attracting students into their courses because the courses were seen as leading to certain employment. Because the latter is no longer the case, neither is the former. Most ICT faculties have recently been involved in significant down-sizing.

- Fewer ICT jobs for graduates may have the effect of increasing the perceived value of having acquired some real-life learning along the way.

- The advisability of being able to provide such real-life learning in a course may convince academics that it is to be valued. Some may even be so bold as to take the next step and acquire it.

VIRTUAL CORPORATE TRAINING SYSTEMS
Defining Criteria and Indicators for Evaluation

Marina Keiko Nakayama, Christine da Silva Schröeder, Bianca Smith Pilla, Daniel Garcia Haro and Erlaine Binotto
PPGA/EA/UFRGS – Universidade Federal do Rio Grande do Sul Rua Washington Luiz,– Porto Alegre/RS – Brazil marina@ea.ufrgs.br, christine@ea.ufrgs.br, bspilla@ea.ufrgs.br, dharo.ez@terra.com.br and erlaine@ufrgs.br

Abstract: The objective of this study is to identify criteria and indicators to evaluate distance education programs used in companies. The choice of this subject is justified by current difficulties companies experience in evaluating training, especially virtual training. It provides a correlation between results of this type of training and organizational results. A theoretical base was built on the following aspects: training perspectives and development, structure and evaluation of virtual training and definition of performance indicators – emphasizing the model of evaluation of four levels by Kirkpatrick (1998) and the Balanced Scorecard by Kaplan & Norton (1997). Starting from this conceptual base, the authors conducted exploratory research using techniques of data collection, interviews with distance education specialists, and an analysis of organizational best practice in virtual training. Eight specialists from Brazilian Universities were interviewed and the best practices of thirty two companies were analysed from papers presented to the Congress on E-learning Brazil in 2004. The preliminary results allow establishment of a relation between criteria and relevant indicators for evaluation of this type of training system. The validation of this model will be through a case study of a company using virtual training.

Key words: Distance education, training, evaluation, results.

1   INTRODUCTION

For many years, administrative theories have evolved and have been concerned with training of organization collaborators, seeking to use activities which minimize operational flaws in the current administration of knowledge as a tool for sustaining competitive advantages. Training and development activities (T & D) of company employees are characterized as strategic issues. Program methods of T & D have started to receive new focus. Distance education has been an emerging solution for training. According to Niskier (1999), distance education offers advantages such as reduction of costs, access for a larger number of individuals, integration of different educational resources and the possibility of constant updating. In this sense, an important subject related to the use of distance education in training activities is the measurement of current organizational results in the application of such a methodology. It is necessary to identify the criteria and relevant indicators for this evaluation process.

"What to measure?", "why measure?" and "how to measure?" are relevant subjects for companies. In this context, the evaluation of results involves not only short term goals, but also long periods of guaranteed sustainability of organizational strategy. Even faced with different methodologies of evaluation, it is believed that many companies have difficulty adjusting to this process. The issue is how to appropriately measure training results, especially in virtual training. This ranges from student reactions to the training program, to the way in which new knowledge alters his/her behaviour and work procedures. The result of the financial return is important, because it is the final product of the improvement process and the intellectual capacity of the company.

It is necessary then to work out a process of measuring performance systems of virtual corporate training, consisting of criteria ("what needs to be measured?") and indicators ("what can be used to measure?"). Starting from this point, the research problem is proposed: which criteria and indicators can be used for the evaluation of systems of virtual corporate training?

2   THEORETICAL REFERENTIAL

The accomplished research is based on the following aspects.

2.1 Training and Development Perspectives

The management of human resources in the last 10 years has had a larger involvement in the executive decision processes aiming for results through the alignment of human potential with the strategic focus of the organization. To Bohlander, Snell and Sherman (2003), the term "training" is frequently used in a casual way to describe the efforts of a company to stimulate its members to learn. However, many specialists make the distinction between training focused on subjects related to performance in the short-term, and development focused on the enhancement of an individual's ability in the long term. According to Marras (2001), training is aligned with tasks, and a development program offers a person an overview of the business. Both have been combined in a single expression - "training and development" - to indicate all of the activities that increase the foundation of employees' abilities in companies.

2.2 Structure and Evaluation of Virtual Training

The structure of a training program can be defined through four basic stages (Bohlander, Snell and Sherman 2003): evaluation of needs, the project, implementation, and evaluation of training. In the last one, the four levels proposed by Kirkpatrick (1998) are reaction, learning, behaviour and results. To Hack (2000) they can also be adopted to training via the Internet:

- **Reaction:** The student is evaluated for participation in learning activities, indicating whether he/she is adapting to the form of the material presented. A positive reaction to training is as important for internal instructors training within the company, as for programs offered to the public, because the future of the program depends on this reaction;
- **Learning:** Learning happens when there is a change in the process of being aware of reality and/or increased knowledge or ability;
- **Behaviour:** New teaching methods are only good when studied in the context of the student's abilities and attitudes. Similarly, this level tries to identify the changes generated after the student has finished the training program;
- **Results:** The object of this level, maybe the most complex level, is to identify if the company has obtained a return on its investment. To provide a more complete idea of the impact of learning within the company, indicators can be added like data for market growth, etc.

2.3 The Importance of Performance Indicators

Organizations are using different systems of performance evaluation focused on their processes and, consequently, their results. There are methods capable of evaluating organizational excellence with a wider view than just the financial one: in other words, the operational environment of participants and stakeholders (people, creditors, suppliers and others who have a direct economical bond with the company). In the process of defining criteria and performance indicators, there are some essential considerations regarding indicators, such as their essential characteristics, criteria and classification which are focus indicators using the Quality approach (Takashina and Flores 1995; Camargo 2000), and especially the indicators of the Balanced Scorecard approach (Kaplan and Norton 1997).

The Quality approach – Takashina and Flores (1995) argue that an indicator should be generated carefully, in a way that ensures the readiness of the data and more relevant results in the shortest possible time and at the lowest cost. To Camargo (2000) there are essential parameters in the generation of the quality indicators: selectivity or importance; simplicity and clarity; comprehensiveness, traceability and accessibility; comparability; stability, accessibility and affordability.

The Balanced Scorecard (BSC) method consists of a model of evaluation of organizational performance. It has come from conflict between highly competitive functions and static analysis of financial accounting of costs. Scorecard has made possible communication of strategies to the organization in creating a holistic model, based on four main perspectives. They are complementary through a cause and effect relationship, through perspectives of financial, customers, internal processes and learning and growth which are translated into strategic objectives, measured through goals and performance factors. These results give the organization important feedback.

3   METHOD OF RESEARCH

This research is characterized as an exploratory and qualitative study. The techniques for collection of data were interviews with distance education specialists and the analysis of cases of virtual corporate training.

The objective of the interviews was to identify relevant aspects in the evaluation of distance education systems used by companies, according to the views of specialists. Forty specialists from universities, consultancies and Brazilian companies were contacted. The sample was characterized by accessibility and convenience. Among the group who were researched, eight interviews took place. To complement the data, 32 papers were analysed describing the operation of distance education systems in Brazilian and multinational companies. Their views were presented during the Congress E-Learning Brazil 2004. The phases of the research were:

a) the first phase was bibliographical research seeking to use theoretical reference for orientation and details of a conceptual model of criteria and indicators;

b) the second phase was a collection of data (analysis of the interviews with the specialists and the business practice cases) to explain a skilled model of criteria and indicators; and

c) the third phase was explanation of final criteria and indicators model.

After these phases researchers intend to continue with a case study in which the proposed model will be applied in an organization. The data used for interviews was analysis of documentary sources and content analysis.

4 DESCRIPTIONS AND ANALYSIS OF RESULTS

After bibliographical research into the definition of criteria and indicators and analysis of interviews with the distance education specialists, it was verified that: distance education specialists place greater emphasis on evaluation of learning, while the managers of Training and Development defined a larger range of criteria and indicators, especially evaluation of the results. However, this suggested that criteria, rather than specific indicators, were easier to evaluate and therefore there were some gaps between the two.

The reaction stage was more easily analysed by the specialists in the context of the business practice cases. In the behaviour phase, it was observed that it was more difficult to examine criteria and indicators.

As a result of the research up to the present moment, a model composed of criteria and indicators of evaluation of virtual training, which structure is based on training evaluation phases proposed by Kirkpatrick (1998): reaction, learning, behaviour, and results. Such arrangement has resulted from a coalition of criteria and indicators of the revision of literature, interviews with the specialists and analysis of the business practice cases.

Reaction	
Criteria	**Indicators**
E-learning technological platform	• Students' satisfaction with technological support (help-desk) • Availability of equipment for the students • Number of requests assisted by support • Service time (average)
Viability of the project	• Expected total workload • Date definition for conclusion of the modules • Cost reduction estimate in trips ($) • Educational material and structure • The relation between total investment and expected benefits ($) • Estimated number of students and public
Organizational involvement	• Percentage increase e-learning courses x Percentage of increase in courses • Percentage monthly growth participation in virtual training • Percentage of employees that participate in virtual training
Previous knowledge on content and on computer science	• Number of people who accessed tools of collaboration • Time dedicated to the course • Time taken to learn how use the system • Grading on previous knowledge • Evaluation on computer use.
Academic and software quality	• Grade of evaluation of initial opinion • Amount of available learning materials

	• Previous research with specialists, final users and help-desk
Motivational/support for the tutor and student feedback	• Students' satisfaction with their tutor
Personalized teaching in agreement with the student's cultural, social, historical and environmental aspects	• Percentage access by collaborators, partners, relatives, customers and other users • Number of students enrolled in virtual training x number of students in training

Learning	
Criteria	**Indicators**
Students performance (content domain, autonomy and goals obtained)	• Test grades of content domain • Analysis of the composition of papers and reports relating to content • Evaluation of the accomplished tasks • Grading of the students' self-evaluation • Simulations, challenges and case studies • Consensus and feedback tools, tests, self-evaluation and tracking progress • Evaluation by the classmates
Participation and students interaction	• Number and quality of participants in interactive tools (chats, forums, discussion lists, e-mails, etc) • Evaluation of contribution levels / articulation of a processed idea
Adaptation of the levels of complexity of content, themes and periods	• Comparative data of the virtual teams for areas and purpose • Periodic evaluation opinion of the participants

Behaviour	
Criteria	**Indicators**
Change verification – relationship / interaction among virtual communities	• Verification of the relationship among classmates • Numbers and characteristics of the interaction between students and teachers during and after training • Use of communication tools for integration of teams and to facilitate the execution of tasks
Change verification – cognitive structure / organizational culture	• Students daily activity evaluation including behaviour • Self-evaluation of the student at the end of the course x periodic self-evaluation during the course
Students motivational aspect / attitude the virtual mode of training	• Periodic evaluation of opinion • Evaluating motivation to undertake new virtual courses • Final Percentage of access collaborators, partners, relatives and other users • Comparison of initial motivation x motivation during the program
Execution of processes	• Process attendance • Ranking of team performance

Results	
Criteria	**Indicators**
Performance analysis	• Self-evaluation and final evaluation • Audit evaluation
Continuous improvement – customers	• Percentage Increase the customer bases • Market share
Continuous improvement – processes	• Number of completed processes • Percentage reduction in mistakes / defects / infringement of procedures • Number of new products and services • Time reduction percentage in the execution of processes • Re-work volume

	• Amount of overtime
Continuous improvement - communication	• Optimization of the use of communication tools and data bases
Practical usefulness on knowledge / student autonomy at the conclusion of this process / personal and professional development	• Percentage of previous knowledge x percentage of the final evaluation of knowledge • Exercise and assembly of experiments • Simulation of situations in the virtual environment • Time taken to answer the tasks • Verification of attitude changes in the daily activities after completion of the course • Index comparison of the use of the environment and students' practical results
Return on the Investment	• Percentage increase in profitability • Percentage loss and gains regarding competition • Percentage reduction in production cost
Improvement of the organizational image / social responsibility / digital inclusion	• Research of the internal and external customer's satisfaction
Value of the human resources	• Number of courses in process and new planned courses • Total number of employees and those who finished virtual training • Percentage of the relation between the retention of employees before and after training

Figure 1:   Final criteria and indicators model for the evaluation of virtual training
(Source: Details from the theoretical reference and the collection of data)

5   FINAL CONSIDERATIONS

The presented model has expressed the effort of listing maximum possible relevant criteria and indicators for evaluation of virtual training in the organizations. It was also established specific indicators related to each criterion, being that some are repeated for different criteria. However, the study has pointed out that the definition of indicators is still inexact for four criteria, as the evaluation of each is more directly linked to the particularities of organizational reality:

- Safety tools - access, authentication, authorization, audit (in the Reaction stage): the safety tools to be implanted in the system depends on the definitions of strategic, tactical and operational training traced by the management of HR with the high managers of the company.
- Scales of classification with behavioural anchor (in the Behaviour stage): the desired levels of behaviour are defined from the organizational mission and vision of each company;
- Attitude related to content (in the Behaviour stage): the criteria of evaluation of the desired attitude will be conceived from the definition the organizational standards of behaviour mentioned previously;
- Alignment with HR subsystems and the integration of platform to other corporate systems and holistic vision of the business (in the Results stage): the definition of criteria is extremely complex as to the

means that broad knowledge on the Strategic Planning of the company becomes necessary, as well as the adjusted virtual structure on processes to other subsystems of HR, like remuneration, positions and salary, benefits, etc.

In this sense, it is suggested a subsequent validation of group criteria and indicators in a company which uses virtual corporate training. At it shows, the model presented a list of criteria and indicators, which can be adapted to the reality and culture of each organization intending to measure its system of virtual training. This way, each organization can define its criteria and respective indicators. This analysis will interact with the criteria and indicators of the global results indicators which need to be adapted to the reality and culture of each organization intending to measure its system of virtual training. The criteria and indicators are evidences of cause and effect. To convert training into results will be a constant challenge for the companies. Next phase of this research is the construction of an evaluation model of a specific company in Brazil respecting its business, culture and reality. The company is the wholesale business segment.

6   REFERENCES

Bohlander, G.; S. Snell & A. Sherman (2003) *Administração de recursos humanos,* Pioneira Thomson Learning, São Paulo.

Camargo, L. L. (2000) *Uso de indicadores da qualidade para o gerenciamento estratégico de empresas do ramo comercial,* Programa de Pós-Graduação em Engenharia de Produção, Universidade Federal de Santa Catarina (UFSC), Florianópolis. [http://teses.eps.ufsc.br/defesa/pdf/4429.pdf]

Hack, L. E. (2000) *Mecanismos complementares para a avaliação do aluno na educação a distância,* Curso de Pós-Graduação em Ciência da Computação, Instituto de Informática, Universidade Federal do Rio Grande do Sul (UFRGS), Porto Alegre.

Kaplan, R. S. & D. P. Norton (1997) *A estratégia em ação* – Balanced Scorecard, Campus, Rio de Janeiro.

Kirpatrick, D. L. (1998) *Evaluating training programs:* the four levels (Second Edition), Berret-Koehler Publishers Inc., San Francisco, CA.

Marras, J. P. (2001) *Administração de recursos humanos:* do operacional ao estratégico, Futura, São Paulo, pp.145-172.

Niskier, A. (1999) *Educação a distância:* a tecnologia da esperança. Edições Loyola, São Paulo.

Takashina, N. T. & M. C. X. Flores (1995) *Indicadores da qualidade e do desempenho,* Qualitymark, Rio de Janeiro.

ISSUES IN THE ASSESSMENT OF REAL-LIFE LEARNING WITH ICT

Anne McDougall
Department of Science & Mathematics Education, The University of Melbourne, Australia
a.mcdougall@unimelb.edu.au

Abstract: This paper examines some aspects of the assessment of the effectiveness of learning with information and communications technologies (ICT) in real-life learning contexts, and looks at the role of ICT as a tool in assisting this endeavour. It argues that real assessment of learning with ICT is a challenging task, and that assessment strategies that are simple and economical to use need to be balanced with use of strategies that acknowledge the complexity of the learning processes and outcomes being assessed. To illustrate the case the paper draws on research work being undertaken by two groups within the Department of Science & Mathematics Education at the University of Melbourne. The first is a group of staff and research students who are examining the learning of students in a postgraduate teacher education course on robotics. One researcher within this group is comparing the learning of novice programmers working in both syntactic and symbolic programming environments, looking at the need to take account of differences in learning styles and preferences among individuals when learning is assessed. The second group is a research team exploring novel and sophisticated uses for ICT itself as a tool in educational research, particularly in the study of the complex learning processes of groups of students. This work, initially devised for studying the learning interactions occurring in classrooms, is being adapted by another researcher in the robotics research group to study the learning by groups of adult learners of scientific concepts such as gearing.

Key words: Assessment, cognitive style, multimedia, group work, research.

1   INTRODUCTION

It is widely acknowledged that assessing learning with ICT is a challenging task (Johnson et al. 1994, McDougall 2001, Harrison et al. 2002, Cox et al. 2003). Throughout the development of the use of ICT for learning extensive work has been undertaken on formative evaluation and assessment of software and of innovative projects, but no similar range of effective and reliable ways of assessing real learning gains attributable to or associated with the use of ICT has so far been developed. Nevertheless it is critically important to develop effective techniques for doing this in the light of the major developments and growing investment in ICT resources for learning, including of course real-life learning.

The difficulty of assessing real-life learning with ICT is the result of a combination of many factors. This paper will focus particularly on three of these, all of which contribute to the challenge of the task. These are: individual differences in cognitive and learning styles among learners; the complexity of what is to be assessed, and the likelihood that existing forms of assessment cannot measure all of the aspects of learning that might occur, when a learner works in a multimedia environment; and the need for assessment techniques that are more sophisticated than the traditional study-and-test approaches, in order to allow for the complexity of learners' interactions and achievements with ICT. This last is particularly important for real-life learning, where much valuable learning is undertaken in discussions with mentors of one kind or another or with groups of learners.

2   INDIVIDUAL DIFFERENCES AMONG LEARNERS

The matter of individual differences among learners has long been an issue in education. Current research is showing that such differences can be dramatically evident and can have a major impact on assessment in settings where ICT is used. Differences in impact on learning are being observed in case studies of students involved in exactly the same ICT activity. These are exemplified by findings from a research project investigating the effects of the use of ICT in students' writing, recently completed by John Vincent at the University of Melbourne. Although this study was undertaken with school students, it raises an issue of major importance for learning beyond school settings as well.

Vincent's project was stimulated by his earlier observation of a small number of students who had great difficulty with writing and other forms of verbal expression but showed astonishing improvement immediately on being introduced to multimedia software such as MicroWorlds. Vincent set writing tasks to be undertaken by his students in various ways – with pen and paper, with a word processor, and in multimedia environments. He collected the students' written work and computer files, administered a questionnaire on their attitudes to writing, made notes of observations and recorded interviews with the students. Conjecturing that in his previous work the students helped by the multimedia software appeared to have a preference for visual rather than verbal styles of working, he also administered a cognitive styles test (Riding & Cheema 1991) to the students.

As might be expected in a mixed ability group, he found a wide range of levels of attainment in writing with pen and paper. Some students wrote freely and with high levels of complexity. Others had enormous difficulty in producing more than a few words; some of these students had been assessed as "at risk" and were receiving remedial help. Of course there were many students performing at levels between these two extremes. The word-processed work produced very similar results. However, given the option of using MicroWorlds for their writing, some of the students for whom the task had previously seemed almost impossible adopted the new environment with enthusiasm and produced longer and often complex pieces in which the writing was integrated in various ways with graphics, animation and sound provided by the multimedia environment. By contrast, some of the students who were highly skilled writers previously, found the requirement to use non-verbal modes inconvenient, complaining that this hindered their work and stopped the flow of their writing. Again there was a range of student responses between these extremes. For some students in the class it was strikingly clear that the multimedia environment enabled vastly enhanced performance, while for others not only was it unhelpful but it actually hindered writing activities (Vincent 2003).

Vincent's work shows some patterns that appear to relate directly to differences in cognitive styles. Since cognitive style is generally acknowledged to be robust over time for individuals, we can expect that individual variations in what is learnt, and how, will occur similarly when learners interact with ICT environments in real-life learning situations.

Assessment of performance of different learners in real-life learning situations might also depend on what kinds of ICT environments are used. Vincent's study found marked individual differences among students who were all using the same software environments – the word processor, then the multimedia environment – for the same tasks. John Murnane, also working at the University of Melbourne, is extending Vincent's work, investigating some similar issues with real-life learners, exploring the hypothesis that different types of software might be preferred by different individuals undertaking the same task.

Murnane is working with teachers in a professional development context undertaking a Masters level subject as part of their study for a postgraduate qualification in Information Technology in Education. Within the subject Educational Programming Environments the teachers learn programming for robotics. Murnane is offering these learners two contrasting robotics programming environments. One is a word-based development of the Logo programming language. The other, RoboLab, uses a completely graphical programming system in which icons representing different elements such as motors, decisions, loop structures and containers are dragged onto the desktop and connected. Using observations and videotaped records of the teachers working, their reflective journals and the cognitive styles analysis instrument used by Vincent, Murnane is investigating how the teachers learn the programming for their robotics activities in each of these environments. He is comparing the ways in which the teachers react, solve problems and learn with these two environments. He is seeking any preferences individual learners might have for either environment for learning programming, reasons for such preferences, and views on each environment for the teaching of programming for robotics in schools. In particular he is investigating whether the cognitive styles of the learners are related to their use and perceptions of each environment. It is anticipated that gaining understanding of individuals' preferences might enable provision of more equitable assessment through offering students a choice of the programming environment to use.

Preliminary analysis of Murnane's data suggests that the teachers do perceive important differences in the learning experiences provided by the two environments. The assessment issues raised by Vincent apply in the setting in which Murnane is working, but at the time of writing it is too early to establish the relevance of these differences for assessment of programming for robotics and the extent to which they might relate to individual differences in the learners' cognitive styles.

3   ASSESSING LEARNING IN MULTIMEDIA CONTEXTS

Vincent described students, almost completely incapable of expression in words, who produced complex and sophisticated narratives when allowed to work in multimedia environments. Judged solely in verbal terms these students appeared to be severely limited in their ability to express their ideas and understandings. However the multimedia artefacts they produced dramatically belie this assessment.

Vincent notes that almost all of the official assessment tools that teachers use are verbally based, so the performance of a learner is judged by skills with words. He used the Writing Assessment instrument of the Victorian Curriculum and Assessment Authority's Achievement Improvement Monitor (VCAA 2003) to assess his students' pieces written with pen and paper and with word processor. However he found that this instrument was completely unsatisfactory for assessing the multimedia products of his students.

Words are only one of a number of semiotic modes that are used in multimedia products. To assess the performance of a learner working in a multimedia environment it is necessary to understand the use of a range of modes, including images, sounds, music, animation, and text, in communicating what the learner intends. Each of these modes may have its own assessment techniques, and thus in a multimedia environment we are presented with a far more complex assessment task.

Vincent developed an approach to assessing the multimedia products of his students, taking account of the range of modes used, how they were used for effect, and the extent to which they were integrated in the piece. While his technique goes some way toward addressing the problem, he acknowledges that it is just a beginning and argues that much more work is needed to develop reliable and complete assessment techniques for assessing the performance of learners working in multimedia environments.

4   ASSESSING LEARNING IN COLLABORATIVE GROUPS

The assessment of group learning activities, like the matter of individual differences among learners, is not an issue peculiar to real-life learning. However it is particularly important in real-life learning contexts as learning through discussions and group activity are very widely used strategies in real-life learning settings.

Assessment of learning undertaken in collaborative groups is one of the issues arising in another study being undertaken in the robotics classes at the University of Melbourne. Debora Lipson is investigating the acquisition of the concepts of gears and gearing by adult learners in a constructionist robotics environment. The subjects for her study work together in small collaborative groups to build and program robots. This group work replicates a range of real-life learning situations in which groups of learners work on open-ended, authentic problem-solving tasks. An essential requirement for effective learning in such situations is good interaction with other group members; there must be clear communication among the learners in the group. How might such interactions be assessed with validity and reliability?

Assessment might be undertaken in substantial periods of observation of each group at work, but this is rarely practicable. Lipson is using video-recording of her groups at work to enable assessment not only of the knowledge gained by the students at the end of the course but of the processes used by the groups to achieve their outcomes, the levels of discussion, and the types of interactions and learning communications within the groups as they work.

While video-recording is currently used quite widely for collecting data for research, the amount and richness of data collected this way and the time taken to analyse it makes it generally impractical for regular assessment purposes. However a technique currently being developed for video data analysis for research purposes may well be adaptable for group learning assessment purposes as well.

A novel strategy for video data analysis that enables detailed research into the interactions in classrooms has been developed by David Clarke and his colleagues at the International Centre for Classroom Research (ICCR) at the University of Melbourne. These researchers argue that studying the complexity of interactions among learners necessitates multi-faceted analysis of classroom interactions to investigate student learning; this is particularly necessary in the context of recent shifts from a view of learning as transfer to a view of learning as constructed in action (Clarke, Sahlstrom, Mitchell & Clarke 2004).

Clarke and his colleagues use three video cameras to record classroom lesson sequences; one camera focuses on the teacher, one on the class as a whole, and the third on a small group of students. Software allows researchers to create codes for lesson events in real-time as they are happening in the classroom. Mixing of the teacher and student camera images into a split-screen video record is undertaken on-site; this can then be used to stimulate participant reconstructive accounts of classroom events. Thus the video recordings can be supplemented by post-lesson video-stimulated interviews with students and teachers, as well as scanned samples of written work, and test and questionnaire data. These techniques are currently being used in a major international study of mathematics classrooms, and aspects of the ICCR strategy are assisting several smaller studies in science and ICT classroom settings.

Techniques for compression, editing, storage and transfer of digitised video and other data, and software tools for sophisticated analyses of these complex data bases have been developed by the group. This has involved working in collaboration with an Australian software company Sportstec to adapt a video analysis software product Studiocode, used in televising Australian Rules football, for use with classroom video data (Mitchell, Clarke, Sahlstrom & Clarke 2004). Classroom events appear as coded instances in a timeline window and are immediately accessible as a video playlist. A matrix editor allows a researcher to view statistics on classroom events in a two-dimensional table format. Events associated with particular cells of the matrix can then be selected in any order, and a video created immediately that can play back all of these instances. Codes can also be exported into Excel spreadsheet files for further statistical analysis.

The approach is proving powerful in examining some of the more complex aspects of student learning in classroom and smaller group situations. High-ICT research techniques such as this, investigating the complex communications within groups of learners, will provide insights into group learning processes and – while I am not suggesting the use of three-camera strategies for assessment – could provide more sophisticated techniques for assessment of the work of groups and communities of learners.

5   CONCLUSION

The paper explores some aspects of the complexity of assessing real-life learning with ICT, focusing on three particular issues. The first is the problem of differences in cognitive styles of learners. Some aspects of this were illustrated with a description of research on school students' writing, and the extension of this work into a current study of adult learners' preferences for different software environments for programming for robotics.

The second is the problem of suitable strategies for assessing learning in multimedia environments. A pioneering attempt to address this with an assessment instrument taking into account the variety of modes of communication used in a multimedia artifact and the extent to which these modes are integrated was described.

Thirdly the paper raised the possibility that a recently developed sophisticated approach to analysis of video data, currently being used for research into learning interactions in classrooms, could be adapted to assist in the difficult but important task of assessing real-life learning in collaborative groups.

6   REFERENCES

Clarke, D., F. Sahlstrom, C. Mitchell & N. Clarke (2004) Optimising the Use of Available Technology in Educational Research. Paper for presentation at the 7th IASTED International Conference on Computers and Advanced Technology in Education CATE 2004, Hawaii.

Cox, M., C. Abbott, M. Webb, B. Blakeley, T. Beauchamp & V. Rhodes (2003) *ICT and Attainment: A Review of the Research Literature*. London: Department for Education and Skills.

Harrison, C., C. Comber, T. Fisher, K. Haw, C. Lewin, E. Lunzer, A. McFarlane, D. Mavers, P. Scrimshaw, B. Somekh & R. Watling (2002) ImpaCT2: The Impact of Information and Communication Technologies on Pupil Learning and Attainment. A report to the DfES. ICT in Schools Research and Evaluation Series No.7. Coventry: Becta.

Johnson, D.C., M.J. Cox & D.M. Watson (1994) Evaluating the impact of IT on pupils' achievements. *Journal of Computer Assisted Learning* 10, 138-156.

McDougall, A. (2001) Assessing learning with ICT. *Journal of Computer Assisted Learning* 17, 223-226.

Mitchell, C., N. Clarke, F. Sahlstrom & D. Clarke (2004) Optimising the Use of Available Technology in Educational Research. Paper for presentation at the Australian Computers in Education Conference, Adelaide.

Riding, R. & I. Cheema, (1991) *Cognitive Style Analysis*. Birmingham: Learning Assessment Unit.

VCAA (2003) *Achievement Improvement Monitor*. Melbourne: Victorian Curriculum and Assessment Authority.

Vincent, John (2003) Individual Differences, Technology and the Teacher of the Future. In McDougall, A., J. Murnane, C. Stacey & C. Dowling (Eds.) *ICT and the Teacher of the Future*. Sydney: Australian Computer Society, 127-9.

KNOWLEDGE WORK MANAGEMENT
A Framework for Web-based Knowledge Products and Instant-Qualification

Till Becker, Alexander Karapidis
Fraunhofer IAO, Stuttgart, Germany
Till.Becker@iao.fhg.de and Alexander.Karapidis@iao.fhg.de www.pm.iao.fhg.de

Abstract: Industry product life cycles and their technological life cycles are getting shorter and shorter. At the same time these products are getting more and more complex. In consequence, this causes faster innovation processes, new production concepts and client-oriented products. The share of knowledge work increases. There are different concepts to support companies in managing the changes and the higher part of knowledge work using new technologies. One is the idea of knowledge products. They take care of different user groups and give support to search and find of information. They help to improve the product, allow faster and smarter updates for product changes, make product presentations more effective and give the staff more orientation in their highly complex work environment. Another concept is to learn by "Instant-Qualification" just in time. The employee pools special information with his own expertise and can handle the actual specific work tasks immediately. The idea is the combination of knowledge management and learning in one real-time system. The surroundings of the employee are the interface of the learning application. It facilitates intuitive use of information. Learning is integrated into a real working process by using new technologies.

Key words: Personalised learning, individualised learning, work place learning, just in time, knowledge management.

1 KNOWLEDGE WORK MANAGEMENT – THE CONCEPT

Within the discussion about professional training, the term "knowledge work" refers to coping with work tasks which are complex or new at least to the person concerned in professional work. Knowledge work requires a large variety of information and sound knowledge as a raw material. (Nonaka, Takeuchi, 1995; Pine, Gilmore, 1999) It generates new knowledge as a product. Davenport's definition for knowledge work is:

"In our definition, knowledge work's primary activity is the acquisition, creation, packaging, or application of knowledge. Characterized by variety and exception rather than routine, it is performed by professional or technical workers with a high level of skill and expertise. Knowledge work processes include such activities as research and product development, advertising, education, and professional services like law, accounting, and consulting. We also include management processes such as strategy and planning." (Davenport et al., 1996, p. 54).

1.1 The Goals and Visions of Knowledge Work and Learning Arrangements

It is necessary for Europe's enterprises to be more effective and efficient in their work to be more competitive. At the same time the quality of both working life and the working conditions for the employee must not suffer, and these are just some of the aims. So, the main goal is to help to improve working conditions for knowledge and e-workers (Davenport, Beck, 2002):

- **Comprehensive job content**. The job tasks are planned, performed, checked and organised fairly independently by the employees. This makes the tasks attractive and motivating.
- **High individual demand on creativity and independent problem solving**. Knowledge-intensive services are generated and provided in an interaction with the customer or co-operation partner, solutions must be developed spontaneously and on the spot. The job content, therefore, is challenging in a positive sense.
- **Situated, context-related and informal professional learning**. Traditionally, research has focused on the transfer of knowledge from those who know to those who do not know . But most of the learning takes place as informally situated and context-related learning, closely connected to the professional work. The learning arrangement will support this new view of learning.
- **New innovative types of learning**. Some concepts are just-in-time-learning, just-in-case-learning, Instant-Qualification.
- **Work in multi-disciplinary teams of experts**. Actors with different competences, thinking patterns and interests co-operate for a limited period of time. Communication problems, interpersonal dynamics and unease, therefore, have a greater influence on the working processes.

- **High degree of fragmentation and limited possibilities of planning**. Frequently, new job tasks come suddenly and without warning. This forces the employees to reorganise their work sequences. Activities must often be interrupted and resumed later.
- **Job design for knowledge work**: In the field of knowledge-intensive service work the issue is rather to counteract potential overstrain situations – for the protection of the employees as well as for the benefit of productivity.

Knowledge work does not know any frontiers. As a result of growing international co-operation, different corporate cultures and structures are bound to meet and they have to maintain their standing in industrial relations more than ever and prove their economic performance capability.

Successful enterprises, especially SMEs, depend more on their intellectual capabilities than on their physical assets, often specialising in knowledge intensive products. Strategic information and knowledge enable SMEs to recognise chances early and increase competitiveness. The ability to manage knowledge work via situated/ informal, contextualised learning arrangements and to convert it into new innovative products and services is a crucial factor for success. Current trends in European economy are:

- Shift to more and more knowledge intensive products and services
- Company cultures are becoming related to managing knowledge
- Loss of revenue due to missing knowledge exchange between manufacturing and R&D
- Companies cannot afford drain of knowledge due to staff fluctuation
- Continuous outsourcing of manufacturing capabilities opening a wide gap regarding information and knowledge transfer between engineering and manufacturing.

Expected long-term benefits from knowledge work management include cost reduction due to greater efficiency, improved business processes and products due to better use of staff knowledge and more efficient task performance. Knowledge Management methodologies, tools and best practices will be made available to a very wide audience. The results are improvements in efficiency and reduction in costs, which will improve user competitiveness. There will be new product opportunities for developers of tools or particularly software, for a further improving economy.

The bottleneck for the progress in Knowledge Work Management is that research has traditionally focused on enhancing traditional training and transfer of knowledge from those who know to those who do not know. (Becker, Gidion, Rickert, 2002) To solve this problem, the learner has to obtain his knowledge from an individualised learning support which is geared to his individual learning needs (personal and contextual). Informal and competence conductive professional learning must be supported. This means the direction of knowledge transfer as learning is reversed to consider real needs of potential users in companies. New technologies are enablers for knowledge work management in supporting knowledge work more effective and efficient in the described way (Drucker, 1991; Hermann, 2002).

2   KNOWLEDGE PRODUCTS

Knowledge products transfer knowledge from staff and traditional media (like manuals) about "classical" products or service products into multimedia format. So, the added-value lies in supplying all different user groups with information, training and qualification needs. To understand the product at their individual working task. Because products get more and more complex and are designed in short lifecycles they have to be explained.

- Rapid change of markets requires faster introduction of new products
- Lack of developing and handling understandable products just-in-time
- Lack of target group oriented solutions in production support
- Insufficient training and qualification materials

Development of a knowledge product starts simultaneously with the production process and is integrated into the engineering processes. A knowledge product is a service offered in addition to a classic product from any branch of industry. Knowledge products get more popular because companies compete on markets that are very often turbulent. Market entrance barriers against imitators of "classic" products are often very low. Products can be adapted very fast by competitors. So, lifecycles of products are becoming shorter and companies need faster introduction of new products at every position in the supply chain. Additional companies have to face a growing complexity in products. They are getting less transparent for the users. There must be solutions to close the gap between developing and handling new products. The production of knowledge products can be described in three phases.

In the **creation phase** the concept will be defined and evaluated. Content management is the main focus. Two steps are crucial for success of appropriate content management. 1. Relevant knowledge resources must be collected, clustered and evaluated. 2. There must be a criteria-controlled selection process of relevant knowledge.

In the **engineering phase** the knowledge product is designed, produced and piloted. Content transformation and content embedding are the main focus. Four steps are relevant for success for an appropriate content transformation. 1. Content has to be (re)structured so that it fits the product. 2. Development of scenarios for each user group. 3. Knowledge has to be adapted to product requirements. 4. Usability test of embedded knowledge.

In the **management phase** the knowledge product will be delivered and positioned in the market. Content provision for training and qualification is the main focus. Training and qualification have to be provided with the product. It has to be controlled and improved continuously.

In all stages there has to be strong integrated user-producer interaction to implement customer training and qualification needs from a very early stage in product development. (Holzschuh, Karapidis, 2002; Karapidis, 2002). Using knowledge products has the following advantages:

- The product has an added-value by training and qualification sections for all user groups with a content-oriented focus.
- Training and qualification content can be used just-in-time.
- The quality of the product increases by the training and qualification sections and it is not that easy to imitate. Barriers for market entrance for competitors are higher.

3 INSTANT-QUALIFICATION

Hitherto, employees have primarily been regarded as cost factors by their employers. Nowadays, it is recognised that there is an advantage in employing highly qualified and motivated staff. The human resource is the most valuable resource of a company. Human resource management and organisational development grow together and require new concepts to make work more productive and attractive. One possible concept is to enable the employee to learn while fulfilling working tasks. This means arranging work in a way that provides learning incentives and connects knowledge management with learning by using new technologies. (Kerres, 2001)

Traditionally, research has focused on the transfer of knowledge from those who know to those who do not know. But most learning takes place as informally situated and context-related learning, closely connected to the respective activity. The Instant-Qualification supports this new view of learning. For this training form, a new communication scheme is required. (Back, Seufert, Kramhöller, 1998).

The learner cannot anticipate all possible future working tasks. With the new training concept the learner will get his information personalised to his own "position" in the workplace, contextualised in the work process and individualised to his own media competence just in time. He pools this information with his own expertise and, in this way, becomes able to fulfil specific work tasks. He gets the additional information required:

- Everywhere – at the right place,
- Anytime – in the right moment,
- Any media – intuitively usable.

Instant-Qualification makes training calculable: as it is possible to calculate a specific work task / or additional equipment for a product, it is possible to calculate training "bits" necessary to fulfil this task or to mount the equipment. Instant-Qualification provides e-learning capabilities to the individual worker directly by the working task in the actual working environment where knowledge-intensive processes take place. Instant-Qualification fits the technological developments of the future: where the surroundings of the employee is the interface, not only display, keyboard and mouse, where all senses can be used intuitively and the knowledge transfer is not only based on writing and reading; where the knowledge handling is context-based and where more than a word-based information search exists.

Instant-Qualification is a means to produce individualised/customised products with low training costs. Every specific individual working task has its specific individual training content. It is the combination of knowledge management and learning in one real-time system. Learning is integrated into a real-life working process by using new technologies to fulfil the working task effectively. The provision of content and knowledge is context-based. Both content and knowledge can be used intuitively, an instruction is not necessary. So quality of work increases because there is a high level of transparency of content and knowledge. Qualification is also calculable.

4   EXAMPLES OF APPLICATION FIELDS

4.1   Knowledge Product: Considering an Example in Thermo Technique Production

The example is the transfer from a contemporary gas furnace of a global acting company into a knowledge product to satisfy information, training and qualification needs. It shows a new multimedia training and qualification solution for all user groups to support the use of or maintain the gas furnace. In the example, the knowledge products aspects from the maintenance staff are outlined. The maintenance of a gas furnace is hosted by the company's own staff and by third parties. Maintenance staff has to know the functionality of the furnace, the different options for normal operation, the different errors that can occur and has to acquire problem solving competence. One barrier especially for maintenance is different product update releases (up to 40 a year). The challenge of a knowledge product especially for maintenance service staff lies in a rapid and effective mobile support application.

In the creation phase of the gas furnace knowledge product the first step was to identified all relevant knowledge resources. That means, not only the use of manuals or product sheets, also use of experience knowledge of alpha staff and end-users. Second, relevant content was evaluated and selected together with maintenance staff with respect to their specific work processes. The main selection criteria was work process support, not overall information of the gas furnace. Also, the realisation techniques were selected according to the needs of staff with respect of their work situations.

In the engineering phase of the knowledge product the content collected in phase one was restructured in a way that it fit the technological environment and the needs of maintenance staff to support their work. This was the main challenge and most critical for success. Together with the maintenance staff, problem solving scenarios were worked out and the suitability of content for their needs was tested iteratively by different usability tests. At the same time, first mock-ups, such as 3D furnace software trial, error trees, first modules, etc. were prototyped. After the embedding of the restructured content, the embedding of content in the technology platform started. In the final phase, the user-producer interaction was critical for success. By testing usability during the adaptation of the content to media elements, different items were tested such as navigation concepts, integration of different content modules and technical reliability.

4.2 Instant–Qualification: Considering an Example in the Lorry Production

The example is the certification of lorries at the end of a production line. It offers a perspective on new educational environments. The "surroundings" of the employee is the interface. The input is the position of the employee – physically as well as in the working process. The output is a sound instruction on what to do at the lorry at the respective place in the working process. The worker can use all senses intuitively. The learning task is not based on writing and reading. In the example the information is given to the employee as if an expert were standing by his side. It is a work process that provides context-based knowledge. In this section the employees fulfil repetitive work tasks, with differences regarding details. A requirement is to solve critical situations in a more professional way.

The initial situation for the development of a new training method was the launch of a new lorry product line. The employees of the section had to handle certification of the new production line and discontinuation of the old one at the same time. In addition, they had to handle changing instruments and tools for production control, quality control and personnel management. Within the pilot installation the following challenges were identified:

- In the work process, knowledge is more and more important. The need of specific knowledge also expands to manual work processes.
- More individualised products are demanded; therefore the work process gets more complex.
- To manage the complexity, an assistant system for the employee is helpful. But PC-based systems are often unsuitable. The required knowledge has to be integrated into the work process with a suitable media format.
- Cost pressure with production increases. It is not possible to finance expensive preparatory trainings for every product modification.

The solution to this problem was found with the concept of Instant-Qualification. With the new training system the employee receives the required information by a spoken audio signal, generated for the specific lorry model that is handled at the respective moment. This is made possible by technology of cross-media publishing. The checker follows these instructions. If there is a problem with handling a task, he can watch a reference video for that specific task. For the user, in the course of time, the training system develops from an instruction instrument into a routine operating control. The activities of the worker can be controlled by himself by using the inspection sheet. This sheet is also rendered by spatial identification and sound during checking process. While the checker follows all given instructions, the system generates a complete inspection sheet.

5   BENEFIT

The main result of the knowledge product concept is that it works! Installing a prototype of a training and qualification (knowledge) resource for the gas furnace enables workers in maintenance to improve their effectiveness. Yesterday, even alpha teams had problems to find solutions for unusual errors. Today, with access to this work process-oriented knowledge resource with anytime – anywhere accessibility, the service performance of maintenance staff has been much improved. So for the company, the gas furnace knowledge product was a milestone to improve quality and effectiveness of their staff by on-work process-oriented qualification of staff.

The advantages of Instant-Qualification are: Special working tasks can be fulfilled effectively when they occur. There is no learning content "lost". Provision of content and knowledge is context-based and just in time. Content and knowledge can be used intuitively. Instruction is not necessary. The quality of work increases, because there is a high level of transparency of content and knowledge, both can be used in an optimal way. In the end, qualification and training become calculable. It is possible to calculate training "bits" necessary for a specific work task on an individual product.

6 LITERATURE

Back, A., Seufert, S, Kramhöller, S. (1998) Technology enabled Management Education: die Lernumgebung MBE Genius im Bereich Executive Study an der Universität St.Gallen, in: io mamagement, 3, S. 36-42

Becker, T; Gidion, G; Rickert, A. (2002) Didaktische Modelle: Aufbereitung von e-Learning Content. In: Bullinger, H. J.; Weisbecker, A. (eds) Content Mangement - Digitale Bausteine einer vernetzten Welt, Stuttgart: IRB

Davenport, T.H. et al. (1996) Improving Knowledge Work Processes, in: Sloan Management Review, Vol. 37, No. 4

Davenport T.H, Beck J.C. (2002) The Attention Economy, Harvard Business School Press

Drucker, Peter (1991) The New Productivity Challenge. Harvard Business Review 6, S. 69-79

Hermann, S. (2002) Wissensarbeit erkennen und organisieren. In: Personalwirtschaft 6, 49-55.

Holzschuh, G, Karapidis, A (2002) Benchmarking organizational competencies with the dynamic e-assessment tool. In: Service Benchmarking, Ganz, W., Hofmann, J. (eds), IRB-Verlag.

Karapidis, A (2002) Putting the competence card into practice - sample methods from two fit for service clubs. in: Fit for Service report 2002 - Service Benchmarking, Ganz, W., Hofmann, J. (eds), IRB-Verlag.

Kerres, M (2001) Multimediale und telemediale Lernumgebungen, München Wien Oldenburg

Nonaka, I., Takeuchi H. (1995) the Knowledge Creating Company. How Japanes Companies Create Dynamics of Innovation, New York, Oxford

Pine B. J., Gilmore J. H.(1999) The Experience Economy, Harvard Business School Press

COMMUNITIES OF PRACTICE IN HIGHER EDUCATION

Marijke Hezemans and Magda Ritzen
Hogeschool van Utrecht, University for Professional Education and Applied Science, Utrecht, the Netherlands: CETIS, Expert Centre for Educational Innovation and Training
m.hezemans@cetis.hvu.nl and m.ritzen@cetis.hvu.nl

Abstract: Internal and external developments in higher education are leading to transformation of education being placed high on the agenda. This places a great burden on the professionalisation of the staff. In a previous article (Hezemans and Ritzen, 2004) we described the way in which professionals learn and innovate. Communities of Practice (CoPs) were introduced as a 'new' way to learn. In this article we further zoom in on the phenomenon CoP: what are CoPs, what are the success-factors and how can this way of learning and working together contribute to innovation in higher education.

Key words: Professional development, community of practice, on-the-job training, higher education, life-long learning.

1   INTRODUCTION

Academic universities and universities of professional education are currently in the midst of modernising their education to better suit the demands of present and future students. Higher education is becoming more vocational and occupationally-orientated: there is more and more interest in (learning) the application of theories and concepts. This requires a new approach in the coaching of learning processes. Demand-driven, the exchange of experiences and collaborative learning (community-learning) seem to be promising elements when giving shape to modernisation.

This paper describes a way of learning and working when giving shape to educational innovations, given our experiences within the University for Professional Education and Applied Science, Utrecht, the Netherlands. The stronger aspects of the phenomenon community-learning, that has caught on in recent years (also in the business world) are included. First a description of a Community of Practice is given. Learning in a CoP, by definition, is directly related to the personal work-environment, the 'practice' of the participant. Furthermore (learning-) benefits for both organisation and individual are sketched. In conclusion, on the basis of experiences within our university, a number of success-factors are put forward, which can promote collaborative learning and working in a community.

2   WHAT IS A COMMUNITY OF PRACTICE?

A CoP is a group of people who share a (great) interest in a certain subject or theme. They meet to exchange, develop and make explicit knowledge, which arises from questions and problems they have (Wenger, McDermott & Snyder, 2002). CoPs can be initiated by individual staff members, experts or by teams (for example, after completion of a project) and exist thanks to the 'give and take' attitude of the participants. Participants are usually active: formulating a problem or learning-question, giving feedback, asking questions, giving tips or answers, supplying literature, etc.

CoPs can differ in method of working (formal with agendas or informal), accessibility (open/closed) and size. These aspects are related to the extent to which it is important to know one another (trust) and the wish to cooperatively – as a community – apart from sharing experiences, also develop knowledge. Knowledge-development requires trust and this best grows in a small community or in a secluded part of a larger community.

CoPs are in reality their own clients, the participants adopting an open attitude towards each other, with self-organisation forming the basis of the CoPs activities. There are 'free' communities (cooperative relationships, networks, mailing lists etc.) and CoPs which adopt an official relationship with the organisation (sponsored or business-related CoPs). Members of a CoP can, with or without a request by an external body (for example the management), take on a certain job. The members of such a business-related CoP find it fun and useful to work on self-chosen/accepted assignments and by doing so make a direct contribution to the organisation. Such a contribution can in this case be considered an 'educational innovation'.

CoPs know (ideally) three stages of development: individual knowledge sharing, communally making knowledge explicit and communal creation of new knowledge (Andriessen, 2003). Some communities start directly with the ambition of communally creating new knowledge and thereby give shape to educational innovation. In other communities only after a certain passage of time will it become clear that there is a demand for knowledge-development or that sharing experiences is sufficient (for example cooperative relationships, networks, interest group, themed-site, research group, special interest group).

What distinguishes a CoP is that learning occurs in parallel on three different levels: with respect to the content, socially and with respect to the process. Along with the discovery and development of effective approaches and processes, the mutual solidarity with the community grows and the members find better ways of exchanging and combining knowledge (Bood & Coenders, 2004). CoPs differ in this regard to project-teams: in a project-team it is the (quality of the) result that matters.

CoPs are shaped by the members and the goals. There are few 'hard' golden rules that can be given. There are, however, important success-factors to be taken into account; these are elaborated upon later on.

3   COP'S AND THEIR BENEFITS

Communities ought to have a place in every learning organisation. Organisations that support learning score highly on two dimensions (Dankbaar & Oprins, 2002):

1. Organisational dimension: the extent to which the structure and culture of the organisation support and stimulate learning, for example via a clear mission through which learning-processes gain a focus, management offering solid support for methods such as coaching and reflection, being open-minded towards new ideas.
2. Personal dimension: the extent to which staff are self-confident, motivated and able to learn. This can be seen in an open-minded attitude and a willingness to learn.

If both the organisational and personal dimensions turn out to be positive then there is a safe environment within which staff can cooperatively learn from experiences and new ideas can be formed, focussed on the mission and strategy of the organisation. Whenever people come together in the context of their work with such an open-minded attitude, the organisation as a whole benefits. This benefit can be implicit (people help each other) or explicit (shape is given to innovations, new style education in such a way that others are also able to benefit).

In the table below the benefits for the individual and educational organisation are sketched. Examples of CoPs in the University for Professional Education and Applied Science, Utrecht, the Netherlands illustrate these benefits.

Table 1: Benefits of CoPs for individuals and educational organisations

	Short term benefits	Long term benefits
	Optimisation of the learning-environment	*Educational innovation*
Benefits for the organisation	• Environment conductive to solving problems • Multiple points of view with regard to the solution of a problem • Coordination, standardisation and synergy between teams • Sources for implementation-strategies In the CoP ICT and project-work professionals make explicit the aspects that are important in relation to collaboration in projects by students in an ICT rich environment. The results are made accessible to other faculties.	• Retaining talent • Capacity for knowledge-development projects • Capacity for developing new strategies • Raising visibility of undiscovered talent A faculty of our university wants to introduce a portfolio in 2003. The CoP student-mentorship and portfolio is asked to make a contribution.
	Raising the quality of work	*Innovation by the profession*
Benefits for community member	• Help with challenges • Access to a source of expertise • Taking enjoyment from working with colleagues • The feeling of belonging to something Professionals in the CoP Instruments of our university give each other feedback on modules that they have developed in a digital environment.	• Platform for dissemination of skills and expertise • Fortification of professional reputation • Fortification of professional identity In the CoP professional coaches develop a coaching and assessment model, which they also make known to colleagues.

4   SUCCESS-FACTORS COMMUNITIES OF PRACTICE

Within our university there is gradual recognition of the importance of communities in educational innovation: managers approach communities for advice on policy. Staff functioning in multidisciplinary teams seek out communities, depending on their learning needs. They find it helpful to exchange experiences and develop new solutions with colleagues who share their learning needs. The case below will help illustrate the way in which community-forming is stimulated within the university (HvU).

4.1 HvU-Case: Development of Professionals and Innovation

- **Background.** In March 2003 a conference about innovating education and ICT was held for the second time. At the conference staff and students from various faculties showed the different uses they make of ICT. During the conference everyone is very enthusiastic and full of good intentions to meet again after the conference. Usually this does not happen. For this reason the conference commission decided to follow-up the conference with community of practice (CoPs) gatherings.
- **Initiative.** The conference was arranged according to eight themes. Each theme was prepared and chaired by a chairperson. As part of the preparation the chairperson would gauge the level of interest the presenters had in a CoP on 'their' theme. During the conference sessions it was announced that the sessions would be followed-up by CoPs, and the planned kick-off dates were given. Additional questions were collected and would be used as input for the CoP. On the basis of registrations it was decided that four of the eight CoPs would go ahead. These were the four CoPs that were most clearly related to education: 'Testing and Assessment', 'Student coaching and Portfolio', 'Instruments in Education' and 'ICT and project-based education'. CoPs such as 'wireless' and 'quality assurance' were dropped due to lack of interest.
- **Facilitation.** Measures needed to support the CoPs could be realised within the framework of the Information Policy Plan: the theme chair people (content moderators) and 'pullers' (organisers and CoP-experts) could claim a part of their hours. Catering and room hire were payed for by the 'hosts'. IT-support by Lotus Quickplace was – till 1st January 2004 – made possible by the IT department. The chair people and 'pullers' met in the interim periods to exchange experiences and to look at whether the current arrangement of CoPs (domains) was still relevant.
- **Way of working.** Most of the CoPs have approximately eight participants and meet regularly (once every six weeks). Two CoPs had a communal question right from the start (e.g. how can a project-based approach to problems / assignments be best supported by ICT), one CoP decided to let their agenda be composed of participants' questions and another CoP had such a diverse set of questions that progress was severely hampered and eventually only 7 out of 15 participants

remained. This CoP did manage to book communal results, but there is little remaining drive.

- **Benefits**. The participants (staff members) continue to find it worthwhile to attend CoP meetings. They meet, and can consult, people who are working on the same things they are. In all the CoPs problems are discussed and experiences are exchanged, in a few CoPs an attempt is made to make explicit knowledge and ideas (e.g. what are the characteristics of project-based teaching) so that others may also benefit. In this way the CoPs play an important role in the professionalisation of participants and satisfy important success criteria: demand-driven, to the point and on the job.

- **The future**. The evaluation of the CoPs has now taken place. The participants indicate that they found the CoPs beneficial for their work, but that they could be even more beneficial through measures such as: rotating chairpersonship, more accurate description of the domain, merging of CoPs, expansion of participancy through organisation-wide announcement of meetings (promotion), more focus in the agenda, more attention for formulating joint results. The management is also satisfied by the early results and has signalled their intention to reserve money for the expansion and support of the experiment. This support is constituted by a web-site where materials are (made) available which facilitate the CoP process and virtual rooms which can be reserved by the CoPs. Alongside these measures there are also plans for a coordinating CoP which will advise on the CoP process.

4.2 Success-Factors

On the basis of the experiences within our university the following success-factors have been identified (Wenger, 2002, Römgens, 2001 and McDermott, 2001):

- Organise preliminary activities, for example seminars or congresses, so that professionals have the opportunity to meet one another and indicate their communal interest in certain themes or subjects.

- Start with a small group of people who already meet on a regular basis in relation to work problems or themes (existing informal groups). A small core group increases the chance of mutual trust, and an open atmosphere is an important criterion for sharing knowledge.

- Appoint a coordinator of the CoP. This role is very important. He/she talks regularly to various members and makes contact with potential members. In this way the coordinator always has a good picture of what the biting issues are which need to be tackled in order to keep the community alive.

- Give the CoPs a place in the organisation, for example by formalising their role in a policy or professionalisation plan with matching budget.
- Organise a coordinating community, which has and develops expertise in relation to the import of CoPs for organisation and individual, knowledge management and the coaching of communities. This is especially of import in the start-up phase: the coordinating community is knowledgeable about the world of communities, can gear activities to one another and is up to speed on the activities and themes within the various CoPs in the organisation. The community combines (external) expertise with (internal) lessons learned and uses these to develop knowledge about creating and maintaining successful CoPs.
- Raise the question of the benefit of the CoP regularly within the CoP itself: What benefits does the CoP yield as a community/group?; How does the CoP benefit the organisation? The value can be visible (in documents) or invisible (trust and ability to innovate, feeling of belonging, spirit of enquiry). A CoP that doesn't yield any benefits for the respective individuals will not take-off.
- Try to link the community in to the work situation and work related problems the participants have. Sharing a communal issue ensures that it is fruitful to work on problems together (on the job and to the point).

CoPs are for and by the participants and originate in a bottom-up manner. But just like a 'wild' garden cultivation, care and attention have a positive influence. The way in which the organisation carries out this cultivation can vary greatly and depends on the type of, and innovative character of, said organisation. Certain organisations strongly steer towards the form and set-up of a CoP, for example a company such as Unilever that needs new products in order to survive is therefore greatly benefited by 'innovative' communities. But there are also organisations that only create the minimally required preconditions and master the art of working, learning and innovating collaboratively as they go: educational organisations seem to be best catered for by bottom-up initiatives and top-down facilitation (Beijering et al. 2002).

5   CONCLUSION: COPS AS SEEN BY PROFESSIONAL AND ORGANISATION

Above we provided a description of what Communities of Practice are, what benefits they bring for individual and educational organisation and which success-factors can improve learning and working in communities. Communities of Practice can play an important role in the exchange, development and making explicit of new knowledge. A CoP can be a place where the innovative energy of an organisation is bundled: communities then perform an important role in adding value to the process of making the strategic policy operational and creating new and innovative solutions. To make this possible the organisation must accommodate the formation of CoPs: it must have faith in the professionalism of its staff; a culture which creates challenges and chances, but also places demands on the professional development of its employees, including management (van Emst, 1999).

An organisation that wants to grow into a learning organisation would be wise to stimulate and cherish the development of CoPs (from community-like initiatives to innovative CoPs).

The experiences of our university show that Communities of Practice actually are important in the exchange, development and making explicit of new knowledge. HvU-communities perform more and more an important role in adding value to the process of making the strategic policy operational and creating new and innovative solutions. Our communities offer staff a way to both work and learn whilst also shaping educational innovation.

6   REFERENCES

Andriessen, J.H.E. (2003). Kennisnetwerken. In: *Opleiding & Ontwikkeling*, 3, pp. *27-31.*

Beijering, J. e.a. (2002). Eindrapport Virtueel Kenniscentrum en expertisenetwerken: opbouw en verspreiding van expertise. Digitale Universiteit, http://www.digiuni.nl

Bood, R. en M. Coenders (2004). *Communities of Practice*. Utrecht: LEMMA BV.

Dankbaar, M.E.W. en E.A.P.B. Oprins. (2002). Kennismanagement: ervaringskennis delen in werkomgevingen *Opleiding & Ontwikkeling,* 10, pp. 13-18.

Hezemans, M.G.O., & M.M.J. Ritzen, (2004)., The teacher: from a responsible student's point-of-view. In: P. Nicholson, B. Thomson, M. Ruohenen & J. Multisilta (eds), *Etraining practices for professional organisations*. Boston/Dordrecht/London: Kluwer Academic Publishers.

McDermott, R. (2001). *Knowing in Community: 10 Critical Success Factors in Building Communities of Practice,* http://www.co-I-l.com/coil/knowledge-garden/cop/knowing.shtml

Römgens, B. (2002*), Instrumenten voor Communities*, CIBIT, interne publicatie.

Shaffer, R., Koehn, D., *Creating Communities of Practice – The Knowledge Bridge Builders*, juni 2002, http://www.rgsinc.com/publications/pdf/white_papers/Communities_of_Practice.pdf

van Emst, Alex (1999). Professionele cultuur in onderwijsorganisaties, Utrecht: APS/Edukern

Wenger, E. McDermott, R. en Snyder, W.M. (2002). Cultivating CoP's, A guide to managing knowledge. Harvard Business School press, Boston Massachusetts.

Wenger, E., (2001) Supporting communities of practice, a survey of community-oriented technologies, versie 1.3, Shareware, www.ewenger.com/tech

KNOWLEDGE ACQUISITION IN SMALL BUSINESSES
Capacity Building for the Use of IS

Stephen Burgess and Carmine Sellitto
School of Information Systems, Victoria University, Melbourne, Australia

Stephen.Burgess@vu.edu.au and Carmine.Sellitto@vu.edu.au

Abstract: This paper reports a series of research studies that demonstrate how some small businesses have engaged in the task of capacity building to enhance the use of information systems within their business. What we found in each of these situations is reliance by small businesses on the formal and informal networks that they have set up to support their capacity building. A common thread amongst each of these situations is the entrepreneurial nature of the small businesses involved. In all of the cases the business were looking for ways to expand their own markets.

Key words: Capacity building, small business, information systems.

1   INTRODUCTION

Capacity building goes beyond the notion of using training to build business know-how. From a small business viewpoint it is about the use of informal and formal networks to help overcome the barriers they face in adding to their understanding. For purposes of this paper that understanding is related to how best to build capacity to know how to effectively employ their information systems. This paper examines, through a series of research studies conducted by the authors, how some small businesses have tackled the task of capacity building to enhance the use of IT.

1.1   Definitions

Small Business - When studying the use of Information Systems (IS) in small business, the definitions used to describe 'small business' varies across international boundaries. This range can make it extremely difficult for researchers to 'match up' different small business studies. A 2003 study by worldwide members of the Information Resources Management Association Special Research Cluster on Small Business and Information Technology (Burgess, 2003) found that definitions of 'small business' ranged from less than 20, 50 and 100 employees (with some definitions including requirements for annual turnover and asset levels). In this study we will treat any organisation with 20 employees or less as a small business.

Information Systems – comprise hardware, software, people, procedures and data, integrated with the objective of collecting, storing, processing, transmitting and displaying information (Tatnall et al, 2002). Such a system does not require use of a computer.

Capacity Building – There are many definitions of capacity building. The Australian Government (2004) suggests that it is about increasing the abilities and resources of individuals, organisations and communities to manage change. Capacity building can occur at an organisational, local, regional and even national level. The important thing is that it is about building knowledge and understanding through avenues such as training and social networks: in this case for the use of IS within small businesses.

2   BACKGROUND

In 1994, a study of 358 small business in New Zealand (Igbaria et al, 1997) suggested that many small businesses cannot afford to employ specialised IS staff. The authors concluded that potential system users should be made aware of its functionality, and that this can occur through internal training, management support and external support. Although the computing environment has altered since the study the premises still appear to be applicable today. In fact, the literature contains what is now a fairly accepted list of 'barriers' to the successful implementation of IS in small businesses. These barriers typically include (Management Services, 1997; Igbaria et al, 1997; Pollard and Hayne, 1998; McDonagh and Prothero, 2000):

- The cost of IS.
- Lack of time to devote to the implementation and maintenance of IS.
- A lack of IS knowledge combined with difficulty in finding useful, impartial advice.
- Lack of use of external consultants and vendors.

- Short-range management perspectives.
- A lack of understanding of the benefits that IS can provide, and how to measure those benefits.
- A lack of formal planning or control procedures.

These barriers form a dangerous combination of factors that can affect the ability of a small business to add to its knowledge base of how to use information systems effectively. A lack of formal IS training usually leads to a lack of formal IS knowledge. Managers are reluctant to send employees on training courses as they either cost too much or will take employees away from their 'real' work. There is a mistrust of external consultants, either because they charge too much or because it is felt that they do not fully understand the business. There is also a lack of understanding within the business of the strategic benefits that IS can provide (Burgess, 2002).

One technique that small businesses often adopt to overcome these barriers to capacity building is to become part of informal or formal support networks. These can support relationships and allow swapping of ideas or useful contacts (Fink, 2002) or can just involve use of family members or friends for advice (Burgess, 2002). The latter, of course, can be an approach fraught with danger; depending on credentials of the person offering advice.

3   SMALL BUSINESS STUDIES

The next section describes the nature of capacity building adopted by different types of small businesses in a number of recent studies by the authors. For each study a short description of the research method will be provided, followed by a description of how the study participants faced the challenge of capacity building for their IS.

3.1   Australian Bed and Breakfasts (2003)

This study examined 10 instances of Website adoption by small Bed and Breakfast accommodation providers operating in the Bendigo region: a rural area in Victoria, Australia (Burgess, Sellitto and Wenn, forthcoming). Bendigo was selected because early projects on awareness/adoption of electronic commerce technologies were undertaken in this locality – research that actively involved some of the region's businesses. The subsequent formation of the E-Commerce Association of Central Victoria (EComCV) after these early formative studies has been instrumental in alerting local businesses to lessons learned and impacts of adopting Internet technologies (EcomCV, 2004). Hence, it was felt that this group of small accommodation providers, having been exposed to a proactive environment promoted by and associated with EComCV, would most likely be relatively early adopters of a business Website. Moreover, it was assumed that they would be advanced along the technology learning curve when it came to using the Internet and implementing their Website. From a Rogers (1995) diffusion of innovation perspective this group of early adopters would have utilised the Internet for competitive advantage and provided examples and leadership for others to look to. As such we expected that these small businesses would be a little more 'IT savvy' than comparative ones elsewhere.

In all cases the individual business owners were the initiators behind establishing their website – the main motivation for establishing the Site was to provide relevant information content for clients. Two of the businesses had adopted a website in the preceding twelve months, six businesses within one to two years and two businesses had set up a website between three to five years ago. All businesses were using email and a website as part of their business communication and promotions strategy.

From a capacity building viewpoint we were interested in determining how businesses built their knowledge of how to establish their websites. All the businesses relied on some type of advice or information when setting up their websites. This came from consultants (70% - mainly Bendigo Web Central, see below), friends (40%), magazines and newspapers (20%), relatives (10%) and business associates (10%). This is consistent with the idea of using informal networks as a support base for building capacity. Consultants were mainly used for setup and maintenance of websites and it was observed by a number of respondents that it was important that the *business retain control of content.* There were quite a few instances where the website took longer to set up than the business anticipated and only 60% of the providers actually looked into the cost of the website before they made the decision to implement it! Comments in relation to setup included:

- The cost blew out beyond expectation. We had no idea how demanding it would be. We went for the middle quote.
- We didn't ask about cost. We only got a quote for pictures and text, not the development.
- We had problems with unwelcome marketing approaches.
- We just wore the cost because it had to be done. We negotiated and took best price although picture transfer was messy.
- We already had photos so saved on cost.

Some of these comments indicated that the businesses felt that they had made mistakes when trying to determine the cost of the websites and the process of setting them up, even though we had anticipated that they may have 'advanced' knowledge compared to other small businesses. There were indications that they would do things differently if they had their time over again, although for most it was considered a good learning experience.

3.2   Australian regional wineries (2003-2004)

This study investigated the regional relationship between wineries that came together to implement a small winery based portal website to collectively promote their businesses and foster wine tourism. The site was identified from a broader study (Sellitto and Martin 2001; Sellitto 2002; Martin and Sellitto 2003; Martin and Sellitto 2003a) that examined Internet adoption by Australian wineries. This site was identified as an important conduit that allowed a group of regionally based Australian wineries to collectively use Internet technology to facilitate information dissemination.

The website was aimed at enhancing wine sales, marketing wineries as tourism entities and fostering an environment for dissemination of electronic information. Rheinegold (1993) describes virtual, or Web, communities as they are sometimes called. Today this concept takes various forms including newsgroups, chatrooms and Web sites on which they are accessed (Dyson 1997; Schneider and Perry 2001). Web communities, as well as fostering social interaction, are able to assist companies, customers and suppliers to transact, collaborate and interact in ways that benefit all (Schneider 2002). Thus, the wine portal can be considered a representation of a virtual or Web community with various functional features. The group had obviously been in communication beforehand, and with help from one of their members being a 'champion' of the collaboration they started the portal.

It has been suggested that Internet technologies can be used by regional groups to create a global identity by establishing themselves as virtual business entities that can involve sharing of resources and services (Fitzsimons and Styles 2001). As a result of the wineries using the Internet to form a virtual community as well as being able to achieve consumer sales, they have also enhanced communication between members, allowing a type of *corporate culture* to develop. Thus the implicit success of the site appears to be due to preparedness of participants to collaborate and cooperate through both formal and informal networks – which is represented by a cohesive and integrated presence on the site. The success of the site is even more significant when one considers that members are usually competitors – each selling their own types of wine products.

In this instance, a major part of capacity building for each business has been centred on online collaboration. In fact this has even enhanced informal networks that exist between businesses. It has been the basis for knowledge sharing, not only in relation to the website, but to marketing strategies associated with regional tourism and engaging with other businesses.

3.3   Small Import/Export businesses (2002)

A study of successful individual small and micro firms located in six Asia Pacific Economic Co-operation (APEC) member economies was commissioned in early 2002 by the Asia Pacific Economic Cooperation to provide an overview of the contribution of small and medium enterprises (SMEs) to trade in the APEC region (Breen et al, 2004). The study 'Small Business and Trade in APEC' was tendered for and conducted by the Small Business Research Unit at Victoria University and was coordinated through the Australia Department of Foreign Affairs and Trade (DFAT)[i]. The purpose was to promote discussion and understanding of barriers, enablers and needs of SMEs involved in intra-regional trade and investment. This was particularly in relation to technological, financial and regulatory factors. The study involved in-depth interviews with 6 businesses – 3 micro businesses (from Australia, USA and Mexico) and 3 small businesses (from Philippines, Japan and Malaysia). The number of cases was determined by APEC.

As a general rule the smaller a business in terms of number of staff then the less likely it will have access to a broad range of skills and expertise. Frequently operators have to provide the range of skills as best they can or access the skills and expertise from a range of sources, at minimum cost. Family members can often be one source of that low-cost expertise, while in some instances governments can provide specific support. The participants in these businesses, which were all viewed as being 'successful' by nature of their longevity, took advantage of a number of family members and friends for their IS advice. Others did look to other areas, such as government for support. Interestingly, each of the business owners indicated that they would benefit from IS related training, recognising a lack of such expertise within the business. This was the case even with two businesses that felt they had IS skilled staff – they both indicated that if the 'expert' left or fell sick there would be problems as there was no-one with 'backup' skills. Thus – the capacity was there, but was not spread widely enough through the business. One important difference that came out of this study was the entrepreneurial nature of the owners. This seemed to be linked with a real recognition of a need to build capacity within their businesses, (and not just in the IS field).

4   DISCUSSION

What we find in each of these (quite distinct) situations is reliance by small businesses on formal and informal networks that they have set up to support their capacity building. In the case of the bed and breakfasts much of their IS support came from consultants and friends. In the winery case they already had an informal network which was further strengthened by the online collaborative venture. The APEC small businesses all realized the importance of training and were looking to family members and friends and government for support. The one common thread amongst each of these situations is the entrepreneurial nature of the small businesses involved. In each case the businesses were looking for ways to expand their own markets. It is interesting that the only group that really relied on formal support for capacity were the Bed and Breakfasts. Remember that we had commented that these were in an area that had been supported by EComCV.

5   CONCLUSION

The task of capacity building in small business is not an easy one. This paper has shown three research studies into the use of IS by small businesses and discussed the various ways in which they approached their capacity building. Although each of the situations involved small businesses that seemed to be entrepreneurial in nature and keen to grow, there was still quite a healthy reliance on the informal networks that had been a traditional source of knowledge (but perhaps not skilled in the use of IS) as the major source of advice for the use of IS within their businesses.

6   REFERENCES

Australian Government, (2004) *Capacity Building for Innovation in rural Industries*, Rural Industries Research and Development Organisation, Canberra, http://www.rirdc.gov.au/capacitybuilding/, [27/8/04].

Breen, John; Bergin-Seers, Susan; Burgess, Stephen; Campbell, Gordon; Mahmood, Muhammad and Sims, Robert, (2004). 'Formulating Policy on E-Commerce and Trade for SMEs in the Asia Pacific Region: An APEC study', in Al-Qirim, Nabeel and Corbitt, Brian J (eds), *eBusiness, eGovernment & Small and Medium Enterprises*, Idea Group Publishing, Pennsylvania, USA, pp.134-155

Burgess, Stephen, (2003). *A Definition of Small Business*, Information Resources Management Association Special Research Cluster on Small Business and Information Technology, www.businessandlaw.vu.edu.au/sbirit/research_issue_Results.htm , [29/704]

Burgess, Stephen, (2002). 'Information Technology in Small Business: Issues and Challenges' in Burgess, Stephen (Ed.), *Information Technology and Small Business: Issues and Challenges*, Idea Group Publishing, Pennsylvania, USA.

Burgess Stephen; Sellitto Carmine, and Andrew Wenn, (2005, forthcoming). 'The perceived value of Web site features: An exploratory study of small regional accommodation providers in Australia', International Journal of Mgt & Entrepreneurship Development.

Dyson E. (1997). *Release 2.0: A Design for Living in the Digital Age*, New York: Broadway.

EcomCV, (2004), *E-Commerce Association of Central Victoria*, (EComCV): About Us [Online]: http://www.ecomcv.asn.au/aboutus.html, [15/1/2004].

Fink, (2002) 'Building the Professional Services E-Practice', in Burgess, Stephen (Ed.), 2002, *Information Technology and Small Business: Issues and Challenges,* Idea Group Publishing, Pennsylvania, USA.

Fitzsimons C. and Styles K. (2001). *Using ICT to Develop Sustainable Business Clusters in Gippsland.* Proceedings of the 5th Information Technology in Regional Areas Conference. 5-7 September 2001. Rockhampton. Central Queensland University. pp. 321-325.

Igbaria, Magid; Zinatelli, Nancy; Cragg, Paul and Cavaye, Angele L. M., (1997) 'Personal Computing Acceptance Factors in Small Firms: A Structural Equation Model', *MIS Quarterly*, Minneapolis, Vol.21, Iss.3, September, pp.279-305.

McDonagh, Pierre and Prothero, Andrea, (2000) 'Euroclicking and the Irish SME: Prepared for E-Commerce and the Single Currency?', *Irish Marketing Review*, Dublin, Vol.13, Iss.1, pp.21-33.

Management Services, (1997) 'Computers Fail to Click with Small Businesses', Enfield, Vol.41, Iss.9, p.4

Martin B. and Sellitto C. (2003). *Investigating a Knowledge Dimension in eBusiness models within the Victorian Wine Industry.* Paper presented at the 3rd International eBusiness Conference. January 3-7, 2003. Sheraton Towers, Melbourne. University of Ballarat.

Martin B. and Sellitto C. (2003a). *Wineries as Knowledge-Intensive Enterprises: Internet Adoption in the Australian and Victorian Wine Clusters.* Proceedings of 4th European Conference on Knowledge Management. Oxford University, UK. pp. 645-656.

Pollard, Carol E. and Hayne, Stephen C, (1998). 'The Changing Faces of Information Systems Issues in Small Firms', *International Small Business Journal*, London, Vol.16, Iss.3, April-June, pp.70-87

Rheingold H. (1993). *The Virtual Community: Homesteading on the Electronic Frontier,* New York: Harper Collins.

Rogers E., (1995). *Diffusion of Innovations,* 4th edition. New York: Free Press.

Schneider G. P. (2002). *Electronic Commerce,* 3rd edition. Boston, MA: Course Technology.

Schneider G. P. and Perry J. T. (2001). *Electronic Commerce,* Boston, MA: Course Tech.

Sellitto C. (2002). *Perceived Benefits of Internet Adoption: A Study of Regional Wineries.* Proceedings, 4th Information Technology in Regional Areas Conference. Rockhampton. Central Queensland University. pp. 319-328.

Sellitto C. and Martin W. (2001). *Diffusion of the Internet in the Victorian Wine Cluster: Wineries are the Laggards.* Proceedings of the 4th Western Australian Workshop on Information Systems Research (WAWISR) on CD-ROM. 26 December 2001. Perth, Australia. University of Western Australia. pp. 1-13.

Tatnall, Arthur; Davey, William; Burgess, Stephen; Wenn, Andrew and Davison, Alistair, (2002), *Management Information Systems: Concepts, Issues, Tools and Applications,* 3rd. Edition, Data Publishing, Melbourne.

---

[i]   The final report of the study, **Small Business and Trade in APEC,** is available from the Australian Department of Foreign Affairs and trade (www.dfat.gov.au).

EXPERIENCES AND PRACTICES IN MODELING DISTANCE LEARNING CURRICULA FOR CAPILLARY APPROACHES AND LIMITED ICT RESOURCE SCENARIOS

Martins, Joberto S. B. and Quadros, Teresinha
University Salvador – UNIFACS Salvador – Bahia - Brazil
joberto@unifacs.br ; t.quadros@terra.com.br www.unifacs.br

Abstract: Actual curricula design and development for distance learning courses have been challenged by constraints such as the absence of conventional face-to-face (F2F) (Keeton 2002) class communication, the required student's autonomy and the need for ergonometric interfaces, just to mention some. In general, both the extensive use and the focused application of ICT components (Felder & Silverman 1988) may provide some significant contributions to overcome these drawbacks. The objective of this paper is to describe a distance learning curricula design and implementation strategy considering a capillary approach with limited ICT resources. It highlights the approaches undertaken and the obtained results. The implementation scenario is an undergraduate level course for active high-school teachers requiring certification for improving their pedagogical methods. The numbers, methods and implementation aspects presented are based on a real-life ongoing course.

Key words: Curricula design and structure, ICT resources and constraints, capillary approach.

1   CURRICULA IMPLEMENTATION CHALLENGES – THE SCENARIO

Actual curricula design and development for distance learning courses have been challenged by constraints such as the absence of conventional face-to-face (F2F) (Keeton 2002) class communication, the required student's autonomy, active participation and highly interactive engagement, the need for ergonometric interfaces, just to mention some. In this context, both the extensive use and the focused application of ICT components (Felder & Silverman 1988) may provide some significant contributions to overcome these drawbacks, typically existent in distance learning conventional approaches.

The real-life learning challenge effectively discussed in this paper consists in providing high quality education services and finding scalable solutions constrained by ICT limited resources (limited bandwidth telecommunication resources, limitation in computer capacity, others). This scenario will typically happen when a capillary approach, not restricted to main urban centers and densely digitalized areas, is considered. Beyond that, lecturers and students profiles are such that, for instance, familiarity with computers and the cognitive learning paradigm are not completely developed and, as such, have to be packaged in the course methodology itself.

The targets are undergraduate level courses in diverse knowledge areas. The basic approach discussed is focused on modeling curricula development by using interdisciplinary learning (Martins et al. 2002) and fully computer-assisted pedagogical, collaborative and self-learning approaches.

2   THE DESIGN PRINCIPLES

The design principles adopted in the curricula design are the *capillary* approach, the adoption of a *web-centric solution* as the basis for the mediating process and a *highly flexible implementation* approach which corresponds to an intensive use of multimedia, ICT resources and multiple content formats.

The capillary approach is intended to provide higher education services in rural areas, underdeveloped regions and other unassisted remote locations where they are scarce and have limited options. By adopting this principle, attendees do not need to move away form their home locations and, beyond that, they may keep their activities while following courses.

The web-centric option is due to its intrinsic characteristics such as, a high capillary and modern solution with worldwide presence, its ability to ergonomically integrated different media types which are fundamental for the distance learning process and, finally, its support to human interaction and mediation processes. These characteristics are valuable assets to overcome the classical problems found in distance learning courses such as student isolation and the difficulties found in providing a more personalized follow-up.

Delivering contents in multiple medias and multiple formats is one of the most important design principles followed by the curricula modeling process

(Figure 1). In effect, the flexible implementation approach is such that courses are created with multiple media formats and intensive use of ICT resources. In addition, the course logistics are adapted to the socio-economics of the target public and region and, as such, the technological infrastructure available has to be taken in account.

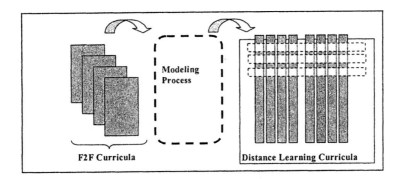

Figure 1. Distance learning curricula adaptation process

In summary, the discussed approach to develop distance learning curricula needs an adaptation process that is dependable on ICT resources available, considers the capillary approach and is dependable of curricula content specific constraints. Additional guidelines for curricula development are provided by the pedagogical model adopted.

3 THE PEDAGOGICAL MODEL

The pedagogical model adopted for curricula development preserves the design principles discussed and, in addition, is based on principles such as autonomous cognitive learning process, interdisciplinary methods, collaborative and meaningful learning.

By adopting an autonomous cognitive learning process as one of the pedagogical model principles, the curricula, through its pedagogical practices, stimulates the student autonomy and contributes to overcoming the isolation typically found in distance learning courses. The systematic research activities realized using networked communication tools, the huge amount of information available with instant access and the friendly web interfaces contribute to the development of the autonomous cognitive posture of learners.

The interdisciplinary learning method is achieved by having disciplines grouped in knowledge areas and having a curricula managing system that articulates knowledge when executing the disciplines.

Collaborative learning means to explore systematically within curricula the interaction among students by using the virtual tools provided by information and communication technologies. The web-centric approach is particularly helpful for this purpose. By this principle, experience sharing is instigated, the collaborative and interdisciplinary work is stimulated and the learners' autonomy is developed.

Meaningful learning is a pedagogical principle in which applied learning materials use learner's experience as an asset. The daily experience of each one is used as the point of departure and continuous reference for the learning process.

The proposed pedagogical model defines a curricula structure implementation (Figure 2) based on "learning core unities" which are grouped in "thematic matrixes" and distributed in temporal units called "flows". The "disciplines/ modules" respond to the learning process itself and are grouped in cores units, thematic matrixes and flows (temporal arrangement). They correspond to the skills and competences to be developed during each step of the construction process leading to the professional profile expected.

The pedagogical model establishes that all curricula have an "integration matrix" in its structure that has its focus on practices and evaluation. As the name suggests, its objective is to integrate the course contents developed by the disciplines in a flow by using an interdisciplinary approach and the student's experience as reference. The integration matrix is the effective way to assure the pedagogical principles defined (interdisciplinary, collaborative work, autonomy and meaningful learning).

In summary, the adopted design model is based on a *collaborative pedagogy*, reinforces the idea of *actors cooperation* in the pedagogical process, considers the *knowledge exchange* as part of the learning process and *integrates the lecturer* in the learning community (Vygotsky 1984) (Wallon 1982).

Matrix 1	Matrix 2	Matrix 3	Matrix 4	Matrix 5	Flow	
Module 1	Module 1		Module 1	Module 1	Flow 1	Core 1
Module 2	Module 2		Module 2	Module 2	Flow 2	
Module 3	Module 3	Module 1		Module 3	Flow 3	Core 2
	Module 4	Module 2		Module 4	Flow 4	
		Module 3	Module 3	Module 5	Flow 5	
		Module 4	Module 4	Module 6	Flow 6	Core 3
				Module 7	Flow 7	

Figure 2. Curricula structure

The curricula structure by itself does not guarantees the principles proposed for the pedagogical model and effectively corresponds to an implementation plan and reference for the pedagogical practices. The curricula execution has to guarantee consistent practices such as professors developing interdisciplinary contents, tutors being able to act as mediators and, in addition, the adequacy of the technological infra-structure should support the necessary interactive level.

4 PRACTICES, METHODS AND EXPERIENCE

The discussed design principles, pedagogical model and curricula development are in practice intended to support real-life, limited ICT resources and high capillary scenarios. In effect, a broad coverage (Portuguese speaking countries like Brazil, Portugal, Angola, others) and a significant numbers of students (thousands) are the course targets. A pilot project as described is the experimental basis for analysis and discussion:

- Undergraduate course: Portuguese and English Language (2.940 hours – 03 years).
- Course coverage: state of Bahia (Brazil), 198 provinces (about 2.000 Km range), most of them with very difficult terrestrial access and very limited ICT and computational facilities.
- Attendees profile: 500 students, most of them beyond 40 years, active lectures on various teaching subjects, having very limited computer abilities.

4.1   ICT media choices and infra-structure

The course implementation scenarios are restrictive with respect to ICT resources and have to be considered case-by-case by indicating the media options and compatible procedures. The proposal is to have a web-centric approach coupled with a rich set of ICT media facilities that could be adapted to real-life and capillary restrictive scenarios.

The basic media choices and ICT facilities adopted for all curricula to be implemented are:

- ❑ The platform: TELEDUC, an open-source web-based distance learning supporting tool;
- ❑ Synchronous tools: chat, video-conferencing (dedicated network), web-based conferencing and free callback service (0800);
- ❑ Asynchronous tools: forum, electronic mail, broadcasting conferences, mail (postal service) and faxing;
- ❑ Contents distribution options: web distribution, printed material, multimedia CD (web content copy for off-line access).

The platform has characteristics and features such as security mechanisms, student follow-up tools, interactive mechanisms, ergonomic interfaces, and intuitive navigation, among others.

The synchronous and asynchronous tools should support the interactive processes in different circumstances in terms of the available ICT resources and student's time availability to follow the course. Asynchronous tools are the predominant option for most of the implemented courses (90% asynchronous – 10% synchronous).

The complete set of media options and communication facilities considered for all courses are indicated in Figure 3.

4.2   Capillary and ICT Constraints Mappings

The constraints applied to the basic implementation setup (set of medias and communication facilities) are related respectively to the student profile, the network access facilities and the computer equipment available.

An attendee is considered to be qualified to follow a distance learning course if he has minimum computer handling abilities (basic informatics concepts: commands, peripheral manipulation, others) and, beyond that, he has minimum understanding of the autonomy, self-learning and other characteristics necessary to undertake a distance learning program.

A minimalist acceptable condition for network access corresponds to having either permanent or dialup access independently of their quality. Dialup access is low-speed and, as such, is a permanent restriction for multimedia and lucidity facilities incorporated in web pages (course material). Additionally, connectivity may be "occasional". Connectivity is considered occasional when it represents a financial cost for the attendee (access is paid and attendees income is predominantly low-level) and/or the connection has very low quality. In effect, strong ICT restrictions do exist for the majority of cities and provinces covered by the course. As an example, dialup connections are typically 33Kbps and the "high-speed" ADSL connections (256Kbps) availability is rare.

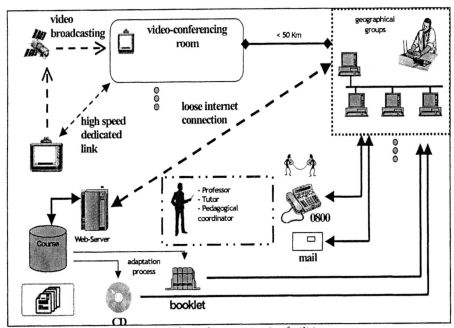

Figure 3.Media and communication facilities

Minimum quality computers are those available and capable of running multimedia applications. Unavailability condition corresponds to a situation where the computer is effectively unavailable and/or has unacceptable low-performance.

As such, the potentially available mappings that have to be considered in a large-scale implementation are as follows:

1. Case "A" corresponds to a potentially qualified distance learning scenario. There is a minimum quality computer, the network access is available and attendees profiles are satisfactory. We have then a potential online student.
2. Case "B" corresponds to a less qualified attendee situation where computers are available but there is no satisfactory network access

and/or attendees do not have the necessary abilities to follow a distance learning program.

3. Case "C" is a worst-case situation where computers are unavailable and, beyond that, combinations of network access and attendees abilities unavailability are present.

The target is to promote distance learning in all the above scenarios and provide the practices methods, adaptation approaches and strategies in order to achieve a high quality course.

4.3   Practice Methods and Pedagogical Strategies

The described constraints mappings "B" and "C" are the focus of the practices methods and pedagogical strategies defined to deal with the challenges resulting from a capillary approach and they do represent a real-life implementation issue.

The main guidelines and practices followed in order to overcome the restrictions imposed are:

- ❑ To provide attendees with computer skills training and introduce distance learning working principles as part of the course package itself;
- ❑ To always adopt a consistent and integrated set of flexible multiple media content distribution (course material);
- ❑ To guarantee multiple redundant interaction channels between the professor, tutors and students.

The reason to include the teaching of computer skills (digital insertion) and introduce distance learning working principles as part of the course itself has strategic and economical reasons. The adoption of this approach allows an immediate increase of the potential number of attendees in rural areas and underdeveloped economic regions and, as such, is fundamental for a capillary approach. Certainly, this argument is not valid worldwide and, eventually, would be applied only for underdeveloped and 3rd world countries.

The distribution of the course content by multiple media (web server, booklet – printed material and CD) requires an integrated approach. The web server content distribution is focused on scenarios where connectivity is satisfactory. The CD and printed material have a dual purpose:

- ❑ For scenarios with satisfactory connectivity, they just complement the web content distribution mechanism.
- ❑ For scenarios where web connectivity is compromised, both the CD and printed material are the content distribution mechanism itself.

This dual approach requires from the pedagogical point of view a certain care in the sense that each media requires a specific language and different evaluation methods. Due to that, students moving their condition (online to offline and vice-versa) do require specific and extra attention from professor and tutors in terms of the pedagogical model.

The guarantee of multiple interaction communication and feedback channels has multiple purposes. A key factor for the course quality and success is the promotion of the interaction, collaboration, student autonomy and assistance (tutors and professor). This is achieved by two different mechanisms.

The first mechanism corresponds to the course contents and activities being structured on the different media types and the second fundamental mechanism corresponds to the mediation action promoted by professor and tutors with respect to student's interaction.

In this sense, the use of postal service, callback, and faxing as the student feedback channel should be considered as complementary and temporary resources. They should be used only for a limited period to overcome the ICT resource limitations.

In terms of the *pedagogical strategies* that should be adopted we have:

- The intensification of the tutorial action using telephony services and video-conferencing resources complemented with ICT supported interaction by fax and call-back service;
- The stimulus for group leadership among students in order to promote experiences sharing and reduce the isolation resulting from the limited ICT resources;
- An increase in the amount of face-to-face meetings with respect to those previewed in case "A" scenario;
- The guarantee of prompt feedback to students in terms of their activities results and evaluation.

Although discussed in this paper as isolated practices or strategies, all the discussed guidelines are grouped in a broader planning document denominated *"fidelity plan"*. The fidelity plan is targeted to guarantee overall *course quality* and, as far as the pedagogical and technological solutions are concerned, it consolidates a list of integrated case-by-case solutions according with the implementation scenario considered.

4.4   Course Quality as an Consolidation Approach

Course evaluation is a key quality factor and, as such, the fidelity plan defines the evaluation procedures, the quality metrics, the relation among pedagogical and practical actions for distinct scenarios, the timing constraints involved when upgrading attendees and, finally, computes a "quality rank".

The discussion about the fidelity plan details is beyond the scope of this paper and, in terms of the practice methods, technological solutions and pedagogical strategies discussed, it just organizes them. This is realized by scenario (cases "A", "B" and "C") and an upgrade time schedule (case "C" → "B" → "A") is defined. The ability to accomplish the defined schedule is one of the metrics contributing to the overall course quality rank. Figure 4 illustrates a set of typical time constraints as defined for a course having part of its attendees being upgraded among levels.

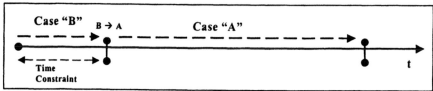

Figure 4. General schedule for upgrading attendees

The fidelity plan overall objectives are, firstly, to keep attendees satisfied by evaluating the course and providing feedbacks in order to achieve the best possible course quality (quality verification and assurance) and, secondly, to bring in a pre-defined time-schedule at least 90% of all attendees to the fully qualified implementation scenario (case "A").

In other words, one objective of the flexible and adaptable approach being used is, on route, to provide an "upgrade" in terms of necessary attendees background and to point out and propose alternative solutions for the limited computational resources.

The basic set of premises behind the flexible and adaptable pedagogical and technological solutions proposed are:

- ❏ ICT limitations should not interfere on course quality results;
- ❏ Transition between scenarios are "transparent" to course execution; and
- ❏ Transition between scenarios occurs at specific and pre-defined time frames.

5   CONCLUSIONS AND CONSIDERATIONS

The design principles, implementation issues and practices adopted for a real-life distance learning course considering a capillary approach and limited ICT resources have been briefly described.

It is argued that for a huge volume of attendees spread over less developed areas, a highly flexible and adaptable set of practices have to be applied. The general issues to consider consist in, firstly, to overcome the classical problems faced by distance learning curricula (autonomy, interactions, other) and, additionally, to articulate the pedagogical practices in order to deal with different student's profiles and execution scenarios. The pedagogical model proposed, the multiple media tools and content distribution mechanisms, the mapping of the existent constraints and associated pedagogical strategies to handle deficiencies are, all together, an alternative to pursue good quality course results. It is also argued that a high quality course objective may be achieved by having specific actions to "upgrade" student's abilities and overcome permanent ICT resources restrictions.

6 REFERENCES

Decina, M. and Trecordi, V. (1997) Convergence of Telecommunications and Computing to Network Models for Integrated Services and Applications. Proceedings of the IEEE. Special Edition - The Global Information Infraestructure. pp. 1887-1914.

Felder, R. M. and Silverman, L. K. (1988) Learning and Teaching Styles in Engineering Education. Engineering Education, n° 78, Vol.7, pp. 674 – 681.

Keeton, M. Sheckley, B. and Krejci-Griggs (2002), J. Effectiveness and Efficiency in Higher Education for Adults. Council on Adult and Experimental Learning. Chicago: Kendall-Hunt.

Martins, J. S. B. et alli. (2002) Interdisciplinary and Flexible Curricula Practices in Electric and Telecommunications Engineering – A Case Study, IFIP Working Group 3.2 Conference – Informatics and ICT in Higher Education – ICTEM 2002.

Vygotsky, L. S. (1984), A formação social da mente. São Paulo: Martins Fontes.

Wallon, Henri. (1982), La vie mentale. Paris: Éditions Sociales.

THE USE OF ICT IN THE DELIVERY OF ONLINE SERVICES
and its impact on student satisfaction at RMIT University

Kevin Leung, John Byrne, France Cheong
School of Business Information Technology, RMIT University, Melbourne, Australia
kevin.leung@rmit.edu.au

Abstract: With the changing role of the student from participant to customer, universities should examine their level of customer service. Using a questionnaire adapted from the Student Satisfaction Inventory (SSI), this study assessed the differences in expectations, as examined by importance scores, satisfaction scores, and performance gap scores of RMIT Business undergraduate students in regard to the technological services provided by the university. A random sample of final year Business undergraduate students was surveyed and an analysis was performed to determine how student satisfaction was affected by student online services delivered through the use of Information and Communication Technologies (ICT).

Key words: Higher education, satisfaction, online services, technology.

1 INTRODUCTION

In recent years, one of the main concerns in universities has been student satisfaction. The concept of student satisfaction is becoming increasingly important among institutions of higher learning. The customer service approach towards students that universities are using today focuses on meeting demands and expectations of students and fostering overall satisfaction (Astin 1993; Orpen 1990).

Product and service marketers know that in order to keep customers, they must offer high quality service (Dabholkar, Shepherd & Thorpe 2000). This is the reason why student services must keep abreast of changing student needs in order to provide quality services and ensure continued student satisfaction. Moneta (1997) has found that today's students are 24 hours, 7-day-a-week customers who reject the service disadvantages of traditional 9-5 business practices and expect campuses to become a 24 hour domain.

The integration of technology in student services (e.g. admissions, advising, financial aid, orientation, etc.) has the benefit of improving service delivery. Tinto (1987) explained that integrating student service processes will allow the coordination and efficient grouping of often disparate activities to produce services which are in effect, greater than the sum of their separate parts. Moreover, Beede and Burnett (1999) argued that the traditional model of functional silos, lines and multiple offices, limited access and bureaucratic paper-driven process will have to be replaced with the new model of anytime-anyplace (24/7) access and one source of electronic data.

It is clear that technology plays an important part in the delivery of student services. It is equally clear that institutions will need to have a strategic plan for integrating technology in student services. But what should remain first and foremost in every decision made is the institution's commitment to the student (Karla 2002). As such, the mission of higher education is not only to impart knowledge but also to provide reliable, student-oriented services in a way to enhance the student's total development (Astin 1993). One of the ways higher education institutions accomplish this mission is by continuously collecting information on student satisfaction.

2   METHODOLOGY

2.1   Questionnaire

In order to evaluate the levels of expectations and satisfaction of RMIT Business students, a questionnaire was designed. It was based on the Student Satisfaction Inventory (SSI), which was produced by USA Group Noel-Levitz (2000) and whose purpose is to collect basic demographic information about respondents and measure student perceptions regarding both the importance of, and satisfaction with, key student services and campus experiences in traditional campus environments. However, since the SSI is designed for traditional higher education settings, not all of the scales or survey questions may be relevant to student online services. Five SSI scales (out of twelve) are composed of items that most directly address student services and they were further classified into three different dimensions as shown in table 1.

Table 1. Dimensions and SSI Scales

Dimension	SSI Scales
Course Related	Academic Advising and Counselling Effectiveness
Academic Administration and Registration	Registration Effectiveness
General University	Recruitment and Financial Aid Effectiveness
	Service Excellence
	Campus Support Services

2.2 Population and Sample

The target population for this study consisted of RMIT business undergraduate students. However, participation in the survey was restricted only to final year students due to the fact that they had adequate experience to rate the statements in the questionnaire.

To appropriately conduct tests of statistical significance, the issue of sample size is important (Hinkin 1995). The results of many multivariate analysis techniques depend significantly on sample size. Considering these arguments and also time and resource constraints, the sample size chosen for this study was 135 respondents. The sample was obtained using a stratified sampling method. In this method, the sample is not only chosen randomly, but it is also made to reflect the population in some specified characteristic (Petocz 1990). Table 2 shows how the sample size was obtained.

Table 2. Sample Size

School	Business Programs	% Target Population	Size of Random Sample
Accounting and Law	Accountancy	19%	26
Business Information Technology	Business Information Systems	34%	46
Economics and Finance	Economics and Finance	19%	26
Management	Business Administration	9%	12
Marketing	Marketing	11%	14
	Transport and Logistics Management	8%	11
	Total	**100%**	**135**

2.3 Email

The questionnaire was emailed to 135 students by using their university student email addresses. Along with each questionnaire, each respondent was given an informed consent form outlining the research study and indicating that their participation was completely voluntary, their responses would be confidential and anonymous, and that results would only be reported in aggregate form. If the student agreed to participate in the study, he/she was expected to send back the completed questionnaire to the researcher via email. A response rate of 49.6% was obtained.

2.4   Data Analysis

2.4.1   Expectation and Satisfaction Scores

The data that was obtained from the questionnaire were the "course related", "academic administration and registration", and "general university" expectation and satisfaction scores. The sum and average of these scores were then calculated.

2.4.2   Weights of Dimensions

The weights of the three dimensions, were obtained by a process called the analytic hierarchy process (AHP), which was developed by Thomas (1980) and designed to solve complex problems involving multiple criteria. This process requires the respondents to provide judgments about the relative importance of each dimension and then specify a preference on each dimension for each decision alternative (Anderson, Sweeney & Williams 1994). "Pairwise comparisons are fundamental building blocks of AHP" (Anderson et al. 1994;pp. 664). In establishing the priorities for the three dimensions, respondents were asked to state a preference for a dimension when the dimensions were compared two at a time (pairwise).

3   RESULTS

An examination of the level of expectation of respondents based upon their gender revealed that females had higher expectation level than males in all three dimensions. Also, the data analysis indicated that the level of expectation increased with age and this was, indeed, what Hess (1997) discovered in his study of first year and older students. It could be concluded that the respondents viewed these student online services as an integral part of their university experience and that there was a current changing role of student from participant to customer.

With regard to the respondents' level of satisfaction, it could be concluded that most participants were at least satisfied with the RMIT student online services. This is also important for administrators to note because with the respondents' perception in this range, the university may need to make only small changes to its student online services to improve the level of satisfaction of students.

The performance gap score is important because it provides information about unmet student expectations. When using this questionnaire in this study, it is important to note that the smaller the performance gap score, the more effectively the institution (RMIT University) is meeting its students' needs. In this study, the data analysis indicated that the smallest performance gap score (5.01) was recorded for Business Administration students while the largest performance gap score (8.66) was obtained for Business Information Systems (BIS) students. The reason why BIS students recorded a larger performance gap score compared with the others could probably be explained by the fact that BIS students are more used to technology, and as such have higher expectations and lower satisfaction.

4 CONCLUSION

In general, RMIT students have higher level of expectation than satisfaction, meaning that students' needs are not being fully met. Within the past few years, the general public has been bombarded with advertising that stresses customer service. Typically, higher education institutions do not treat their students as customers, but rather as partners in the educational process (Carilli 2000). This may be one of the reasons that students are not as satisfied as one would hope with their experience at RMIT University. As Levine (1999) stated in his keynote address at the First-Year Experience Conference:

> "Students want a different relationship with their universities. They want convenience, and efficient and friendly service, similar to what they receive at a bank."

A limitation to this study is that it focused on only one faculty, that is, RMIT Business Faculty and as such, the conclusions of this study cannot be generalized to other faculties of the university. The results of this study may also be the product of a perception that students may have regarding their peers and the institutions they choose to attend.

Finally, it is hoped that this paper would stimulate more research in the antecedents and consequences of student satisfaction on universities' online services. A qualitative study as a follow-up would be useful as it may provide additional information about the impact of student online services on student satisfaction.

5   REFERENCES

Anderson, DR, Sweeney, DJ & Williams, TA 1994, *An Introduction to Management Science: Quantitative Approaches to Decision Making*, Seventh edn, West, New York.

Astin, AW 1993, *What matters in college?*, Jossey-Bass, San Francisco.

Beede, M & Burnett, D 1999, *Planning for student services: Best practices for the 21st century*, Society for College and University Planning, Ann Arbor, MI.

Carilli, V 2000, 'Student Satisfaction at Southern Illinois University Carbondale', Southern Illinois University Carbondale.

Dabholkar, PA, Shepherd, CD & Thorpe, DI 2000, 'A comprehensive framework for service quality: An investigation of critical conceptual and measurement issues through a longitudinal study', *Journal of Retailing*, vol. 76, no. 2, pp. 139-73.

Hess, EC 1997, 'Students' satisfaction with college life and implications for improving retention through counseling and institutional change', Doctoral dissertation thesis, Walden University.

Hinkin, TR 1995, 'A Review of Scale Development Practices in the study of Organizations', *Journal of Management*, vol. 21, no. 5, pp. 967-88.

Karla, JM 2002, 'Optimal integration of technology in student services', Pepperdine University.

Levine, A 1999, 'Today's college students keynote address', paper presented to First-Year Experience Conference, Columbia, SC.

Moneta, L 1997, 'The integration of technology with the management of student services', *New Directions for Student Services*, vol. 78, pp. 5-16.

Orpen, C 1990, 'The measurement of student satisfaction: A consumer behavior perspective', *Journal of Human Behavior and Learning*, vol. 7, no. 1, pp. 34-7.

Petocz, P 1990, *Introductory Statistics*, Thomas Nelson Australia.

Thomas, LS 1980, *The Analytic Hierarchy Process*, McGraw-Hill, New York.

Tinto, V 1987, *Leaving college: Rethinking the causes and cures of student attrition*, University of Chicago Press, Chicago.

USA Group Noel-Levitz 2000, *Student satisfaction inventory*, Author, Lowa City.

FROM GRADUATE TO UNDERGRADUATE
Translating a Successful Online Graduate Model for Undergraduate Teaching

Paul Darbyshire and Geoff Sandy
School of Information Systems, Victoria University, Australia
Paul.Darbyshire@vu.edu.au Geoff.Sandy@vu.edu.au

Abstract: Online teaching has not as yet penetrated too deeply into the undergraduate culture, and most successful programs are targeted towards vocational or postgraduate courses. It is often argued that postgraduate students are more likely to have the skills necessary to survive in an online environment. However, there is a large cross-section of undergraduates, which would find benefits in the flexibility of online delivery and will also possess the skills necessary to successfully complete online courses. Anecdotal evidence indicates a changing profile for undergraduate students where many continue to work part-time while studying. The work-experience gained by these students can give them experiences, which can be used to construct their learning experience in a synergistic manner by utilization of an appropriate online paradigm. This paper details the experiences of translating a successful online teaching approach used in a fully online postgraduate course to an undergraduate program.

Key words: Online learning, online model, undergraduate teaching, feedback loop.

1   INTRODUCTION

Despite initial opposition, online teaching is now becoming a component of many university courses, and in some cases is the only delivery paradigm implemented. Online teaching has not as yet penetrated too deeply into the undergraduate culture, and most successful programs are targeted towards vocational learning or postgraduate courses. Postgraduate students, particularly those who are working and trying to obtain their qualification at the same time, benefit from the flexibility that a fully online course can offer. Additionally, postgraduate students are more likely to have the skills necessary to survive in an online environment, where it can be argued that undergraduate students are obtaining these skills. However, not all undergraduate students are alike, and there is a large cross-section which would find benefits in the flexibility of online delivery and possess the skills necessary to successfully complete online courses.

This paper details the experiences of translating a successful online teaching paradigm used in a fully online postgraduate course to an undergraduate program. The online teaching model is based on a semi-Socratic paradigm and is largely constructivist in nature. This model is successfully used in the largest international fully online Master of Computer Science course, and targets working professionals too busy to attend the traditional classroom environment. By implementing this model, the School of Information Systems at Victoria University successfully conducted an online pilot in for its Faculty core subject in semester 1 2004 for undergraduate students. The pilot deliberately targeted part-time students who were self-motivated and willing to share personal experiences to make best use of the paradigm. These students, while not possessing all the proficiency of a postgraduate student, generally possess the motivation and skills necessary to survive in the online environment.

In the following sections, a brief literature review is presented on teaching and learning paradigms and online approaches. This is followed by a description of the approach translated from a graduate program for use in the undergraduate subject. A description of the implementation of the approach is then given and the results from the pilot online subject are presented.

2   LITERATURE REVIEW

The dominant paradigm for teaching and learning at Universities has been described as Pedagogy (KIT 2003; Heuer and King 2004). An emerging paradigm suitable for online teaching and learning has been referred to as Andragogy (KIT 2003; Heuer and King 2004). The major differences between the paradigms are summarized in Table 1, Two Teaching and Learning Paradigms (KIT 2003; Pelz 2004). The emerging paradigm prefers the term facilitator or moderator to that of teacher or instructor. In an online environment the term is e-facilitator or e-moderator (Salmon 2000; Heuer and King 2004).

Table 1. Two teaching and learning paradigms

Pedagogy	Andragogy
Learner is dependent on the teacher	Learner is self directing
Teacher initiated transmission of information	Welcomes the learners experience as a valuable contribution
Learning is subject centred	Learning is more life centred or task oriented
Assumes if a student is not ready then no learning will take place	Students will be ready to perform more effectively in some aspects of their lives
Assumes students are motivated by external pressures	More emphasis on internal motivation

There are a number of approaches to the facilitation or moderation of an online class. Bedore et al. (1998) suggests a useful classification of Interactive, Bounded Interactive, Consultative, Independent and Special Configuration. The role of the facilitator varies with each approach principally because of the different levels of interactivity required. In the case of the Interactive approach where a class size is about 10-15 students and each student is expected to send 10-12 meaningful messages a week high level skills are required of the facilitator. However, for the Consultative approach where there are about 40-60 students the facilitators role is primarily used by the students as a subject matter expert. Such a model has greater similarity to some approaches belonging to the Pedagogy paradigm.

Despite initial opposition to online teaching and learning it is increasingly being adopted by Universities. Opposition usually criticizes the high demands and commitment together with the need for excellent time-management skills required by both facilitator and students (Haddad 2000; DiPaolo 1999). Again criticism is also made about the need for students to work independently and in isolation and with a lack of face-to-face personal interaction that results in impaired teaching and learning (Haddad 2000; DiPaolo 1999). Finally, criticism is made that students must be technologically literate and have access to the relevant technology (Haddad 2000; DiPaolo 1999).

In contrast the major benefits claimed for online teaching and learning stress the convenience and flexibility for the students and less interruption to careers from the learning (Davis 2001; FCIT 1999). Further it is claimed that online classes are richly diverse in terms of age and ethnicity and students are usually highly motivated (Davis 2001; FCIT1999). Proponents of online teaching and learning freely acknowledge that it is not suitable for everyone but will provide educational outcomes at least equal to similar offline environment (Dutton et al 2002; Neuhauser 2002).

As mentioned previously this paper reports on the use of a hybrid online teaching and learning approach for undergraduate students in an Australian University, Victoria University. This approach is now described.

3   AN ONLINE LEARNING APPROACH

The online teaching and learning approach reported on here is based on a semi-Socratic ontology and is largely constructivist in epistemology. In terms of the approaches referred to previously it is a hybrid of the Interactive and Bounded Interactive. The approach is successfully used in the largest international fully online Master of Computer Science course of the University of Liverpool and its partner Laureate Online Education B.V. (formerly K.I.T. eLearning). It targets working professionals who find it difficult to attend the traditional classroom offline environment. These students are usually highly motivated, technologically literate and are willing to work independently and meet the high demand of time to be successful in the learning. They welcome the convenience and flexibility such approach gives them and view the interaction with a richly diversity classmates as a positive experience. The Masters course adopts best practice criteria as outline in MSACHE (2001)

The main features of the approach adopted here are described in Bedore et al (1998). The approach limits the class size to 15-20 students so as to achieve a high level of dialogue. However, the level of dialogue should be such that it does not impose an unreasonable load the students and is at a level that can be processed by the facilitator. As a rule of thumb if the message rate is in excess of 200 messages per workshop then this limit is reached. Messages represent a student's individual input including papers/ project work, assignments, responses to discussion questions as well as comments related to other students' input. Each student is expected to read all messages. This is a major reading and response load for students and for the facilitator who must manage this load while providing appropriate leadership and comments. This requires high-level facilitation skills.

Because of the strong partnership between Laureate and the University there is a strong commitment to the students' success. Each student is assigned a Program Manager who acts a personal contact throughout the course. The University exercises close quality control over the course content, quality of students and quality of facilitators. Faculty staff (facilitators) are supported by both Laureate and the University on both academic and technical dimensions. All facilitators must undertake and perform satisfactorily in an online training module before they can take a module. The first time a staff members takes a module the facilitator is mentored and evaluated. An unsatisfactory performance means no certification.

Students are admitted to the course after extensive consultation, verification of previous studies and a two-week orientation period where an online class is simulated. Students are clearly informed of assessment procedures as they are well documented and a through, transparent and fair grading process is used. Both student and staff are formally involved in the evaluation of each subject module given and a process is in place to evaluate the feedback and act

4 IMPLEMENTATION OF THE APPROACH

This successful approach was used by the authors from the School of Information Systems at Victoria University for a group of part-time students undertaking the core business subject titled Information Systems for Business. All students of the Bachelor of Business must take this core subject along with a number of other core subjects like Economics, Accounting and Management. This was a pilot study that deliberately targeted part-time students who were self motivated and willing to share work and life experiences to make a success of the opportunity to learn with this approach. However, the authors were conscious that there were differences between this group and those normally taking the Master of Computer Science. Specifically, they were younger and consequently had less work (and life) experience to draw upon together with the obvious differences and expectation associate with Undergraduate and postgraduate studies. The online learning software is WebCT Campus Edition, which is licensed to Victoria University and mandated for use by recipients of a Curriculum Innovation Grant (CIG). The authors are recipients of a CIG although they are also experienced in the delivery of PG courses using FirstClass software.

The existing undergraduate subject lectures were extensively rewritten to construct ten self-contained textual based seminars to relay the subject matter. Discussion questions were written for each of the seminars to initiate discussion on the seminar topics. Additionally, assignments were selected from the on-ground subject to complement the seminars. The length of the online pilot was reduced from the normal 12 week semester to 10 weeks, as online subjects are typically more intensive and of shorter duration. During the re-enrolment period, a self-evaluation survey was distributed to part-time students to enable them to determine if they were suitable for online learning. Finally, twenty students were selected from the respondents on a first come first serve basis, and the group was brought together for one meeting. During this meeting, all details of the conduct of the online class were explained, and an orientation was conducted on the use of the virtual class software.

5   PILOT PROGRAM RESULTS

The pilot online subject ran in semester 1 2004, in a fully online asynchronous mode. The initial class size of 20 students stabilized to 14 students after the first three weeks. This represented a retention rate of 70%, which is reasonable in a fully online class where the participants had not experienced the online paradigm previously. Only part-time students were actively recruited into the pilot online class, though the class did include two full-time undergraduate students. The class ran for 10 weeks, and a two week break was inserted after week 5 to break the online semester into manageable tasks. At the end of week 10, each student was sent a subject feedback form so data could be gathered concerning satisfaction with various components of the online subject.

The feedback consisted of 18 questions requiring a Likert scaled response of a number from one to five. A response of one indicates a poor or negative opinion of the point raised in the question, a response of five indicates a strong positive opinion of the point raised. The 18 Likert type questions are given in Table 2.

Table 2. Feedback Likert scaled questions

1 The instructors involvement in the online class
2 The instructors responses to your questions
3 The lecture notes
4 The assignments
5 The convenience of WebCT
6 The help-desk response (if applicable)
7 The resolution of any technical issues (if applicable)
8 The resolution of any personal issues with the instructor (if applicable)
9 The consistency of the subject with the syllabus (course guide)
10 The text book
11 The usefulness of the online discussions
12 The online subjects flexibility
13 The achievements of the subjects aims
14 Any contribution to professional knowledge (if applicable)
15 Satisfaction with the instructors performance
16 Satisfaction with the subject
17 Would you recommend this mode of learning to another student
18 What is your evaluation of the pace of the subject

At the end of the feedback form, there are three open ended questions where the students are invited to comment further on other aspects which they were either happy of unhappy about. These questions are:

- Please describe in a few words one aspect of the subject you were most satisfied with.
- Please describe in a few words one aspect of the subject you were least satisfied with
- Is there anything else you would like to add regarding the online program?

At the end of the pilot in Semester 1 2004, a total of five questionnaires were returned so no concrete conclusions can be drawn. However, the pilot experience is promising. The results from the Likert scaled questions of the questionnaire are shown in Table 3 along with comparative data from 4 classes of a graduate subject. The graduate subject is taught via Laureate through the University of Liverpool as part of the MSc in Computer Science. The figures from Laureate were collected from the subject feedback throughout 2002. The shaded column represents the averages for the Likert-style questions for the undergraduate subject piloted at Victoria University. The same questionnaire was given to the undergraduate and Masters students, except the undergraduate questionnaire had two extra questions.

Table 3. Questionnaire Likert scaled responses

Questions	Pilot Class averages	Comparative Graduate data (4 classes)				
		averages	class 1	class 2	class 3	class 4
1	4.4	3.9	4.1	3.7	3.5	4.4
2	4.2	4.3	4.6	3.8	4.2	4.6
3	4.2	4.5	4.6	4.1	4.5	4.8
4	3.6	4.5	4.4	4.1	4.9	4.5
5	5.0	4.0	3.9	4.0	3.8	4.1
6	3.5	4.2	4.3	3.8	4.2	4.5
7	4.0	4.0	4.1	4.0	4.0	4.0
8	5.0	4.3	4.5	4.0	4.4	4.4
9	4.4	4.2	4.3	4.1	4.3	3.9
10	3.8	4.2	4.0	4.2	4.5	4.1
11	5.0	4.0	4.2	3.8	4.1	4.0
12	5.0	3.6	4.2	3.3	3.0	3.8
13	4.6	4.2	4.5	3.9	4.1	4.4
14	4.4	4.4	4.5	4.1	4.4	4.4
15	4.4	4.2	4.7	3.6	4.0	4.6
16	5.0	4.2	4.6	3.8	4.1	4.3
17	4.6					
18	4.0					

A brief analysis of the data displayed in Table 3 can quickly highlight some of the differences between the graduate and undergraduate experience.

5.1   Undergraduate Experience

The undergraduate students responded more negatively to questions four and six, in the questionnaire, representing questions regarding the class assignments and the WebCT help-desk system. As the online class received assignments from the same material as the equivalent on-ground students, the response may indicate a lack of confidence in performing assignments by remote instruction. However, unless the on-ground students are similarly polled, it is difficult to speculate. Additionally, as there is not yet an online teaching culture established at Victoria University, the help-desk aspect of the online experience is not mature, and a poor result would have been expected.

There were a number of questions where the undergraduate response represented a more positive experience than the postgraduate one. These included: the instructors involvement in the class, the convenience of WebCT, the instructors help, the usefulness of the discussions, the flexibility of the subject, and the overall satisfaction of the subject. Of these points, question 12, '*the flexibility of the subject*' stood out as the most significant positive difference between the undergraduate and graduate feedback. This is surprising given the similarity in the demographics of the students from both programs. The MSc program conducted by Laureate and the University of Liverpool is specifically targeted to working professionals; while in the pilot undergraduate subject at Victoria University, we intentionally targeted part-time students. The part-time students are normally in paid full-time employment and thus represent a group of students with similar demands on their time as the graduate students. However, as this pilot represents the first fully online class the students have participated in throughout their degree, the flexibility inherent in the subject design would have a great impact on their experience. The corresponding postgraduate subject would normally have been studied after a number of other online subjects, and thus at this stage, the postgraduate students would be more experienced and discerning of online class conduct.

As the undergraduate subject is designed around the online discussions, it is satisfying to see the relevant question ranking high in the student's perception. Above all else, it is the discussions of the paradigm we have adopted that drive the learning process. Thus satisfaction with the usefulness of the discussions would also directly relate to the overall satisfaction with the subject. This question also ranked very highly. Again, the lack of experience in online classes would most likely artificially inflate these figures until more experienced was gained. One of the more traditional methods of measuring the outcomes of the subject is of course the success rate of the students and the frequencies of the various grades received. This data is shown in Table 4.

Table 4. Final grade frequencies

N2 (0-39)	N1 (40-49)	P (50-59)	C (60-69)	D (70-79)	HD (80+)
0	0	3	6	5	0

At first glance, the grades received seemed skewed towards the high end, but this reflects a common experience in online learning. Generally, online learning, while far more flexible, is also far more demanding. When the class numbers settle down after the initial drop-outs have taken place, those left are usually in for the long-haul, and represent those students more suited to the online paradigm. Such students tend to be self-motivated and hard working and will do well in the online or on-ground environment. This is usually reflected in the grades. It is interesting to note that although we intentionally targeted part-time students in the pilot online subject, we did have two full-time students participating. Two of the three pass (P) grades were allocated to those students. While we cannot draw conclusions based on two students, the follow-up class online class in Semester 2 is composed mainly of full-time undergraduates. It will be interesting to compare the performance levels between the two classes.

Although the grades shown in Table 4 represent an overall good performance, this was also one of the points of contention raised a number of times. At the end of the questionnaire, students were asked to comment on the thing they were least satisfied with in the subject. A number of them raised the question of the marking scheme...

I was going to moan about the marking system, but I see that's already been done, so I won't bore you any more ... actually, I will... it was a bit of a pain when everybody handed in their DQ's and stuff on the last night of the week...

... the grading scheme seemed a bit harsh. You had to work very hard every week to had a hope of getting a HD, and the marking scheme made this very difficult...

In retrospect, we adopted the same grading scheme as the one used in the online MSc. This represented a requirement for a level of work that overly harsh in order to receive a high grade in an undergraduate first year subject. The grading scheme has been reviewed and adjusted for future classes and we will shortly have results from the next class due to finish in Semester 2 2004.

5.2 Instructor's Experience

The experience of an instructor is always subjective, but from an instructors' perspective, the online class performed well in comparison to the experience of the graduate class. There were a number of notable differences, but these were mainly at the beginning of the semester when the students were becoming familiar with the online paradigm. More motivation in terms of instructor postings was required to initiate discussions early in the semester. There was more reluctance to discuss personal experience; however as the semester progressed, the students became more responsive to the questions. Towards the end of the semester, the discussion frequencies and quality of the postings reached very satisfying levels.

One of the concepts that seemed more difficult for the undergraduate class to grasp was that of synergy generated from the postings. The paradigm works well when student discuss regularly over a period of days. In fact, while this was a requirement, it was difficult to impress on many that it was imperative for the paradigm to work effectively. There was a particular cohort that seemed to post everything on the last night of the week, and technically, while meeting the required number of postings, didn't add to the synergy of the group during the week. Unfortunately, the only thing to change the behaviour pattern was the allocated marked for the week.

6 CONCLUSIONS

Many of the successful online programs are directed towards the graduate market. It is argued that at the graduate level, students have the commitment and the skills necessary to survive in the online environment. An online subject can be as, or more, demanding than the equivalent on-ground subject. However, the flexibility inherent in online approaches is attractive to people with busy life styles and demands made by family and career. There has not been a deep penetration of online learning into undergraduate culture, and it is uncertain if successful approaches used in graduate programs will be successful in undergraduate programs.

This paper has presented the results of translating a successful online approach used in a fully online MSc to an undergraduate subject. The subject was specifically marketed to part-time undergraduate students. This represented a section of the student population that would have a similar demographic to those undertaking the MSc, but with far less academic background. The outcomes for the students undertaking the online subject were promising, despite criticism of the marking scheme that was retained from the MSc program. The feedback from the end-of-subject questionnaires overall showed a more positive response to many of the aspects of the online subject, particularly the flexibility and overall satisfaction. However, given the number of returns and the first-time experience for the students, it may be difficult to draw concrete conclusions.

Given the positive outcomes for the students and the flexibility offered to an often-neglected sector of the student population, the pilot subject seemed very successful. However, to judge effectively the success of this particular paradigm for undergraduate teaching, classes need to be conducted with a more representative cross section of the student population. Currently, such a class, with full-time students making up the majority is due for completion in semester 2, 2004.

7 REFERENCES

Bedore G, Bedore M and Bedore G (1998) Online Education: The Future is Now, Art Press.

Davis A (2001) Conversion from Traditional Distance Education to Online Courses, Programs and Services. International Review of Resaerch in Open and Distance Learning, January.

DiPaolo A (1999) Online Education: Myth or Reality? The Stanford Online Experience, Proceedings on Online Education, Berlin.

Dutton J, Dutton M and Perry J (2002) How do Online Students differ from Lecture Students. JALN, Vol. 6, No. 1.

Florida Center for Instructional Technology (FCIT) (1999) Benefits of Distance Learning. A Teachers Guide to distance Learning, Chapter 3.

KIT (2003). Seminar Week 2, Online Training.

Knowles M (unknown) Andragogy. http://www.dmu.ac.uk/~jamesa/learning/knowlesa.htm Date accessed 18 Octber 2004.

Haddad W (2000) Higher Education:The Ivory Tower and the Satellite Dish, TechKnow Logia, Vol. 2, No. 1.

Heuer B and King K (2004) Leading the Band: The Role of the Instructor in Online Learning for Educators, Journal of Online Education,

Holocomb L, King F and Brown S (2004) Student Traits and Attributes Contributing to success in Online Courses: Evaluation of University Online Courses. Journal of Interactive Online Learning, Vol. 2, No. 3.

MSACHE (2001) Best Practices for Electronically Offered Degree and Certificate Programs. Commission on Higher education, Middle States Association of Colleges and Schools.

Neuhauser C (2002) A Comparative Study of the Effectiveness of Online and Face-to-Face Instruction. The American Journal of Distance Education, Vol 16, No 2.

Pelz B (2004) (My) Three Principles of Effective Online Pedagogy, JALN, Volume 8, Issue 3, pp. 33-46.

Rivera J and Rice M (2002) A Comparison of Student Outcomes and Satisfaction between Traditional and Web Based course Offerings. Journal of Distance Education Learning Administration, Vol.5, No. 3.

Salmon G (2000) E-Moderating: The Key to Teaching and Learning Online, Kogan Page.

ENCAPSULATING REAL-LIFE EXPERIENCE

David Kelly & Bill Davey
RMIT University, Melbourne, Australia
David.Kelly@rmit.edu.au Bill.Davey@rmit.edu.au

Abstract   In this paper we discuss experiences with work-situated learning and difficulties that commonly arise. The alternative of encapsulating real life experience in hypermedia based materials is then presented using a number of case studies. Finally a model is presented for producing these "real life" encapsulations which overcomes the problems of lack of structure in individual experience without losing the advantages of common lifelike experiences. Some testing of the model is presented. The model involves the steps of:

- Determine real life skills commonly required
- imagine a context rich enough (and having the case study design team with enough knowledge of the context that they can draw from their experience to fill in the holes)
- structure (partition) the case so that team work is possible without too much overlap between tasks. Identify the overlapping points that will force the level of teamwork between students that is intended
- identify parts of the solution development where students can be synchronised using a published solution to part of the problem
- create answers for each skill point starting from the top
- tag each part of the answer with the essential component of information required for an answer
- determine the most likely format that the tagged information would be found in real life
- create the set of tagged information using unskilled labour to provide detailed data
- write the project brief so that an appropriate level of guidance is given for navigating the information sources.

Keywords: Data model, business context, case study, virtual organisation, system analysis.

1   INTRODUCTION

Weisman and Anthony (1999) concluded that there are four ways that knowledge is transferred: involvement (participation in learned organizations such as trade societies), association (formal or informal interactions with others), experience (knowledge acquired through implicit learning), and direct education (formal learning pursuits). A study by Simmonds et al. (2001) concluded that: "In general, results suggest that the primary source of management concepts for practicing managers is experience, followed by association and involvement. The least identified knowledge source for practicing managers was direct education."

If we are to make this last and least effective learning environment more effective we must make the learning environment more closely reflect real experience. One aspect of learning through experience is that all learning "on the job" is, by definition, useful.

Usefulness implies ways of resolving a problem through clarification, alternation, or actual solution and is based on an attitudinal perception of the effectiveness of applying specific information to resolve a problem or to make a decision. Other views of usefulness of education included those of Mangaliso and Choo. "Information is useful if it is appropriate for the situation in which it is used" (Mangaliso, 1995). Choo (1998) contends that "selection of information depends on the degree of relevance the user attributes to the information."

Using these views of education the designer of learning experiences is convinced to have at least some aspect of their delivery through a simulation as close to real as possible. There is a long history of using computers to provide simulations of learning situations where the real experience is not available or too expensive or dangerous. These are often linear experiences for students. Maddux has pointed to the essential weakness of linear experiences encapsulated in a computer delivered experience. "But typically, behavioural models of computer programmed instruction have several weaknesses: first, isolating factual information; second, learning in isolation; third, a linear structure that cannot match some learning activities; and fourth, lack of flexibility and user-friendliness" (Maddux et al., 1997, p.76-77).

2   SYSTEMS ANALYSIS AS A TOPIC

Teaching of systems analysis often is reduced to identifying specific skills and then designing tasks based on text descriptions of a case to be analysed. These text-based case studies can degenerate into a written comprehension test. Students can achieve the intended result by "finding the answers" in the text. Systems analysis in a real life situation involves obtaining information about the site in a number of ways. These include the project brief, interviews, document analysis and observation of the current system. These applied tasks can be described as the capabilities of a graduate of a systems analysis course. If we are to teach real life capabilities then we must prepare assessment tasks that incorporate these real life characteristics. In real cases the information required to properly specify the problem will come from a mixture of these sources. Clearly a simulation of the process of systems analysis is fertile ground for use of multimedia delivery of the case study. A basic assumption of the techniques reported here is that "Knowledge is defined as a dynamic concept: Knowledge is only knowledge when it can be applied" (Weert 2003). Here we address the possibilities of encapsulating real life experiences in a web-based hypermedia experience for students and argue that the benefits of a controlled environment outweigh the lack of reality still inherent in the hypermedia.

3   SYSTEMS ANALYSIS AS AN EXEMPLAR EDUCATIONAL AREA

At RMIT University in Australia the teaching group charged with delivering education in systems analysis hit this need for relevance and experience as a major hurdle. Systems analysis involves searching through the miasma of complexity of a normal human organization to discover problem definitions that are amenable to analysis. Often the skills involved are required to be learnt by undergraduate students with superficial understandings of organizations typical of the consumer rather than even a junior employee of an organization. Skills such as recognising raw data to be relevant, obtaining data from a wide variety of sources including interviews and document analysis can be taught in isolation, but the transfer of these skills in a real situation seemed very poor. Transfer of knowledge to real situations was studied. Crucial factors that were not components of the learning experience were identified. These included:

- In real life different members of an organization see a given problem in different ways. The analyst is often presented with conflicting views of what the job is that they have been asked to analyse.
- Information in real organizations is "hidden" in a multitude of places and formats; in employee memory, in documents, in procedure manuals, in policy statements, in daily practice.

- The information needed for analysis is "hidden" amongst large amounts of data that is of no relevance to the problem to be analysed. None of the data is tagged "relevant" or "not relevant"
- Real problems have a time and resource limit that has no bearing on the size or complexity of the problem. Problems are not tailored for a certain amount of time that is reasonable in terms of a thorough solution. This forces a problem solver to compromise quality of the solution to the resources available

4   HYPERMEDIA AND THE WEB

Gayeski defines hypermedia as a classification of software programs which consist of networks of related text, graphics, audio-files, and video clips through which users navigated by browser (Gayeski 1993). Such a definition of hypermedia seems to include all the facilities that allow a learning environment to reflect the complexity of real life. This advantage is in addition to those claimed by the literature for all hypermedia-based learning. For example (Liaw 2001) makes three claims for the advantages of hypermedia: "In the building of hypermedia instruction, four advantages of this learning environment emerge: multiple perspectives, collaborative learning, learner-orientation, and interdisciplinary learning." The use of collaborative learning environments provides a means to create more engaging and dynamic instructional settings (Slavin 1992). Collaboration can help individuals to make progress through their zone of proximal development by the activities in which they engage (Vygotsky 1978) Authors have also recognised the potential for hypermedia-based systems to show the dynamism that characterises real life situations. Typically, in formal schooling, much content quickly becomes "inert" while processed and integrated (Gagne et al. 1993), as it has little relevance to the life circumstance of the learners.

5   COMPLEXITY AND HYPERMEDIA

An underlying assumption of our work here should be stated explicitly. The teachers of systems analysis are in common accord as to one of the underlying requirements of professionals. The very need to perform systems analysis assumes that real systems have very detailed complexity. This complexity defeats many of the reductionist attitudes to classroom experience design. In a classroom of the past a teacher would attempt to look into a situation with a view to determining the simple principles to be attained by students. Experiences would then be designed that present those principles in as stark a situation as possible. Teaching of systems analysis is the antithesis of this process as students must be trained to find the principles from amongst the vast array of complex detail, most of which will be discarded deliberately in the systems analysis process. Liaw has expressed this essential skill of the real life partitioner. "Today, the problem is not so much in finding information but sifting through the huge amount that is readily available and locating the particular pieces that are of most interest at the moment" (Liaw 2001).

6   WHY PRODUCE CASE STUDY SIMULATIONS

The systems analysis team started in 1989 producing traditional case study material on paper in text. These "case studies" were descriptions of organizations where the text description contains ALL the information a student needs to produce the analysis and in approximately the right order. The team was dissatisfied with the process of learning that students demonstrated. A study of the literature found many principles that might be included in a new approach. For example Lee had concluded that "The modern computer technology has made possible a new and rich learning environment: the simulation. In an instructional simulation, students learn by actually performing activities to be learned in a context that is similar to the real world" (Lee 1999). A study of the simulations available indicated that it could be valuable to include simulation ideas in presentation of material. These factors were recognised in 1992 and a slow process of developing computer-based case studies was started. Until the emergence of the web these were largely text-based and delivered on the student network. Only recently have multimedia components been added and delivery made so that students can access the case studies from any web connection.

7   THE DESIGN PROBLEM

The creation of case studies for students of systems analysis has been an arduous task for many academics. A common strategy of those that produce their own case studies is to write about a fictitious business from personal experience of a real business. This often leads to the case study being structured around memories of the operations of a business rather than providing a rich environment in which the student can find use for skills they are developing.

Our early case studies were small. This meant that several students would be given identical tasks to complete. Apart from a natural tendency of students to solve the problem by waiting for a good student to "find the answers" and then using that knowledge for their own solution, a small single case does not promote communication. We would like students to be saying "I have this problem with my area, did you have a similar problem and, if so, how did you approach the solution?"

A small case also has the problem that there is not much room for co-operative group work which is typical of real systems analysis projects.

Our "from memory" case studies were often realistic enough but segmenting the larger ones to allow for group work lead to some members of a group being given very trivial tasks with not much challenge in them. Our memories returned case studies with a single problem in them in one area: the area we solved when doing the real problem the first time.

Our early case studies had the designer clearly anxious to put information in that could be quickly put into one of the design diagrams we were teaching. Attempts to add sample data and other detail were difficult to achieve and normally were included not as sample data would normally occur, but to make sure students were guided to produce a particular "answer".

8   TEAM WORK, CASE STUDY SIZE AND COMPLEXITY

A particular constraint of case studies in systems analysis is the issue of teamwork. Systems analysts almost always work in teams due to the size and complexity of real life problems. It is our belief that teamwork can be taught, but can only be learned by working in a team and experiencing the problems of teams that are mentioned in the teaching.

It is unrealistic and unfair to expect students to learn new behaviours, form new relationships, and learn about new topics and methods in a short period of time, with the pressure of assessment and without guidance on social aspects of technology use, particularly when the technologies and the networks on which we rely for collaboration do not always function optimally.

9   THE DESIGN STRATEGY

Our solution which has evolved over a number of years involves the following activities:

1. *Clearly identifying the concepts to be addressed in the case study.*
   In this case: Basic entity modelling including identification of entities, attributes and relationships. Relationships to be one to one, one to many and many to many. Mandatory and optional relationships. Entity modelling involving supertypes and subtypes. Entity modelling involving recursive relationships.

2. *Create a solution incorporating examples of the concepts.*
   In this case: We created an ER model containing 5 entities one of which contained subtypes and one of which contained a recursive relationship. The solution produced can also be used as the basis for the correction of student work.

3. *Duplicate several possible solutions to essentially similar problems so that you can reduce the number of students working on the same problem thus reducing the ability to copy other student's solutions.*
   In this case: We created an ER model containing approximately 25 entities (5x5) covering five functional areas. Students could then be given one of 5 sets of data.

4. *Work backwards from the solution to create the problem.*
   In this case: We needed to give broad hints as to the existence of entities, attributes and relationships particularly in regard to recursive relationships and super and sub types.

5. *Problem definition to incorporate as much realism as possible through the use of multimedia components.*
   In this case: We used video tapes and still images for definitions and processes, audio tapes for business rules and forms for attribute identifications. Clues to identification of entities could be found in all four.

6. *Create an interface which necessitates the use of investigative techniques to gain access to above components.*
   In this case: We use a simple web-based interface. This is the next step for improvement.

7. *Allocate duplicate problems in a manner to minimise copying.*
   In this case: Final assignment consisted of a group assignment where each member would contribute their component to the construction of the whole. This required that each group member be working on a separate component thus essentially requiring each member of the group to be working on a different component than their closest friends normally the most common target for copying. Groups tend to be friendship based.

8. *Investigate Web based delivery if appropriate.*
   In this case: All components were placed on the Web.

10 THE RESEARCH

Over a two year period approximately 300 students were exposed to a hypermedia-based business case study delivered through the web. The case study underwent three iterations during this period, each time increasing the complexity of the business environment simulation. In the first case, "DD real estate" was a business using photographs of properties, scanned images of documents, Excel and Word documents and a web interface with almost no intelligence. The final case study includes video and sound files and has been fully designed using the structured approach outlined above.

Structured interviews of students, the teaching team and analysis of student results was used to gather data. This data sought to determine the extent to which the format of the business environment supported the establishment of systems analysis skills. Staff input was also used to test the effectiveness of the design strategy in producing the case study material.

11 OUTCOMES OF THE RESEARCH

Case study production has now been carried out over several courses in systems analysis for over 10 years. In this time we have measured the amount of learning in several ways, chiefly including teaching staff reflections and assessment material analysis. We have also measured the amount of output and time taken to produce that output in terms of total size of the case study.

In that time we have found a number of clear outcomes
1. Students respond to their assessment tasks in a different way from the past. Students show an involvement with the cases of much greater depth. This shows clearly in questions asked of the tutorial staff and the types of activity undertaken during construction of their systems.
2. Students produce solutions with a far greater depth of detail, more closely reflecting common business practice.
3. There are some indications of better learning. This can be seen in the level of difficulty in examination questions. This measure of success is difficult to quantify as pass rates for examination are kept fairly constant.
4. Since the start of this research in 1989, several new staff members have been involved in subjects in which the techniques here have been used. Without exception the new staff report a greater satisfaction with the case studies produced and with their ability to contribute to the case study production.

12 CONCLUSION

Sample problems can be placed on a web site for students to test and develop their learning. In the case of learning systems analysis this is particularly apt as the web is an ideal environment in which to encapsulate the complexity and fragmentation of information normally found in a business environment. Here we describe a technique for ensuring that a web site with this aim encapsulates all the aspects needed to ensure that a student is able to learn those skills intended to be included by the teacher.

1. Clearly identifying the concepts to be addressed in the case study.
2. Create a solution incorporating examples of the concepts.
3. Duplicate a number of possible solutions to essentially similar problems so that you can reduce the number of students working on the same problem thus reducing the ability to copy other student's solutions.
4. Work backwards from the solution to create the problem.
5. Problem definition to incorporate as much realism as possible through the use of multimedia components.
6. Create an interface which necessitates the use of investigative techniques to gain access to above components.
7. Allocate duplicate problems in a manner to minimise copying.
8. Investigate Web based delivery if appropriate.

13 REFERENCES

Choo, C. W. (1998). The Knowing Organization: How Organizations Use Information to Construct Meaning, Create Knowledge, and Make Decisions. New York, NY: Oxford University Press.

Gagne, E., Yekovich, C. W., & Yekovich, F. (1993). The cognitive psychology of schooling learning. New York, Harper Collins.

Gayeski, D. M. (1993). Multimedia for Learning: Development, Application, Evaluation. NJ, Educational Technology Publication.

Jong, T. D. (1991). Learning and instruction with computer simulations. Education & Computing, 6, 215-227

Lee J; (1999); Effectiveness of computer-based instructional simulation: A meta analysis International Journal of Instructional Media; New York;

Leidner, D. E., & Jarvenpaa, S. L. (1995). The use of information technology to enhance management school education : A theoretical view. MIS Quarterly, 19(3), 265-292.

Liaw S., (2001) Designing the hypermedia-based learning environment International Journal of Instructional Media; New York ,28(1)

Maddux, C. D., Johnson, D. L., & Willis, J. W. (1997). Educational Computing, Learning with Tomorrow's Technologies. 21 Edition. Allyn & Bacon. Needham Height, MA.

Mangaliso, M. P. (1995). "The Strategic Usefulness of Management Information as Perceived by Middle Managers." Journal of Management 21: 231-250.

Simmonds P G ; Dawley D D; Ritchie W J ; Anthony W P; (2001) An exploratory examination of the knowledge transfer of strategic management concepts from the academic environment to practicing managers Journal of Managerial Issues; Pittsburg; Fall 2001;

Slavin, R. (1992). Cooperative learning. Encyclopedia of Educational Research. M. C. Alkin. New York, Macmillan: 235-238.

Vygotsky, L. S. (1978). Mind in Society. Cambridge MA, Harvard University Press.

Weisman, D. and W. P. Anthony (1999). "Strategies of Executive Learning: An Executive Learning Model." Proceedings of the Academy of Management, Chicago, IL.

Weert, T. J. V. (2003). Life-Long Learning in Virtual Learning Organisations. *TelE-Learning: The Challenge for the Third Millenium.* D. Passey; and M. Kendall;. London, Klewer Academic Publishers: 135-142.

GETTING INTERACTIVE MEDIA INTO SCHOOLS
Experiences from a Pilot Project in Austria

Stephan Schwan, Anton Knierzinger, Caroline Weigner
Institute for Education and Psychology, Johannes Kepler University, Austria and EDUCATIONHIGHWAY Innovation Center For School And New Technology; Linz, Austria
stephan.schwan@jku.at   a.knierzinger@ist.eduhi.at   c.weigner@ist.eduhi.at

Abstract: The introduction of new types of audiovisuals - streaming videos, hypervideos, and video-based E-Lectures – into classroom was addressed in a nationwide Austrian school project, in which a large number of digitized audiovisual media were provided. The aim of the project was to create an Internet-based platform which allows teachers to access a large database of digitized educational movies, equip it with convenient tools for searching, ordering and downloading, and gain some empirical insights in its acceptance by teachers and students, its feasibility for classroom teaching, and its appropriate instructional scenarios. Details of the project and its empirical evaluation are described in this paper. The main part of the article is devoted to a discussion of three conceptual issues whose relevance can be deduced from theoretical grounds and which also have been found important in the empirical evaluation of the project. Finally, some general considerations about the educational future of audiovisual media will be made.

Key words: Real-life learning, media-on-demand, e-learning, e-lectures, changing role of teachers.

1   INTRODUCTION

Currently, the field of New Media, including its interactive variants, is characterized by a growing usage of film-like modes of presentation (Manovich, 2002). This trend is partly motivated by a number of technological developments which enable the production, storage, dissemination and usage of dynamic audiovisual materials with reasonable effort and at low cost. It includes the availability of cheap and easy to use digital cameras and editing software, increased and cheaper computational power and storage capacities as well as the possibility of streaming audiovisual material at relatively low bandwidth with few losses in quality. But it is also motivated by the increasing demands for audiovisual materials on part of the users, as indicated by the success of video or computer games, video on demand services or net-based videophones.

This overall trend is also mirrored in the field of educational applications of New Media. A growing number of collections of educational movies is being digitalised and made available via Internet databases. Additionally, new types of digital videos appear, including Hypervideos (Zahn, Schwan & Barquero, 2002; Zahn, Barquero & Schwan, in press), which structure the video-material in a non-linear fashion, or E-Lectures, in which the video record of a speaker giving a lecture is synchronized with his or her presentation slides, a table of contents and eventually a written transcript of his or her talk (He, Grudin & Gupta, 2000). By means of the vividness and authenticity of its content presentation, both traditional video in its digitized form and new types of nonlinear or interactive videos promise to enrich classrooms with diverse kinds of real-life experiences – be it exchange of knowledge with external experts, producing and analyzing records of field trips, or visualisation of everyday situations as a starting point for discovery learning.

2   THE AVD PROJECT: AUDIO-VISUAL SERVICES FOR CLASSROOM TEACHING

AVD stands for "AudioVisuelle Dienste" which translates "audiovisual services". It is a nationwide project funded by the Austrian Federal Ministry of Education Science and Culture (bm:bwk) and Austrian telecom. Basically, it comprises of a network of tools and services, by which digitalized educational movies are produced, stored in a searchable database, delivered via Internet and satellite, and flexibly integrated into classroom education in an interactive manner. The AVD project consists of three main components:

- AV media: A web-based database which contains about 400 professional educational movies in digitalized form. The videos cover a wide spectrum of topics, ranging from physics to geography, and also address different age groups of students. The database possesses a range of features which allow for a very flexible use, including extended searching possibilities, detailed content description as well as the possibility to preview the videos and to order them for classroom usage. These features are described in more detail below.

- AV academy: A learning platform by which video-based live lectures may be attended to via the Internet in an interactive fashion. The live lectures are recorded and stored in a second database with characteristics comparable to the aforementioned one. Again, these "e-lectures" may be searched, previewed and ordered in a largely self-regulated manner.
- A technical infrastructure by which the chosen and ordered videos or e-lectures are transmitted to the server of the respective school via broadband satellite technology.

After its components had been designed, implemented, and tested, AVD was made available via WorldWideWeb and all Austrian schools were given an opportunity to participate in a field trial. Overall, 89 schools took part in the trial, which lasted over one year and was free of charge. After resolving most of the technical problems during the first few months, the teachers were encouraged to try out these new possibilities in their classroom.

During the last three months of the first project stage, an extensive empirical evaluation was conducted. The questionnaire contained 36 items, including both closed and open questions. In particular, it addressed the following topics: differences between AVD and traditional use of media, benefits and problems, strategies of use in classroom, attendances of e-lectures and overall acceptance. Conducting the questionnaires was complemented by gathering in-depth interview data. Its main focus was on the integration of the AVD material into the classroom and the reactions of the students, as witnessed by the teachers, therefore providing a number of important additional insights.

3 INTRODUCING AVD INTO CLASSROOM: THEORETICAL CONSIDERATIONS AND EMPIRICAL FINDINGS

In retrospect, analyses of the fate of rather short-lived media like videodiscs suggests that a number of preconditions must be met in order to ensure a more successful introduction of film-like learning material into classroom (Wetzel, Radtke, & Stern, 1994). This includes:

- Technological and organizational barriers should be minimized. The process of searching, selecting and using relevant video material should be kept as simple and convenient as possible. Therefore, use of digitized audiovisual material in school should be supported by an appropriate technological infrastructure (Collini-Nocker, Knierzinger & Weigner, 2002).

- Empirical studies show that teachers often restrict video use in the classroom to a mere presentation of a whole video without any interactive or collaborative instructional intervention. Teachers should thus be encouraged to appropriately integrate these new types of media into regular classroom education in a more variable manner.
- Most importantly, the use of audiovisual material must promise some advantages with regard to knowledge acquisition. This includes not only an added value in terms of increased learning effectiveness or efficiency. Additionally, such dynamic and interactive pictorial media should also overcome the cognitive drawbacks of traditional video media which have hindered its widespread use in regular education.

4   NEW FORMS OF AUDIOVISUAL MEDIA: OVERCOMING THE DRAWBACKS OF TRADITIONAL EDUCATIONAL VIDEOS

Whereas the technical and organisational context and the instructional modes set the stage for its appropriate utilization, the most important question is whether computer-based, digitized videos indeed promise to foster learning and understanding of a given topic. In other words, their use in classroom teaching can only be justified if they possess clear learning advantages in comparison with less complex media like text or static pictures in terms of increased effectiveness or efficiency.

For some types of content and types of learning tasks, this can be affirmatively answered. In general, films and videos possess a number of specific features which clearly distinguish them from other media like texts or pictures. Firstly, they comprise of a mixture of different symbol systems, namely pictures, spoken words and sounds, which are simultaneously presented. Secondly, with regard to pictorial quality, they do not only capture shape, colour and layout of objects and scenes, but also their dynamic changes over time. Therefore, in comparison to other media, films and videos are characterized by a high degree of realism in their spatiotemporal depiction of state of affairs.

But films and videos should not be reduced to the notion of maximum realism. Instead, compared to real-life experiences, they possess the additional advantage of allowing customization of the presentation to the cognitive needs of its viewers. As an example, Schwan, Garsoffky & Hesse (2000) show that film depictions of complex activity sequences could be made more intelligible through the placement of film cuts, thereby facilitating the process of cognitively segmenting the stream of activity into comprehensible units. Therefore, audiovisual media are not merely valid reproductions of real facts, but should be conceived as *instruments for information processing*. They give its authors and producers a great degree of freedom for shaping the presentation of information, which may even be greater than for a common observer under conditions of natural, everyday experience. For example, a film director can record a given event simultaneously from multiple viewpoints, and can subsequently choose the best, "canonical" view for each part of the event. In contrast, everyday observers typically are restricted to their particular standpoint (Garsoffky, Schwan & Hesse, 2002).

Despite these advantages, videos do not play the role in the context of school teaching which they deserve. Besides problems of finding appropriate video material, acquiring it and integrating it into classroom education, audio-visual learning material has been additionally shown to possess the danger of being more shallowly processed than printed materials. This lack of mental elaboration, which is manifest in fewer inferences and a lesser degree of activation of prior knowledge, may be attributed to at least three potential causes. Due to its high degree of realism, viewers tend to interpret them as mere reproduction of reality instead of being a communicative device, whose fundamental meanings and intentions must be actively deciphered by means of elaborating its surface content. Additionally, due to its dynamism, the cognitive processing must proceed within a restricted amount of time. This problem may get worse, if no special attention is paid for an appropriate relationship between spoken commentary and pictorial presentation, leading to dangers of cognitive overload (Mayer, 2001).

Another severe drawback of traditional types of educational films or video is that they do not allow for much control over the viewing process, thus not supporting self-regulated learning. Whereas reading a text is a highly self-regulated activity, watching a video is typically not. During text reading, learners may adapt their reading speed to the complexity of the text and their own cognitive demands. Large texts can be browsed quickly, unimportant or uninteresting passages may be skipped while relevant paragraphs may be reread several times. In contrast, watching a video is typically done in a passive fashion with only few video-related activities.

Taken together these problems of shallow cognitive processing and lack of possibilities for self-regulated learning, it comes as no surprise that reading a text on a given topic outperforms watching a respective video in terms of memory and understanding (Salomon, 1984). But with the advent of digitalized, computer-based and networked types of video media, a number of new solutions to tackle these problems have been developed. These solutions comprise augmenting video material with additional, more abstract types of information, allowing for a structured, random access to different parts of the video, as well of providing interactivity in terms of controlling pace and sequence of the video. These aspects will be discussed in turn.

Firstly, computers can be conceived as platforms which allow the integrated presentation of diverse symbol systems within a unified and homogeneous framework. Therefore, one important strategy for overcoming the problem of shallow processing of video data is to augment them with additional presentation types like written texts or animations. Thereby, the videos become part of a larger network of hypermedia information sources, which in turn affords a more elaborated cognitive processing, because it requires the user to integrate these various information particles into a homogenous mental representation. This augmentation may be done defining navigable "hot spots" within the videos, which directly link to other information sources (Zahn et al., 2002; Zahn et al., in press). Another solution, which was pursued in the AVD project, is to add a repository to each video which contains various additional information sources like texts, animations, simulation or links to relevant WWW sites.

Secondly, digital videos which are presented via computers can be accessed in a random fashion, thereby facilitating a number of self-regulated learning processes like acquiring an overview over its content before watching the complete video, or searching and selecting particular parts of the video according to ones own motivation, prior knowledge and interests. In the AVD project, several functions provide such kinds of access. In the case of educational films, viewers can read and search a written transcript of the spoken commentary. Additionally, a sequence of keyframes of important scenes, which give a visual overview over the video is presented and allows for skipping through. In the case of electronic lectures, a structured list of the presentation slides is provided, which also can be navigated and used as entry points into specific parts of the lecture. Studies of electronic lectures have shown that viewers make heavy use of these navigational possibilities.

Thirdly, computer-based videos also allow for types of self-regulated learning which to date were primarily provided for static media like texts, pictures or graphics, including the interactive control of sequence and pace of the presentation by means of entry points, stop and pause, and video sliders. Again, in a recent empirical study it could be shown that viewers make heavy use of such controlling devices and that their provision leads to more effective and efficient learning (Schwan & Riempp, in press).

To sum up current empirical evidence, computer-based types of video media have the potential of keeping the advantages of authenticity and customization while reducing its drawbacks, leading both to a more self-regulated acquisition and a deeper elaboration of its contents. These advantages were also acknowledged by the teachers who participated in the AVD project, who made heavy use of both of the extended navigational possibilities and the supplemental repositories. In particular, they used keyframes and interactive navigation through the videos in order to select appropriate material (91%) and to get an overview of the content of the video (48%). Compared to traditional types of video navigation (i.e. rewinding), these new types of interaction were considered easier and more efficient by 86% of the teachers. Similarly, the supplemental repositories of learning materials and didactical suggestions were used for classroom preparation (86%), for making work-sheets (47%), and to a lesser extent for search tasks for the students during phases of self regulated learning (32%).

All in all, and most notably, in contrast to common reservations against videos in classroom, only 9% of the teachers indicated that AV media had led their students to a more passive and receptive mode of learning. Instead 25% saw AV media as an appropriate mean of inducing a more active and self regulated learning style.

5 SUMMARY AND CONCLUSIONS

Educational movies, at least in their traditional forms, face a number of barriers which have hindered their widespread and regular use in the classroom. These barriers include the complicated and laborious process of finding and obtaining appropriate videos material, the difficulties of utilizing videos in more student-oriented and self-regulated instructional scenarios as well as the tendency of the students to view videos in a rather passive manner without deeper cognitive processing.

As the results of the Austrian-wide AVD project have shown, most of these barriers can be substantially reduced by a compound of new media technologies - including video digitization, access by means of user-friendly databases, distribution via Internet and satellite, as well as provision of supplemental multimedia material. The consequences of these technologies can be traced in the infrastructural-organisational, the instructional, and the cognitive realms of using video at school.

With regard to infrastructure, providing a convenient way for selecting and accessing the video material seems to be of special importance, as the comparison of AV media with AV academy, its live lecture counterpart, makes clear. Whereas AV media with its stock of videos received positive to enthusiastic evaluations, the reactions to AV academy were more mixed. In particular, the teachers stressed the conflict between their regular classroom schedules and the spatial and temporal restrictions imposed by the live broadcasting format of the lectures. This has to be considered a severe problem for e-Lecture streaming: Whereas all participants of the evaluation study used AV media on a more or less regular basis, 41% of them did not use AV academy at all, and of the remaining, only 33% used it in live mode, whereas the rest accessed the lectures only in their recorded form.

As a consequence, and most importantly, AVD media led the participants to a change in their teaching strategies. The majority (54%) reported an increase in their usage of audiovisual media in the classroom lessons. But media use did not only change in quantity, but also in quality, ranging from "chalk and talk" modes to learning projects and group work. Thus, in sum, the strategy of providing such material in a digitalized and easy-to-access manner seems to be a promising contribution of new media in the endeavour of introducing more enriched and varied teaching styles at school.

6   REFERENCES

Collini-Nocker, B., Knierzinger, A., Weigner, C. (2002). Streaming Technology – How does it effect education? Report from a Project using Satellite-Based Communication. In: Passey, D. & Kendall, M. (eds): TelE-Learning. The Challenge for the Third Millenium . IFIP WCC 2002 Montreal.

Garsoffky, B., Schwan, S. & Hesse, F.W. (2002). The viewpoint dependency of recognizing dynamic scenes. *Journal of Experimental Psychology: Learning, Memory, and Cognition, 28 (6),* 1035-1050.

He, L., Grudin, J., & Gupta, A. (2000). Designing presentations for on-demand viewing. *Proceedings of CSCW 2000* (pp. 127-134). Philadelphia: ACM.

Manovich, L. (2002). The *language of new media.* Cambridge, Mass.: MIT Press.

Mayer, R.E. (2001). *Multimedia learning.* Cambridge: Cambridge University Press.

Salomon, G. (1984). Television is „easy" and print is „tough": The differential investment of mental effort in learning as a function of perceptions and attribution. *Journal of Educational Psychology, 76,* 647-658.

Schwan, S., Garsoffky, B., & Hesse, F.W. (2000). Do film cuts facilitate the perceptual and cognitive organization of activity sequences? *Memory & Cognition, 28 (2),* 214-223.

Schwan, S. & Riempp, R. (in press). The cognitive benefits of interactive videos: Learning to tie nautical knots. *Learning & Instruction.*

Wetzel, C.D., Radtke, P.H. & Stern, H.W. (1994). *Instructional effectiveness of video media.* Hillsdale, N.J.: Lawrence Erlbaum.

Zahn, C., Schwan, S., Barqureo, B. (2002). Authoring Hypervideos: Design for learning and learning by design. In R. Bromme & E. Stahl (eds.), *Writing Hypertext and learning* (pp. 153-176). Pergamon Press.

Zahn, C., Schwan, S. & Barquero, B. (in press). Learning with hyperlinked videos – Design criteria and efficient strategies of using audiovisual hypermedia. *Learning & Instruction.*

INTELLIGENT LEARNING OBJECTS
An Agent-Based Approach of Learning Objects

Ricardo Silveira, Eduardo Gomes and Rosa Vicari
Universidade Federal de Pelotas, - UFPEL, Campus Universitário, s/n° - Caixa Postal 354
Pelotas - RS -Brazil rsilv@ufpel.edu.br
Universidade Federal do Rio Grande do Sul Av. Bento Gonçalves, 9500 - Campus do Vale -
Bloco IV Porto Alegre - RS –Brazil. ergomes@inf.ufrgs.br rosa.@inf.ufrgs.br

Abstract: Many people have been working hard to produce metadata specification towards a construction of Learning Objects in order to improve efficiency, efficacy and reusability of learning content based on an Object Oriented design paradigm. The possibility of reusing learning material is very important to designing learning environments for real-life learning. At the same time, many researchers on Intelligent Learning Environments have proposed the use of Artificial Intelligence through architectures based on agent societies. Teaching systems based on Multi-Agent architectures make it possible to support the development of more interactive and adaptable systems. This paper proposes an agent-based approach to produce more intelligent learning objects (ILO) according to the FIPA agent architecture reference model and the LOM/IEEE 1484 learning object specification.

Key words: Learning Objects, Real Life Learning Environments, Artificial Intelligence.

1   INTRODUCTION

This paper addresses the integration between Learning Objects and Multi-Agent Systems. A Learning Object according to Downes (2001), (2002), Mohan and Brooks (2003), Sosteric and Hesemeier (2002), is an entity of learning content which can be used several times in different courses or in different situations. The use of reusable learning objects to create learning environments improves quickness, flexibility and economy. According to Downes (2001), the cost of developing learning materials for on line learning can be large, but as the content of related courses taught at different universities and organizations often tend to be similar, the cost of developing the learning material can be shared among its potential users. The object learning approach promises to reduce significantly the time and the cost required to develop on line courses. A specific content can be used for different courses, in different places, and for different purposes.

A learning object must be modular, discoverable and interoperable, in order to be reused. To achieve these features and improve efficiency, efficacy and reusability of learning objects, many people have dedicated long hours of hard work. The majority of the efforts focus on the definition of standardization. Organizations such as IMS Global Learning Consortium (2004), IEEE (2004), ARIADNE (2004), and CanCore (2004), have contributed significantly by defining indexing standards called metadata (data about data). Metadata structures contain information to explain what the learning object is about, how to search, access, and identify it and how to retrieve educational content according to a specific demand.

These features of learning objects are very useful in designing learning environments for real-life learning applications. However, Downes (2002) points out that a lot of work must be done in order to use a learning object. First, it is necessary to build an educational environment in which they can function. It also becomes necessary to locate these objects and then arrange them in their proper order according to their design and function. In certain cases – as for example when the object is a Flash animation or a chunk of streaming media, you must arrange for the installation and configuration of appropriate viewing software, and the objects must be delivered in some appropriate context like a problem solving environment. Although all of this seems to be easier to deal with, we need smarter learning objects.

Mohan and Brooks (2003) point out several limitations of current learning objects. According to them, an instructional designer must carefully examine each learning object in which the task of finding the right object may be quite time consuming. In addition, the current learning object metadata standards are not very useful to support pedagogical decisions.

In order to improve the use of learning objects in real-life learning we propose the convergence of this technology with Artificial Intelligence. The state of the art in Intelligent Tutoring Systems (ITS) and Intelligent Learning Environments (ILE) fields points to the use of Agent Society-Based Architectures. The fundamentals of the multi-agent systems have been demonstrated to be very appropriate to designing tutoring systems, since the teaching-learning problem could be handled in a cooperative approach (Johnson & Shaw, 1997). Using a multi-agent systems approach to designing intelligent tutoring systems can result in faster, more versatile and low costs systems.

We believe that the convergence between learning objects and multi-agent systems can produce *Intelligent Learning Objects* (ILO). We propose a learning object with agent characteristics, such as autonomy, knowledge about itself and its environment, sociability and goals. Such a learning object can be more useful than current learning objects and can help to overcome some limitations presented above.

2 WHY TRANSFORM LEARNING OBJECTS IN AGENTS?

There are many benefits in integrating learning objects and agents. An Intelligent Agent is a software entity that works in a continuous and autonomous way in a particular environment, generally inhabited by other agents, and able to interfere in that environment, in a flexible and intelligent way, not requiring human intervention or guidance (Bradshaw, 1997). An agent is able to communicate with others by message exchange using a high level communication language called Agent Communication Language (ACL), which is based on the Speech Act Theory (Searle, 1981).

The most complete current learning object model, the SCORM used in real-life learning (see next section), performs the communication by calling methods (functions) and passing parameters, according to the Object Oriented Programming paradigm. Using ACL for communication among learning objects, the learning environments can perform a more powerful communication rather than this approach.

With an ACL, it is possible to supply a more powerful semantic in communication using a formal protocol and a formal Content Language (CL) based on some logic formalism to express the messages content. Using an ACL the learning objects can communicate not only variable values, but also facts, rules, mental states and others. The result is that communication using ACL and CL is potentially better than communication using the object oriented approach, like the current learning object models do.

Another interesting useful capability of intelligent agents is their potential learning ability. This feature gives to an ILO the ability to acquire new knowledge and perform different behaviours during its existence, according to its own experience. Thus, by interaction with students and other ILO, the ILO is able to evolve. It is not static like current learning objects.

The possibilities are great: an ILO can summon others to promote a learning experience that can help students in specific points; get students preferences and adapt the content presentation with the student; perform sophisticated evaluation methods, and others.

There are also many researchers addressing coordination and cooperation mechanisms among agents that help the agent society to achieve its goals. Such work can be very useful due to the possibility of a self-organizing ILO society where it can promote richer learning experiences. The coordination and cooperation mechanisms enable complex behaviours and interactions among the ILO and, as a consequence, more powerful learning experiences.

Some types of agents deliberate and make plans based on a set of mental states. These types of architecture, called BDI (Belief, Desire and Intention – Shohan 1993), can be very useful to model complex behaviours. The ILO modelled through BDI architectures can implement advanced learning objects.

Other agent features that can be interesting are autonomy, pro-activity, sociability and benevolence. The autonomy of an ILO gives it the capability to act based on its own behaviour and knowledge with no external intervention. The pro-activity feature assures that the ILO must act in order to satisfy its own objectives. The sociability and benevolence features address the capability of social and cooperative behaviour.

3 DEVELOPING THE INTELLIGENT LEARNING OBJECTS APPROACH

Some researchers concerning learning objects, (Mohan & Brooks, 2003) propose an object-oriented approach. This architecture has a class of objects called LearningObject, which is the superclass of all learning objects. Every learning object is an instance of this class.

The Sharable Content Object Reference Model (SCORM®, 2004) is currently the most complete model of reference for learning content reuse, and it is very useful in real-life learning. In the SCORM model, the learning resources (assets) are added in packages (SCO). Each SCO has an archive (manifest file) with information about the content that it loads and on how it must be used. Besides such information are the SCO metadata and the assets metadata. There are also references for assets and sequencing rules.

Communication between the SCO and a Learning Management System (LMS) is made through a function call of an Application Program Interface (API) implemented for the LMS. These calls are made in JavaScript and can involve information about the students. This information is stored in a Data Model, which allows one standardized communication between SCOs and LMSs. To construct an SCO means to build the manifest file and add together all the learning resources in an archive. The SCO must be able to call upon the API methods.

To follow the SCORM run-time model, an Intelligent Learning Object must be able to manipulate information such as metadata, references to learning resources and rules for sequencing these learning resources. They must have a way of communicating between Intelligent Learning Objects and LMSs.

To achieve agent capabilities the Intelligent Learning Objects must communicate through message exchange using an Agent Communication Language (ACL) and a Content Language (CL). The Foundation of Intelligent Physical Agents (FIPA, 2002), a non-profit organization, produced standards for the inter-operation of heterogeneous software agents. Two important contributions of FIPA are an agent communication language called FIPA-ACL and a content language called FIPA-SL. There are several frameworks that allow the construction of FIPA complaint agents. They provide a set of JAVA classes and services for communication between the agents. Thus, we will use one of them as a reference to implement the Intelligent Learning Object model.

4 INTELLIGENT LEARNING OBJECTS MULTI-AGENT ARCHITECTURE

The proposed multi-agent architecture (Fig 1) encompasses two types of agents: Intelligent Learning Objects and LMS agent. The LMS agent represents all the features of the learning environment which are not performed by ILO. The Intelligent Learning Objects are our object of study in this work. The agent environment that these agents inhabit is a FIPA complaint environment provided by FIPA Operational System (FIPA-OS) Framework (FIPA-OS 2002).

Figure 1. Intelligent Learning Objects multi-agent architecture.

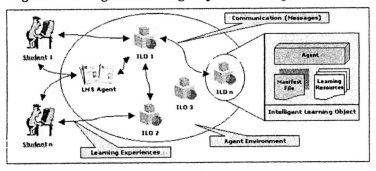

Students interact with an LMS agent in order to gain learning experiences. The LMS agent searches for the appropriate ILO and invokes it. The ILO is then is then responsible for generating learning experiences for the students. In this task, it can communicate with the LMS agent along with other agents in order to promote richer learning experiences. All the communication is performed by message exchange in FIPA-ACL.

The LMS agent task is to manage student interactions with the learning environment where the ILO society is working. Thus, it provides a way for the students access to the ILO, stores information about the students, and passes to the ILO all the student information. The LMS agents must be able to communicate with the Intelligent Learning Objects.

An **Intelligent Learning Object** is an agent that is able to play the role of a learning object. However, it is also a special type of learning object that contains agent features. These two definitions are correct. The responsibility of the ILO is generating learning experiences to the students. The ILOs are agents that can generate learning experiences in the sense of learning objects, that is, they must be modular, discoverable, inter-operable, and, most important of all, reusable.

5   AGENT ARCHITECTURE FOR AN ILO

The Intelligent Learning Object model is composed of an agent, a Manifest File, and Learning Resources. The agent is able to interpret the Manifest File, which has information about how the agent should work. The Manifest File contains references to learning resources (content packaging information). Learning resources are actual files containing learning content. The ILO is able to deliver these learning resources to students. The Manifest File also has information on how the learning resources should be delivered to students (Sequence Rules) and about what the learning experience generated by the ILO is about (Metadata). The internal architecture of this type of Intelligent Learning Object is as shown in Figure 2.

Figure 2. Internal architecture of ILO

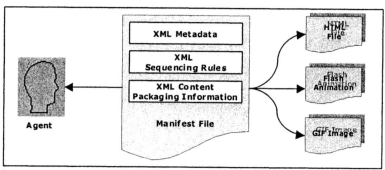

The metadata information is used to describe the learning content that the Intelligent Learning Object loads. Metadata information enables the search and discoverability of the ILO model. The most complete current metadata model to describe learning content is the P1484.12.1 IEEE Standard for Learning Object Metadata (IEEE 2004), an adopted metadata model. The metadata information is described in XML using the P1484.12.3 Standard for XML binding for Learning Object Metadata data model (IEEE 2004).

The content packaging information provides the functionality to describe and pack learning materials. Content packaging addresses the description, structure, and location of the learning resources and the definition of some particular content types. The content packaging uses the IMS Content Packaging Information (IMS 2004). This is described in XML using the IMS Content Packaging XML Binding Specification.

Sequencing rules define a method for representing the intended behaviour of an authored learning experience so that the ILO can sequence the Learning Resources. The specification defines the required behaviours and functionality that a conforming ILO must implement. It incorporates rules that describe the branching or flow of instruction through content according to the outcomes of a learner's interactions with content. We are using the IMS Simple Sequencing Information and Behaviour Model described through the IMS Simple Sequencing XML Binding (IMS 2004).

The Learning Resources represent the actual files referenced by the content packaging information. These files may be local files that are contained within the ILO, or they can be external files that are referenced by a Universal Resource Indicator. They can be of any type that can be represented in a Web Browser. This possibility is very important for distance learning applications.

6   CONCLUSIONS

At this point, we quote Downes (2002): We need to stop thinking of learning objects as chunks of instructional content and to start thinking of them as small, self-reliant computer programs. This means more than giving a learning object some sort of functionality, more than writing Java calculators or interactive animations. When we think of a learning object we need to think of it as a small computer program that is aware of and can interact with its environment.

Intelligent Learning Objects are able to improve the adaptability and interactivity of complex learning environments built with these kinds of components by the interaction among the learning objects and between learning objects and other agents in a more robust conception of communication rather than a single method invocation as the object-oriented paradigm use to be.

7 REFERENCES

Advanced Distributed Learning (ADL)a. (2004) *Sharable Content Object Reference Model (SCORM ®) 2004 Overview.* [www.adlnet.org].

Alliance of remote instructional authoring & distribution networks for Europe. (2004), ARIADNE, [http://ariadne.unil.ch].

Bradshaw, J. M. (1997)An introduction to software agents In: Bradshaw, J. M. Ed. *Software Agents.* Massachusetts: MIT Press, 1997.

CanCore (2004) Canadian Core About. [http://www.cancore.ca/about.html].

Downes, S. (2001), Learning objects: resources for distance education worldwide. in *International Review of Research in Open and Distance Learning,* 2(1). 2001

Downes , Stephen (2002) *Smart Learning Objects.*

FIPA: The foundation for Intelligent Physical Agents (2002). *Specifications.* [http://www.fipa.org}..

IEEE Learning Technology Standards Committee (2004) *Specifications.* [http://ltsc.ieee.org].

IMS Global Learning Consortium. (2004) *Current specifications.* [http://www.imsglobal.org /specifications.cfm].

Johnson, W. Lewis; Shaw, Erin. (2000) Using agents to overcome deficiencies in web-based courseware. In: World Conference on Artificial Intelligence in Education, AI-ED, 8., 1997. *Proceedings...* [www.isi.edu/isd/johnson.html.].

Mohan, P.and Brooks, C. (2003) Engineering a Future for Web-based Learning Objects. *Proceedings of International Conference on Web Engineering,* Oviedo, Asturias, Spain.

Searle, John R. (1981) *Speech Acts - An Essay in the Philosophy of Language.* Coimbra: Livraria Almedina.

Shoham, Y (1993) Agent-oriented programming. *Artificial Intelligence,* Amsterdam, n.60, v.1, p.51 – 92.

Sosteric, Mike, Hesmeier, Susan (2002) When is a Learning Object not an Object: A first step towards .a theory of learning objects *International Review of Research in Open and Distance Learning* ISSN: 1492-3831

ACKNOWLEDGEMENT

This project is granted by Brazilian research agencies: CNPq and FAPERGS.

USING ICT IN A PROBLEM-BASED LEARNING APPROACH
A student and teacher perspective

Gina Reyes and Roger Gabb
School of Information Systems and Centre for Educational Development and Support, Victoria University, Australia
Gina.Reyes@vu.edu.au   Roger.Gabb@vu.edu.au

Abstract: This paper discusses the problem-based learning (PBL) approach used in a subject called "Issues in Tertiary Teaching and Learning" that forms part of a Graduate Certificate in Tertiary Education at Victoria University. The first author took the subject as a student while the second author taught the subject and views the experience from the viewpoint of both student and teacher to show how ICT and the PBL approach can support real-life learning. The paper first discusses the PBL approach and then describes the problem-based learning approach used in the subject. The use of ICT was a central component in the approach, and a discussion is presented on how the characteristics of the technology assisted in delivering quality learning experiences. The overall discussion shows that (1) the approach has the potential to encourage deep learning, but this seems to be dependent on the degree of relevance of the problems posed to the individual student; (2) real life learning, in this case, did not revolve around finding "one right answer" to a situation or to developing expertise in a subject area, but being able to approach a situation using systematic problem solving skills; (3) real life learning implies responsibility on the part of the student to both "own" and manage their learning; and (4) the use of ICT in this instance supported the process and was an integral part of the learning environment and learning activities.

Key words: Problem based learning, real life learning, deep learning, student, teacher.

1   INTRODUCTION

This paper takes the perspective that a person experiences real life learning when he engages in learning a skill or applying a concept to a real-life situation because of a "need to know," which is accompanied by a sense of relevance. In other words, a student approaches learning saying, "I want to learn this because it will help me understand and deal with what I am going through now (or may go through) in my life."

This "engagement" with the object of learning can be observed in what is called the "deep approach" to learning, resulting in a student's cognitive development.

Recent literature on this approach (Biggs 2003; Cope 2003) describe students as developing a personal interest in the subject matter so that there is a desire to seek relationships between, and beyond, different aspects of the subject matter. It involves relating the content to one's own experience, developing an understanding of the underlying laws, rules, processes, relating the content to one's own experience and understanding and thus bringing onto oneself, new insight and perspectives.

The deep approach to learning is differentiated from the surface approach to learning, where a student only considers aspects of the subject matter in isolation; there is no commitment to seek out relationships between these aspects beyond what is required in assessment tasks. There is no personal interest or sense of relevance in what is being learnt, and whatever is learnt can easily be forgotten.

As there are significant similarities in the concepts of "real life learning" and the "deep approach to learning," this paper will use the phrase "deep learning" to refer to both concepts.

This paper will first discuss the PBL approach and its characteristics and highlight how it can encourage deep learning. It will then describe the case study subject where PBL was used, supported by an ICT system. A summary of the reflections from both authors will follow demonstrating the extent of the real life learning supported by the approach.

1.1   Limitations of the paper

There are many issues surrounding the use of PBL (Schwartz et al, 2001), some including: (1) developing acceptance of the approach, (2) developing students' responsibility for their own learning and for teachers to facilitate that learning; (3) developing assessment methods consistent with how students are learning in the PBL approach; and (4) understanding that PBL does not focus on developing expertise in content but in developing specific skills useful in problem solving.

While resolving these issues are important in promoting the use of PBL as a way to developing deep learning approaches, this paper only shows how in one case, the benefits of using this approach does have a significant impact on real life learning and on professional development.

2 PROBLEM-BASED LEARNING AS A DEEP LEARNING APPROACH

Problem-based learning (PBL) has been generally described as a learning approach whereby students are presented with problem, and then they undertake a systematic, student-centred process of inquiry (Barrows and Tamblyn, 1980). Schwartz et al (2001) argue that "although the purpose of using problems in PBL is to stimulate learning of information and concepts brought about by the problems, PBL does teach both a method of approaching and an attitude towards problem solving," (p.2). In this approach, students typically work in small groups. The learning process is facilitated by a tutor, who acts as a moderator of discussions rather than a direct source of information. The learning process is student-centred in that the direction and content of learning, as well as the process of gathering information, is controlled and undertaken by the students themselves. The process can be described as follows (Schwartz et al, 2001, p. 2), where students:

1. are presented with a problem without any preparatory study in the area of the problem;
2. interact with each other to explore their existing knowledge as it relates to the problem;
3. form and test hypotheses about the underlying mechanisms that might account for the problem;
4. identify further learning needs for making progress with the problem;
5. undertake self-study between group meetings to satisfy the identified learning needs;
6. return to the group to integrate the newly gained knowledge and apply it to the problem;
7. repeat steps 3 to 6 as necessary; and
8. reflect on the process and on the content that has been learnt.

Boud (1985) identifies characteristics of problem-based learning subjects, some of which are:

1. Students draw upon their current base of experience in order to make a contribution their learning.

2. There is an emphasis on students taking their own responsibility for their learning as they are expected to plan, organise, search for information, and evaluate their learning.
3. The nature of problems require that the approach to the problem-solving is multidisciplinary or transdisciplinary and thus staff and students are draw into areas outside their expertise.
4. The approach involves having to use theory for practice: theory is drawn naturally into knowledge through the demands of problem-solutions (Argyris and Schon 1974).
5. Students are confronted with the need to know how to approach a problem and acquire new knowledge (Woods 1983).
6. The role of staff changes from that of instructor to that of facilitator. Less emphasis is placed on the presentation of information, more on assisting students to acquire skills of learning and problem-solution (Knowles 1975).

Cope (2003) presents a framework that identifies the factors that are associated with deep learning. These factors are categorised into: factors describing the learning environment, and factors describing the nature of learning and assessment activities. For example, some factors in the learning environment would be (1) the subject is well organised and has clear goals, (2) the student has responsibility for their own learning including some control over the content and approach to learning, (3) the teaching is stimulating and demonstrates the lecturer's personal commitment to the subject matter and stresses its meaning and relevance to the students, and (4) assessment feedback is appropriate and timely. Some factors in the nature of learning and assessment activities are (1) the tasks should be active and experiential, (2) the tasks should encourage the student to reflect on the content and the learning process, and (3) assessment tasks expose students to different perspectives on a topic. He used this framework to identify how ICTs can be used to support deep learning. His argument is that if the technology is able to support a learning environment and a set of learning and assessment activities that adhere to these factors, then deep learning is possible. As a result, there is a perceived higher quality of learning outcomes. He presents the factors as a framework to justify the development of certain learning systems. His framework is presented here to show the ICTs, in and of themselves, do not promote quality or deep learning. It is how these technologies are used.

The following case study describes a subject whereby WebCT was used, and in comparing it to the framework shows that it can serve as an example of how technology can be used to support deep learning.

3   CASE STUDY

The subject used in this case study is called "HEG1706 - Issues in Tertiary Teaching and Learning." The class is conducted over a 12-week period and is offered to teaching staff at Victoria University, Melbourne as part of a 3-subject Graduate Certificate program in Tertiary Education. The subject typically has about 20-25 students in a class, broken down into two groups of 10-15 students.

The subject is designed to explore some contemporary problems in tertiary education and training within the Australian tertiary education and training system. These problems are used to explore tertiary education policy and practice in the classroom and workplace. As a PBL approach is used, it is also designed to introduce participants to this method of learning.

3.1   Learning Outcomes

The subject is designed to enable students to achieve the following learning outcomes:
- Respond to changing environments in tertiary education and training
- Develop information literacy skills in the field of tertiary education and training
- Understand key features of the Australian tertiary education and training environment
- Interpret and implement tertiary education policy; and
- Understand the potential and limitations of problem based learning within tertiary education and training.

The subject is taught using a mixed-mode approach. It includes lecture/discussions, regular face-to-face problem based learning group sessions, individual and group research, and online communication using WebCT. There are three assessment tasks:
- Report of one PBL cycle (40%)
- Contribution to online discussion (20%)
- Submission for a change to local policy or practice (40%)

Students are assessed using a framework called the Structure of the Observed Learning Outcome (SOLO). It is an approach to assessment originally developed by John Biggs and Kevin Collis (1982). At its heart is the specification of desired learning outcomes in terms of a hierarchy based on the *quality* of student response. It is a form of criterion-referenced assessment, where the criteria for achieving a grade are pre-defined. In SOLO assessment, learning outcomes are pre-defined for each grade level, with the expected learning outcomes becoming more complex at each level.

SOLO assessment depends on the *quality* of the student response rather than the *quantity* of the student response. It depends on the assessor making a judgement about the quality of student work using pre-defined criteria at a number of different levels rather than counting the number of correct facts in that work. It is therefore a qualitative assessment rather than a quantitative assessment.

3.1.1 Problem-based Learning cycle

The class was conducted as follows:

1. In the first meeting, the problem-based learning approach was first explained to the students. An overview of the problems to be used in the class were presented, and assessment was explained. WebCT was introduced, an brief tutorial was given on how to access class materials and the discussion boards.

2. In the second meeting, the first problem was introduced. The problem was described in two paragraphs, using language that placed the student in the centre of the problem ("You are the course coordinator of this program and you are faced with this situation ..."). The students, with the guidance of the facilitator, identified about five or six key learning issues (the things the students needed to know more about). The students then decided who would be responsible for finding out more information about which issue. The students were given two weeks to research their assigned issue. Over that period they were to send in discussion board postings on their progress.

3. The third meeting was held after a fortnight. Students took turns summarising their findings on each of the issues and then, as a group, discussed the different approaches to a problem. The end aim was not for the students to agree on a solution, but to understand how to approach the problem, and to incorporate this understanding and problem-solving approach to their own professional practice.

4. The succeeding meetings followed the same fortnightly pattern, until all five problems were tackled.

The topics involved in the five problems used are outlined in Table 1.

Table 1. Problems used in the PBL approach for HEG1706
1. Problem-based learning – is a PBL approach appropriate for your course? If so, how would you go about introducing PBL into the course?
2. Core Graduate Attributes – How would you proceed to incorporate the development of information literacy and its assessment in the core subjects in your course?
3. Learning styles – What would you recommend in answer to the issue of using learning style assessment to select students for group work and then matching learning activities to the different learning styles?
4. Quality – How would you go about designing a quality management system that meets the requirements of AQTF, AUQA, and ISO 9001?
5. Assessing group projects – How would you assess group projects in a way that accounts for individual contribution?

4   REFLECTIONS ON THE RESULTS

The authors were both involved in the subject, Roger as the subject coordinator/facilitator and Gina as the student. Both reflected on the results of the subject and answered the following questions:

1. What was your impression of the subject? How would you compare the experience with that of a traditional lecture/class format?
2. How did the subject, in your view, create a learning environment that supported deep learning?
3. How has the subject helped you develop your professional practice?

For brevity, these reflections were synthesised and are presented below in point form.

4.1   The student's perspective: Gina

In Gina's reflection, the following points were made:

1. The difference between the lecture format and problem-based learning format presented a challenge – the student is no longer a passive recipient of information – and thus required a different pattern of study behaviour.
2. "Engagement" or deep learning was not immediate while undertaking online discussion; initially a surface approach to learning was taken.

This was a direct result of Gina's decision to first focus on putting in enough effort just to pass the online discussion component. Engagement was evident only when the problem on group assessment was discussed, as this problem was a key issue in Gina's teaching practice. It was in this problem that Gina derived the most benefit – she retained more information and felt she "learnt something important" as a result.

3. The use of the WebCT discussion board tool was found to be appropriate mainly because of its asynchronous nature. Gina was able to contribute to the online discussion at her convenience. But it was only the medium and not the motivation for learning.

4. There seemed to be an average of about 100 postings per problem. Gina found that this caused information overload, and she felt she did not gain the full benefit of the discussion because she was not able to read and cognitively process everything.

5. In the face-to-face discussions after the online discussions, Gina felt the need to be told what the right answer was, in order for her to "confirm" or "justify" what she felt she knew about the problem's solution.

6. In hindsight, there was the realisation that part of the learning was not just the content generated by the problem-solving process, but the learning was also about how to approach a particular problem using the method of "finding something out using valid literature."

7. In addition, because the problem of group assessment prompted Gina to examine and improve her teaching practice, the learning from the subject launched Gina into a further exploration of practice resulting in further learning. Thus, it is argued that real life learning occurred in this instance with the problem being the starting point for inquiry beyond the classroom.

4.2   The Teacher's Perspective: Roger

In Roger's reflection, the following points were made:

1. In offering the Graduate Certificate in Tertiary Education, it seems the learning and teaching approaches often send more powerful educational messages to participants than the content, in other words that the "how" is more important than the "what".

2. The focus of this professional development course is on developing the broad capabilities that are required of a tertiary teacher to operate effectively in the complex and changing environment. This included strong information literacy skills so that they could locate, evaluate, manage and use knowledge relevant to the situations they faced in the

classroom. Some of this knowledge is to be found in books and journals, much of the practical knowledge that beginning academics need is found elsewhere, experienced colleagues and transient websites being two important sources. We also knew that many of our students had a great deal of difficulty in using the formal tertiary education literature, let alone using it to help them with teaching problems. We also wanted to encourage these academics to come to grips with the policies that impact on their practice, whether those policies are at national, state, university or departmental level. It seemed that these aims could not be achieved with a traditional lecture/ discussion format and so that resulted in a shift to a PBL format.

3. There was a dramatic development in information literacy skills as participants learnt how to access information that is relevant to the learning issues the group has identified.

4. There was a growing realisation of the sense in John Biggs's theory of constructive alignment (Biggs 2003) as it was revisited problem after problem. The results of final assessment task which is a formal submission for change in a policy or practice show that students were able to achieve the learning outcomes of the subject. Some are directed to course leaders, some to heads of school, some to Deans and some to the Vice-Chancellor but they almost all demonstrate that these teachers can now use evidence from the literature to support their arguments for changes in policy and practice aimed at improving student learning.

5. Roger was concerned about the following:
   a) When something that he regarded as important is rejected by the group as inconsequential or unconvincing.
   b) The reliance on websites rather than on books and refereed journal articles, even when they are available online.
   c) Students who actively participate in face-to-face sessions but do not participate online, as they find the work harder in PBL than they expected

5   DISCUSSION AND CONCLUSION

The reflections on the experience highlight the following:
1. The PBL approach has the potential to encourage deep learning, but this seems to be dependent on the degree of relevance of the problems posed to the individual student. This was evident from Gina's reflection that her engagement in the process was maximal when the

problem was directly relevant to her own professional life. In the next year, one group identified the same problem that engaged Gina as the least effective of the five they tackled because they had already thought through most of the issues relating to assessing group projects. This raises the question of whether the problems used should be identified by the participants themselves if they are already practitioners – a further step towards real life learning.

2. Real life learning, in this case, did not revolve around finding "one right answer" to a situation or to developing expertise in a subject area, but being able to approach a situation using systematic problem solving skills. This is evident in Gina's reflection that while she did not perceive herself as an expert in group assessment techniques, she was able to begin a process of systematic inquiry into her own practice, thus developing other, perhaps more effective, means of group assessment. It is clear in this implementation of PBL that "solving the problem" is far less important than using the problem as a stimulus for powerful learning. Returning to the problem at the end of the cycle is almost anticlimactic – it provides a sense of closure but the important learning has already happened by this stage.

3. Real life learning implies responsibility on the part of the student to both "own" and manage their learning. The benefit of the learning to the student is dependent on the student's approach to the learning activity: unless a student "engages" with the material, then quality learning is not achieved. This has implications for the student (the student has to have a desire to learn) and for the teacher (the problems posed need to be relevant to the student in order for the student to want to engage). The challenge for the teacher is to develop a series of practice-based problems that raise important learning issues while at the same time engaging all (or most) learners. Effective problems are, to some extent, intriguing puzzles with no obvious solution rather than well-defined problems with one correct answer. Problems like this are not only pedagogically effective but also mirror what practitioners face in real life.

4. Finally, the use of ICT in this instance supported the process and was an integral part of the learning environment. It supported deep learning in that it provided a convenient means to interact and communicate ideas, which is a central component of the problem-based learning approach. In following Cope's (2003) framework of factors affecting deep learning, the technology had the potential to provide quality learning because (a) it provided a means to obtain feedback in an appropriate and timely fashion, (b) it supported a process of inquiry that was active and experiential, (c) the discussion boards exposed

students to different perspectives on a topic, (d) the asynchronous nature of the technology gave the student a sense of responsibility over their own learning, and (e) having students search for information using the Internet provided some control over the content and approach to learning.

6   REFERENCES

Argyris, C., & Schon, D. (1974). *Theory in practice.* San Francisco: Jossey-Bass.

Barrows, H. S., & Tamblyn, R. N. (1980). *Problem-Based Learning: An approach to medical education.* New York: Springer.

Biggs, J. B., & Collis, K. F. (1982). *Evaluating the quality of learning: the SOLO taxonomy (structure of the observed learning outcome).* New York: Academic Press.

Biggs, J. (2003). *Teaching for quality learning at university: what the student does,* 2nd ed. Buckingham: Society for Research in Higher Education and Open University Press.

Boud, D. (1985). Problem-based learning in perspective. In D. Boud (Ed.), *Problem-based learning in education for the professions.* Sydney: Higher Education and Development Society of Australasia.

Cope, C. (2003). A framework for using learning technologies in higher education to enhance the quality of students' learning outcomes. In G.Crisp, D.Thiele, I.Scholten, S.Barker and J.Baron (Eds), *Interact, Integrate, Impact: Proceedings of the 20th Annual Conference of the Australasian Society for Computers in Learning in Tertiary Education.* Adelaide, 7-10 December 2003.

Knowles, M. (1975). *Self-directed learning: a guide for learners and teachers.* Chicago: Follet.

Schwartz, P., Mennin, S., & Webb, G. (Eds.). (2001). *Problem-Based Learning: case studies, experience and practice.* London: Kogan Page Limited.

Woods, D. R. (1983). Introducing explicit training in problem solving in our courses. *Higher Education Research and Development, 2,* 79-102.

REAL-LIFE LEARNING IN HIGHER EDUCATION
Embedding and modelling the effective use of ICT

Paul Nicholson and Geoff White
Faculty of Education, Deakin University, Australia
pauln@deakin.edu.au and geoffw@deakin.edu.au

Abstract: While real-life learning is commonly identified with workplace or lifelong learning outside of an individual's initial pre-workforce education, this does not preclude real-life learning experiences occurring within Higher Education programs. This paper describes a program that aims to integrate real-life learning experiences into a pre-service teacher education program in a way that provides rich, contextualised learning experiences, provides a basis for meeting the requirements of external certification criteria that focus on evidence-based performance rather than on academic competencies, and provides students with authentic learning experiences in the effective use of ICT in their professional roles and classroom-based work.

Key words: Teacher education, higher education, practicum, problem-based learning.

1   INTRODUCTION

While 'real-life' learning is commonly identified with workplace or lifelong learning outside of an individual's initial pre-workforce education in the school and Higher Education sectors, this does not preclude real-life learning experiences occurring within Higher Education programs. In particular, in those programs that focus on the development of performance-based expertise in professional practice – such as in teaching, the Arts, and in medicine – the use of real-life workplace-based learning experiences has the potential to greatly enrich and enhance learners understandings and skill development. Putnam & Borko (2000) argue that such contextualised experiences are critical for the effective development of teachers' thinking. These may also form the basis of reflective praxis (Kane, 1999) and life-long learning around pedagogy and educational practices (Levin, 2003). The common lack of connection between school and post-school learning (Fig, 1) often means that learning in schools is seen as an end in itself, with little relevance to subsequent life. However, Walsh & Cripps Clarke (elsewhere in this volume) have shown that connections between work contexts and formal education are important in the development of expert teachers.

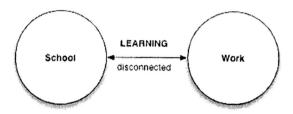

Figure 1. Traditional school to work learning development

The use of workplace contexts and real-life learning helps to ensure that such programs accommodate learners' concerns and contemporary developments, and that they meet learners' expectations of acquiring practical and up-to-date knowledge that is applicable in their workplace – something very important to learners involved in ongoing practicum programs. Countering this possible advantage is the need to ensure that such programs also provide learners with a wide range of professional and academic knowledge about conceptual, practical and policy issues that can be applied to a wide range contexts – and not just those developed in or around one particular context or practicum experience. It is therefore necessary to ensure that such programs are designed around a blended learning model that provides learners with workplace, professional, and academic perspectives.

By providing overlap between school-based and real-life learning, learners have the opportunity to reflect on the relationships between them and to develop rich understandings of the reciprocal relevance and application of their school-based learning to the workplace. Such contextualised self-reflective processes are a central element of lifelong learning and foundational to the development of effective teaching (e.g., Berliner, 1991) and the development of praxis at an early career stage. It is hoped that this will be a useful foundation for the learners' lifelong professional learning (both formal and 'real-life'). Curiously, the PBL is not widely used in teacher education programmes, where didactic approaches and traditional curricula seem to be resilient to change (cf. Nicholson, 1995, 2004; Nicholson & deWacht, 2002).

2 THE CONTEXT

The context of this paper is the semester-long unit 'Creating Effective Learning Environments' (CELE) — one of six units of the 'Education Studies Major' (ESM) program in the Faculty of Education at Deakin University. The ESM aims to provide students with a broad range of academic and professional knowledge and skills that meet the diverse needs of graduate teachers. Other units in the ESM cover developmental and learning issues, curriculum models and influences and the development of particular curricula. Methodological issues in particular content areas are addressed in a separate series of 'methods' units. Students also undertake an extensive practicum program over the duration of their degree. Students in the ESM include recent school graduates, mature age learners making a career change to teaching, and international students. The ESM program is delivered face-to-face on three campuses at Burwood, Geelong Warrnambool. It is also offered in off-campus mode.

The focus of CELE is on educational policy, classroom management and planning, and to develop the students' ICT skills and their awareness of its educational potential for supporting engaging and inclusive learning environments (cf. UNESCO, 2004). Its overall aim is to prepare students to be able to create safe, supporting, challenging, engaging and inclusive learning environments across a wide range of socio-economic and cultural contexts. It also has an explicit brief to support the students' practicum. These foci reflect a crowded tertiary curriculum resulting from a prior institutional reorganisations that reduced the time available to systematically address these topics elsewhere in the curriculum.

In the process of operationalising the unit, two key decisions were made: first, to adopt a problem-based learning (PBL) model and second, to base the PBL program in and around real-life learning experiences to the extent that the course and practicum structures and requirements allowed. These decisions were made separately and independently at different times.

2.1 Why PBL?

The decision to adopt a PBL approach was based on the belief that in a program about effective learning environments, it was essential to adopt an effective adult learning environment model for the unit itself. PBL provided the opportunity to both create an appropriate student-centred team-based active learning environment, and to provide students with experiences of a different pedagogical approach to learning than those previously experienced in their course – a case of learning by modelling and immersion in which students were to act out the role of teachers developing policy as the basis of their work in CELE and to engage in genuine professional tasks.

While PBL has often been seen as an effective way to engage students in authentic tasks, it has also been criticised by some for its focus on solving 'problems' as opposed to acquiring knowledge through more traditional didactic approaches. However, such criticism fails to acknowledge both (a) the extensive incidental learning that occurs in the process of clarifying the problem, finding possible solutions, and in identifying the optimal solution, and (b) the fundamental importance of situative and contextualised learning (and practice) in supporting teachers' cognitive development and expertise (Putnam & Borko, 1997). The latter point, of course, strongly supports the use of real-life learning experiences to provide the kind of rich, authentic learning that can support the development of meaningful reflective practice and 'validate' the students' coursework.

2.2   The Role of Real-Life Learning

The use of real-life learning experiences arose from the PBL context in three ways. First, the PBL task modelled a range a real-life professional roles; second, students used real school data as the basis of their work; third, by providing them with the opportunity to integrate their PBL task into their practicum program by 'sharing and validating' their developing policy with teachers and administrators in their practicum schools. This often led them to engage in extended discussions with teachers and administrators, and provided the students with real-life learning experiences as teachers and coordinators discussed and reviewed their particular school's policy and development issues – making strong links between their engagement in CELE and their real-life practicum experiences. This constant engagement and 'validation' of the nature and purpose of CELE in their practicum workplace (Fig. 2) provided the students with far deeper insights into the nature, development and purpose of policy than has generally been the case in the previous version of CELE which did not adopt this approach.

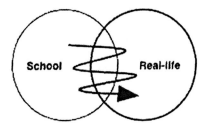

Figure 2. A blended-learning model to accommodate real-life learning

To firmly embed their work in real-life contexts, fictitious school data were provided for students to choose from, each representing a different kind of school based on 'like-school' data generated by a staff team member experienced in school reviews. The variables included in the data included state-wide testing results, the level of funding support for disadvantaged families (i.e., the Education Maintenance Allowance), demographics and cultural backgrounds of the school community, teacher-related issues such as profiles and attitudinal data, transition data and student retention rates. Student teams were required to interrogate the data in order to determine the nature of the 'problems' in their school, to then develop appropriate policy items to address them, and finally to develop and deliver a multimedia presentation of their policy recommendations at a notional school meeting. This presentation was assessed by a panel of university staff members and the students' class peers (Fig.3). The presentation was the only way in which the students' policy development was assessed. This gave the students the experience of evaluating policy in a real-life context.

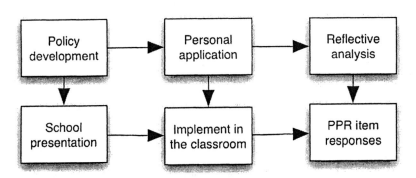

Figure 3. Tasks and assessment items

Later, the students had to demonstrate their ability to implement their policy items. Their ability to do this was peer-assessed by their team members using an evidence-based policy check list developed by each team. Students were encouraged to work closely with their practicum supervisors and other teachers in developing their lesson plans so that there was the opportunity to gain feedback and to learn from them. Finally, the students are required to reflect on their experiences in this program by developing a set of responses to likely annual review questions based on the themes of the unit and as developed in their tasks. Through this multi-stage assessment process, the students have to demonstrate their increasing understanding of policy development in a particular context, to apply it to their teaching, and to be able to justify their decision making to professional peers.

2.3   The Victorian Institute of Teaching

The Victorian Institute of Teaching (VIT) was established in 2001 in recognition of the need to provide a professional body for the teaching profession — one that would serve to enhance the professional status of teachers, to regulate entry to the teaching profession, and to ensure the maintenance of professional standards (VIT, 2004b). Whereas previously, new entrants to the profession could readily gain full registration based on meeting the academic and practicum requirements of their teacher education programme, new graduates are now given provisional registration for a period of 12 months to allow them time to develop and to enhance their repertoire of professional skills and to provide the opportunity to gather evidence of their ability to operate as in independent professional in their educational workplace (VIT, 2004a). All CELE tasks may be used as 'evidence' that can be incorporated into the students' current portfolios.

3   THE USE OF ICT

For the past 40 years, the use of ICT in Teacher Education has been problematic (Nicholson & Underwood, 1996) and only recently have large scale initiatives attempted to provide clear pedagogical guidelines for educators (Cornu, 2001; UNESCO, 2004; Watson, 2001). Whereas many undergraduate students in CELE have basic ICT competencies, this is not necessarily the case with mature-age postgraduate students – those leaving another vocation to become a teacher. In both cases there is a real need to provide them with the basis for engaging in the professional and pedagogical use of ICT (as opposed to developing software skills).

Requiring CELE students to present their policy proposals as a basic multimedia presentation (PowerPoint and digital video) would introduce students to these basic technologies, and provide them with the experience of using them in a professional, as opposed to pedagogical, role. It was also decided that, consistent with the PBL approach, the staff would not provide formal instruction in the use of PowerPoint or iMovie software – student teams would be given a brief introduction to their functionality and a range of web-based support materials. In practice this approach worked well, with most teams having little trouble mastering the software.

The use of an ICT-based presentation in this unit served to force the students to make specific judgments about their materials and the approach to their presentation. They had to make hard decisions about what to focus on, how to represent their policy recommendations, and how to organise their team members presentation skills for an optimal presentation.

Procedural and developmental ICT issues arose in the development of the presentations that were similar to those teachers face in schools.. Some teams attempted to develop their media before their policy content was finished; others had difficulty in fitting their extensive policy recommendations to the confines dictated by the presentation format. There were also significant network and media-based issues.

The real value of the ICT component in CELE lies in its use as a focusing and contextualising tool (in the Activity Theory sense) that mediated the students interactions with peers, with policy issues, and with other team members in ways that forced extensive collaboration and engagement (cf. Roschelle & Pea, 2002) through the need to create and perform, as well as learn the required ICT skills. In many ways it acts like Pea & Kurlands' (1987) cognitive technologies for writing by providing a focusing and filtering mechanism through the dual dictates of media format and presentation context; these helped to drive the pathways between the university and workplace contexts (cf. Fig. 2). The development of a multimedia presentation gave the students a real-word/real-life context for using ICT, and has (anecdotally) given many of them the confidence to explore its further use in their teaching and professional roles.

4 CONCLUSIONS

The use of a real-life context, along with the use of ICT, to foster and model engagement and collaboration appears to have been effective in helping students to see both the importance of educational policy development in schools and the value of challenging and engaging learning environments. Course evaluation data are highly supportive of the use of both PBL and real-life contexts. This suggests that this focus should be maintained and extended to other units in the ESM. The role of ICT is critical, not because of its nature per se, but because of its use a mediating and focusing tool.

5   REFERENCES

Berliner, D. (1991). Educational psychology and pedagogical expertise: New findings and new opportunities for thinking and training. *Educational Psychologist, 2,* 145-155.

Cornu, B. (2001). *Winds of Change in the Teaching Profession* (Report of the French National Commission for UNESCO). Paris: UNESCO.

Kane, J. (1999). *Education, information, and transformation: essays on learning and thinking.* Upper Saddle River, N.J.: Merrill.

Levin, B. B. (2003). *Case Studies of Teacher Development: An In-Depth Look at How Thinking About Pedagogy Develops Over Time.* Mahwah, NJ: Lawrence Erlbaum.

Nicholson, P. S. (1995). A Curriculum for Teachers or Learners? In D. Watson & D. Tinsley (Eds.), *Integrating Information Technology into Education* (pp. 85-94). London: Chapman & Hall.

Nicholson, P. S. (2004). E-Training or E-Learning? Towards a synthesis for the knowledge-era workplace. In P. S. Nicholson, Thompson, J., Ruhonen, M., Mulitsilta, J (Ed.), *elearning solutions for professional organizations* (pp. 360). New York: Kluwer.

Nicholson, P. S., & deWacht, P. (2002). City to Surf: A peer-to-peer model of online professional development. An On-line collaborative model. In D. Passey & M. Kendall (Eds.), *Tele-learning 2002* (pp. 113-120). New York: Kluwer.

Nicholson, P. S., & Underwood, J. (1996). Teacher education for primary and secondary education. In J. D. Tinsley & T. J. Van Weert (Eds.), *IFIP Windows to the Future* (pp. 93-97). Birmingham: Aston University.

Pea, R. D., & Kurland, D. M. (1987). Cognitive Technologies for Writing. In E. Z. Rothkopf (Ed.), *Review of Research in Education* (Vol. 14, pp. 277-326). Washington DC: AERA

Putnam, R. T., & Borko, H. (2000). What do new views of knowledge and thinking have to say about research on teacher learning? *Educational Researcher, 29*(1), 4-15.

Roschelle, J., & Pea, R. (2002, Jan 7-11). *A walk on the WILD side: How wireless handhelds may change CSCL.* Paper presented at CSCL2002:, Boulder, Colorado.

UNESCO. (2004). *Integrating ICT into Education: Lessons Learned. A Collective Case Study, Thailand.* Bangkok: UNESCO APEID.

VIT. (2004a). *Standards & Professional Learning for Full Registration.* Melbourne: Victorian Institute of Teaching.

VIT. (2004b). *Standards (Professional Practice Standards).* Melbourne: Victorian Institute for Teaching.

Watson, D. (2001). Pedagogy before Technology: Re-thinking the relationship between ICT and Teaching. *Education and Information Technologies, 6*(4), 251-266.

ACKNOWLEDGEMENTS

The unit *Creating Effective Learning Environments* that forms the context of this paper was developed by a cross-campus team of academics who constitute the Education Studies Major team within the Faculty of Education at Deakin University. This paper draws on the program as developed and conducted on the Burwood Campus and chaired by Dr. Geoff White. The positions argued and presented in this paper are those of the authors and may not necessarily represent those of other ESM team members.

HIGHER EDUCATION: LEARNING IN REAL-LIFE

Tom van Weert
Hogeschool van Utrecht, University for Professional Education, The Netherlands
t.vweert@cetis.hvu.nl   http://www.cetis.hvu.nl

Abstract: Higher Education operates in the real-life context of a Knowledge Society
driven by innovation. Students are preparing to become knowledge workers in
that society where ICT, innovation and knowledge work are closely
interwoven. Three elements are essential in knowledge work: creation of
innovative solutions, knowledge creation about these solutions (and how to get
such solutions) and personal development. For without innovative solutions
there are no satisfied customers, without new knowledge there will be no
future customers and without personal development there will be no future job.
Higher education students need real-life learning environments in which they
can learn to deal with processes of real-life knowledge work. Real-life learning
implies solving of key innovation problems in academic or professional
practice, in accepted and acceptable ways. Real-life learning implies implicit
and explicit learning while solving these problems. And real-life learning
implies development of knowledge. Validation and critical reflection form the
key to quality assurance of the problem solving process, to explicit learning
and to knowledge development. Key characteristics of real-life learning
environments that stimulate validation and critical reflection are presented.

Keywords: Implicit learning, explicit learning, learning environment, knowledge
development, problem solving, reflection.

1   WORKING IS LEARNING

A Knowledge Society is developing in which Information and
Communication Technology (ICT) is both a catalyst and a necessity.
Knowledge is an invaluable asset in this ICT-integrated society where

production, services, consumption and trade are rapidly changing. "Technological change and innovation drive the development of the knowledge-based economy through their effects on production methods, consumption patterns and the structure of economies. Both are closely related in recent growth performance. Some changes in innovation processes could not have occurred without ICTs and conversely, some of the impact of ICTs might not have been felt in the absence of changes in the innovation system (OECD 2000). "A knowledge-based economy relies primarily on the use of ideas rather than physical abilities and on the application of technology rather than the transformation of raw materials or the exploitation of cheap labour. Knowledge is being developed and applied in new ways. ... In the knowledge economy, change is so rapid that workers constantly need to acquire new skills. Firms need workers who are willing and able to update their skills throughout their lifetimes". (World Bank 2002, p. ix).

To keep up with developments (knowledge) workers need to adapt continuously and acquire new competences: at the work place new knowledge is created to keep up with developments, both *tacit knowledge* in the heads and hands of the workers and *explicit knowledge* (codified, operational knowledge). The concept of knowledge is changing from scientific, theoretical knowledge ('old knowledge') to more operational knowledge ('new knowledge'). *Human capital* is becoming more and more important and workers are becoming more and more responsible for all dimensions of their work (Weert 2004).

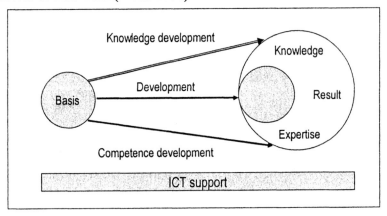

Figure 1. Working is delivering results, learning and creation of knowledge

2   LEARNING IS WORKING

Higher education should help students to become knowledge workers of tomorrow. In their future work 5 key problems play a role (Onstenk 1997):
1.   Problem solving (delivering results in context), involving:
     a.   Decision making
     b.   Design and development
2.   Knowledge development
3.   Construction of meaning (learning)

Only knowledge that is closely connected to an application context, can be transferred to other, comparable, situations and contexts, as literature on 'situated cognition', for example (Larkin 1989), shows. Also implicit knowledge is stored in human memory in direct connection with contextual and situational information. And finally Ryan and Deci (2000; p. 76) conclude that "contexts supportive of autonomy, competence, and relatedness were found to foster greater internalization and integration than contexts that thwart satisfaction of these needs".

It therefore follows that higher education should arrange the learning of students in such a way that this learning is closely connected with the future academic or professional practice of the students: learning is real-life solving of real-life problems.

3   IMPLICIT AND EXPLICIT LEARNING

In potential learning situations persons can react in three ways: not learning, implicit learning and explicit learning (Jarvis 1987). In implicit learning the activities are controlled by what Argyris and Schön (1974) call the *'theory-in-use'*. Explicit learning involves *'espoused theory'*, the activity theory of which we think that we bring it into practice. *'Theories-in-use'* control our behaviour and are mostly implicit (tacit). As Agyris en Schön state: the relation of a *'theory-in-*use' to activities "is like the relation of grammar-in-use to speech; they contain assumptions about self, others and environment - these assumptions constitute a microcosm <of science> in everyday life" (Argyris & Schön 1974: 30). *'Theory-in-use'* is a characteristic of *'experiential learning'* (in the behavioural sense), where learning is a side effect of activities undertaken. *'Espoused theory'* explicitly describes what we do, or what we hope others think we are doing. "When someone is asked how he would behave under certain circumstances, the answer he usually gives is his espoused theory of action for that situation. This is the theory of action to which he gives allegiance, and which, upon request, he communicates to others. However, the theory that actually governs his actions is this theory-in-use." (Argyris and Schön 1974; 6-7).

4   THE ROLE OF REFLECTION IN LEARNING

The concept of *reflection* has several meanings (van Woerkom 2003: 46):
1. '*Reflection*', as defined by Mezirow (1991): an individual activity in a problem solving process, supporting instrumental, mostly implicit learning.
2. '*Reflection in social interaction*': helping to make implicit ('tacit') knowledge explicit in order to achieve quality improvement in problem solving processes; this reflection supports explicit learning.
3. '*Critical reflection*', as defined by Mezirow (1991): an activity in the communication domain aimed at making explicit the value of the problems to be solved and of the problem solving method; this reflection also supports explicit learning.
4. '*Critical self-reflection*': aimed at emancipation, i.e. the development of the individual in the context of the organisation of the problem solving process; this reflection also supports explicit learning.

5   FIRST LOOP, SECOND LOOP AND THIRD LOOP LEARNING

According to Swieringa and Wierdsma (1992) we can distinguish three types of learning:
1. First loop learning: Doing what must be done (rules);
2. Second loop learning: Learning to do what must be done (insight);
3. Third loop learning: Learning to learn to do (principles for organisation and individual).

First loop learning is associated with '*Reflection*' as defined above, which is the '*reflection in action*' of Schön (1983). Reflection in action is based on the actor's own observations and stimulates primarily implicit learning. When the '*theory-in-use*' is supported by own observations there is a situation of non-learning. If there is a discrepancy we have a situation of single loop learning (Argyris & Schön 1974).

Second loop learning is based on '*Reflection in social interaction*' which is '*reflection on action*' as defined by Schön (1983). It is based on external feedback and therefore has a social dimension. This reflection confronts '*espoused theory*' and '*theory-in-use*' and supports explicit learning that influences the regulation of actions. It represents double loop learning (Argyris & Schön 1974) of the *'reflective practioner'* (Schön 1983).

Third loop learning is based on *'critical reflection'* and *'critical self-reflection'* which imply a reflection on method. The method is a fixed, well-thought out way of potential action to gain a purpose. The method makes actions transparent and requires responsible practice (praxis). Praxis refers to actions to which values are attached: human well-being, a quest for truth, and respect for others. Praxis requires that a person "makes a wise and prudent practical judgement about how to act in *this* situation" (Carr and Kemmis 1986; p. 190). Praxis requires a *'reflective professional'*.

6 THE ROLE OF REFLECTION IN PROBLEM SOLVING

In the problem solving process reflection is a tool for quality improvement. However, reflection also brings problem solving and learning together. The *'reflective practitioner'* will, for example, use validation, i.e. *'reflection in social interaction'*, in and at the end of the **project development** phase (Figure 2.) to ensure that the problem is worthwhile solving, that the problem solving method and the cost of the process are acceptable. And at the end of the **project development** phase the *'reflective professional'* will review, via *'critical reflection'* and *'critical self-reflection'*, that the problem solution process and the eventual solution will meet accepted professional standards, that team members know what their professional roles are and are capable to fulfil these roles, etc. Also the process of competence development, with its resulting level of competence will be reviewed, just as the process of knowledge development. The same pattern appears in the phase of **project execution** where the review of 'mid-term' results will be future oriented to enhance quality of the processes involved and the final results. In the phase of **project finalisation** first the project result is validated with the problem owner(s) and after that competence and knowledge development are validated. The project ends with the final project review taking account of the quality of all three project deliverables: effective result, level of competence and re-usable knowledge (how can we do it better next time?). Validation and review are integral part of the problem solving **method** that is used, just as the quality criteria to apply while validating and reviewing.

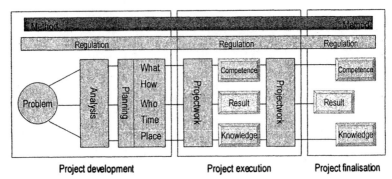

Project development   Project execution   Project finalisation

Figure 2. The problem solving process

7   LEARNING TO SOLVE PROBLEMS

According to Mulder (1997) complexity of a learning task may be characterised in four dimensions: the expertise of the actor, the complexity of the task at hand, the level of support and the external importance of the results. It is "common wisdom" in education that expertise has to be built up by going from the less to the more complex, from a high level of support to lower levels, and from simple, educational tasks to more complex, real-life tasks. However, recent research shows that this approach undercuts motivation and transfer. It is important to let students work in authentic situations with authentic problems as soon as possible (Kearsly & Shneiderman 1999). The addressed problems should be in the zone of nearest development of the students.

According to Ellström (1999) complexity of learning intensive work is decided by the type of work regulation required (Table 1.). He distinguishes four levels:

a) Reproductive learning: solving of routine problems without much attention to regulation which is also routine.

b) Productive learning I: the problems allow for degrees of freedom in the required result with only limited adaptation of the working method.

c) Productive learning II: the problems allow degrees of freedom in both working method and result.

d) Creative learning: Situations have to be analysed, the working method has to be selected, result requirements have to be formulated.

Levels of learning			
	Reproductive	Productive I	Productive II	Creative
Problem	*Given*	*Given*	*Given*	*To be chosen*
Method	*Given*	*Given*	*To be chosen*	*To be chosen*
Result	*Given*	*To be chosen*	*To be chosen*	*To be chosen*

Table 1. Levels of learning; adapted from van Woerkom (2003; p. 72)

Van Weert (2001) uses a typology of learning situations with the same levels of learning as Ellström:

a) *Assignment based*: the student/professional functions in a reproductive role in which standard problems are recognised and solved in a standard way; the student/professional assesses way of working and result against standards.

b) *Task based*: the student/professional functions in an executive role in which typical, task related problems are solved using task oriented methods; the student/professional assesses method selection, way of working and result against standards.

c) *Problem based*: the student/professional functions in a tactical role in which non-standard problems are solved using adapted methods; specifications for the result have to be developed; the student/professional assesses specifications, method selection, application, way of working and result against standards.

d) *Situation based*: the student/professional functions in a context determined, strategic role in which worthwhile problems have to be identified, just as suitable methods for solving; the student/professional assesses selection of problem and methods, application, way of working and results against standards.

In most learning situations team work is implemented to enhance learning. Characteristics of these typical learning situations are summed up in Table 2.

Learning situation	Student responsible for	Available to student	Way of working	Student role	Overall characteristic
Assignment based	Execution Assessment	Problem Result standard Standard method Assessment standard	Prescribed	Reproductive	What Know
Task based	Method Execution Assessment	Problem Result standard Method meta-standard Assessment standard	Adapted	Executive	How Know
Problem based	Result Method Execution Assessment	Problem Result meta-standard Method meta-standard Assessment standard	Dependent on problem and context	Tactical	Why Know
Situation based	Problem Result Method Execution Assessment	Problem meta-standard Result meta-standard Method meta-standard Assessment standard	Dependent on situation	Strategic	Why Care

Table 2. Characteristics of typical learning situations (Weert 2001; p. 49)

8   AUTHENTIC LEARNING ENVIRONMENTS

"In direct contrast to the academic approach, practical problems tend to be characterized by: the key roles of problem recognition and definition, the ill-defined nature of the problem, substantial information seeking, multiple correct solutions, multiple methods of obtaining solutions, the availability of relevant prior experience, and often highly motivating and emotionally involving contingencies" (Sternberg, Wagner & Okagaki 1993, p. 206).

Herrington, Oliver, and Reeves (2002) have defined ten design principles for developing and evaluating authentic activity-based learning environments. Authentic activities must:

1. Have real-world relevance;
2. Be ill defined, requiring definition of tasks and sub-tasks needed to complete the activity;
3. Comprise complex tasks to be investigated over a sustained period of time;
4. Provide the opportunity for students to examine the task from different perspectives, using a variety of resources;

5. Provide the opportunity to collaborate;
6. Provide opportunity to reflect, involve students' beliefs and values;
7. Be integrated and applied across different subject areas and extend beyond domain-specific outcomes;
8. Be seamlessly integrated with assessment;
9. Yield polished products valuable in their own right, rather than as preparation for something else;
10. Allow competing solutions and diversity of outcomes.

9 LEARNING ENVIRONMENTS STIMULATING EXPLICIT REFLECTION

Reflection is a pre-condition for learning. Therefore a suitable learning environment must invite reflection, and specifically explicit reflection ('*reflection in social interaction*', '*critical reflection*' and '*critical self-reflection*'). Argyris, Putnam & McLain Smith (1985) distinguish two different types of learning environment. One that suppresses explicit reflection (Figure 3.) and one that stimulates explicit reflection (Figure 4.).

Model I

Governing values are:
- Achieve the purpose as the actor defines it;
- Win, do not lose;
- Suppress negative feelings;
- Emphasize rationality;
- Primary Strategies are:
  - Control environment and task unilaterally;
  - Protect self and others unilaterally.

Usually operationalized by:
- Unillustrated attributions and evaluations e.g.. "You seem unmotivated";
- Advocating courses of action which discourage inquiry e.g.. "Lets not talk about the past, that's over";
- Treating ones' own views as obviously correct;
- Making covert attributions and evaluations;
- Face-saving moves such as leaving potentially embarrassing facts unstated.

Consequences include:
- Defensive relationships;
- Low freedom of choice;
- Reduced production of valid information;
- Little public testing of ideas.

Taken from Argyris, Putnam & McLain Smith (1985, p. 89)

Figure 3. Learning environment that suppresses reflection

Model I does not stimulate explicit reflection: you can only loose when you make explicit reflections. Model II differs in that validity and public evaluation are core values.

> **Model II**
> Governing values include:
> * Valid information;
> * Free and informed choice;
> * Internal commitment;
> * Strategies include:
>   o Sharing control;
>   o Participation in design and implementation of action.
> Operationalized by:
> * Attribution and evaluation illustrated with relatively directly observable data;
> * Surfacing conflicting view;
> * Encouraging public testing of evaluations.
> Consequences should include:
> * Minimally defensive relationships;
> * High freedom of choice;
> * Increased likelihood of double-loop learning (explicit reflection).
>
> Taken from: (Anderson 1997)

Figure 4. Learning environment stimulating reflection

More specifically van Woerkom (2003) has researched what dimensions influence 'critical reflection' by 'reflective professionals' and which contextual factors influence this reflection. There are seven contextual factors:

1. Reflection (being a reflective practitioner and a reflective professional);
2. Taking part in critical opinion forming;
3. Asking for feedback;
4. Participating in challenging 'groupthink';
5. Learning from mistakes;
6. Experimenting;
7. Perceiving career possibilities.

'Critical reflection' and 'critical reflection on self' are influenced by:
a. Participation (in itself influenced by social integration with peers);
b. Own effectiveness (in itself influenced by variety in tasks and by being informed about tasks to be undertaken), but also by participation.

A learning environment that stimulates critical reflection has the following characteristics (van Woerkom 2003; p. 74-75):

a) Learning climate: characterised by the amount of time available for collective reflection for strategic learning, contacts across the working environment, learning from the experience of others and tolerance for other opinions;
b) Participation in innovation and decision processes;
c) Transparency and integral communication by the management.

10 REFERENCES

Anderson, L. (1997) *Argyris and Schön's theory on congruence and learning.* Retrieved September 2004 from: http://www.scu.edu.au/schools/sawd/arr/argyris.html

Argyris, M. & D. Schön (1974) *Theory in Practice. Increasing professional effectiveness,* Jossey-Bass, San Fransisco.

Argyris, C., Putnam, R., & McLain Smith, D. (1985) *Action science: concepts, methods, and skills for research and intervention,* Jossey-Bass, San Fransisco.

Carr, W. & S. Kemmis (1986) *Becoming critical: Education, knowledge and action research.* Falmer, Philadelphia.

Ellström, P. E. (1999) *Integrating learning and work: problems and prospects.* Contribution to the Forum workshop Learning in Learning Organizations. University of Evora.

Herrington, J., R. Oliver & T. C. Reeves (2002) *Patterns of engagement in authentic online learning environments.* In: A. Williamson, C. Gunn, A. Young, & T. Clear. (Eds.), Proceedings of the 19th Annual Conference of the Australian Society for Computers in Learning in Tertiary Education (ASCILITE) (pp. 279-286). UNITEC, Auckland, NZ.

Jarvis, P. (1987) *Adult learning in the social context.* Croom Helm, New York.

Kearsley, G. & Shneiderman, B. (1999) *Engagement theory: A framework for technology-based teaching and learning.* July 2003: http://home.sprynet.com/~gkearsley/engage.htm

Larkin, J. H. (1989) *What kind of knowledge transfers?* In L. B. Resnick (Ed.), Knowing, learning, and instruction: Essays in honor of Robert Glaser (pp. 283-305). Hillsdale, NJ: Erlbaum.

Mezirow, J. (1991) *Transformative dimensions of adult learning.* Jossey-Bass, San Francisco, CA.

Mulder, R.H. (1997) *Leren ondernemen: ontwerpen van praktijkleersituaties voor het beroepsonderwijs.* Proefschrift. Erasmus Universiteit, Rotterdam.

OECD (2000) *A new economy? The changing role of innovation and information technology in growth.* Organisation for Economic Co-operation and Development, Paris.

Onstenk, J. (1997) *Kernproblemen, ICT en didactiek van het beroepsonderwijs.* SCO Kohnstamm Instituut, Amsterdam.

Ryan, Richard M. & Edward L. Deci (2000) Self-Determination Theory and the Facilitation of Intrinsic Motivation, Social Development, and Well-Being. *American Psychologist* Vol. 55, No. 1, 68-78.

Schön, D. A. (1983) *The reflective practitioner. How professionals think in action.* Basic Books, New York.

Sternberg, R.J., R. K. Wagner & L. Okagaki (1993) *Practical intelligence: The nature and role of tacit knowledge in work and at school.* In: Puckett, J. M. & H.W. Reese (Eds.) Mechanisms of everyday cognition (pp. 205-227). Lawrence Erlbaum Associates, Hillsdale, NJ.

Swieringa, J. & A. Wierdsma (1992) *Becoming a learning organisation: Beyond the learning curve*. Longman Group, United Kingdom.

Weert, T. J. van (2001) *Co-operative ICT-supported learning: A practical approach to design*. In: Reinhard Keil-Slawik, Johannes Magenheim (Hrsg.), Informatikunterricht und Medienbildung INFOS 2001, GI-Edition – Lecture Notes in Informatics (LNI) – Proceedings Series of the German Informatics Society (GI), Springer Verlag, 2001, p.p. 47-61.

Weert, Tom van (2004) *Lifelong learning in the Knowledge Society*. In: Weert, Tom van (ed.) Education and the Knowledge Society, Information technology supporting human development. Kluwer Academic Publishers, Norwell, MA.

Woerkom, M. van (2003) *Critical reflection at work, Bridging individual and organisational learning*. Dissertation. Twente University, Enschede.

World Bank (2002) *Lifelong Learning in the Global Knowledge Economy: Challenges for Developing Countries*. World Bank, Washington D.C. http://www1.worldbank.org/education/pdf/Lifelong%20Learning_GKE.pdf

IN REAL-LIFE LEARNING, WHAT IS MEANT BY 'REAL'?

The Concept of Reality and its Significance to IS Curriculum

Arthur Tatnall

Centre for International Corporate Governance Research, Graduate School of Business, Victoria University, Melbourne, Australia   Arthur.Tatnall@vu.edu.au

Abstract: What do we mean when we refer to 'real' life learning? How do we define the term 'real'? One possibility is that we mean that the learning takes place in actual (real) business organisations. Another is that we are referring to the acquisition of useful skills that have some every-day or employment-related (real) application, or perhaps we mean using technologies and case studies from (real) business organisations. Whether or not a technological artefact, programming language, or systems design concept is considered to be 'real' within the Information Systems community is generally related to its use in industry and commerce. But can a programming language, for instance, be real in education only, even if it is not used in commerce and industry? This rather philosophical paper addresses the issue of 'what is real' in the context of Real-life learning, and especially in regard to the content of IS curriculum, in the hope that this might shed some light on what this learning should involve.

Key words: Real-life learning, information systems curriculum, industry, reality.

1   INTRODUCTION

One of the questions often asked of a new technology or technological concept is whether it is 'real'. By this we often mean: 'is it something that can now be used, or that will be of use to us in the business or consumer world we know?'

"What is REAL?" asked the Velveteen Rabbit one day, when they were lying side by side near the nursery fender, before Nana came to tidy the room. "Does it mean having things that buzz inside you and a stick-out handle?" (Williams 1922 :14)

But the concept of 'real' can be interpreted in many ways, particularly as it applies to information systems (IS) education. One possibility is that we mean that the learning takes place in actual (real) business organisations. Another is that we are referring to the acquisition of useful skills that have some every-day (real) or employment-related application. Maybe we mean that the teaching approach used to deliver the content is based on the use of (real) business problems, or that we use case studies from (real) business organisations. On the other hand, perhaps we mean that educational content being delivered is practically relevant, or that the technologies and concepts we are discussing or using are commonly used outside education. In this paper I will concentrate on the latter: the concept of 'real' in relation to IS curriculum.

2   APPLES, MOBILES, TRAINS, MONSTERS, VELVETEEN RABBITS AND REALITY

The question of whether or not something is 'real' has often also been put of computers and other technological entities (Tatnall 2000). The Apple II computer was briefly popular with business in the late 1970s and early 1980s because it allowed users to run VisiCalc - the first spreadsheet program (Sculley and Byrne 1989). Sculley, CEO of Apple during this period, notes that VisiCalc was responsible for "putting the Apple II on many business desks" (Sculley and Byrne 1989 :207) but that when the IBM PC came along with Lotus 1-2-3 in 1983, business dropped the Apple and VisiCalc in favour of the IBM combination. The Apple II was thus never entirely 'real', except perhaps in education where it was real for several years when many schools made good use of this machine. It was the spreadsheet program that business wanted, and the Apple II was just a means of delivering this. The IBM PC, on the other hand, quickly moved from the status of an expensive toy used only to play games and run Lotus 1-2-3, to being considered a real and useful machine (Sculley and Byrne 1989). Following the IBM PC's successful acceptance by business, other microcomputers of the MS-DOS variety soon also came to be considered real.

In the early to mid-1980s the Apple II was certainly 'real' in many schools as it represented the computer industry and the possibilities available to students when they left school. It was not so much the use of the machine 'across the curriculum' that made the Apple II real in education, but its use in 'computer awareness / computer literacy' courses and the like that taught about what a computer was, how it worked, and how it might be used by business. The fact that it was not the Apple II *itself* that was used by business did not matter. What mattered was that this machine represented business use of computers and could thus be considered to be 'real'. When the Apple Macintosh was released in 1984 it was a long time before it was used enough by business to eventually be considered real, even in a limited way.

'Is it a real ... ?' tends to be a question asked by human actors of non-human actors in an attempt to decide how seriously to take them; to decide whether they are worth further investigation and could possibly be of some use. People asked this question, although probably not in these words, of the first mobile phones, of electronic organisers and of other technological innovations they were unsure whether they could find a use for (Franklin 1990). It is interesting to note that in respect of a given (non-human) actor the question 'Is it real?' is fairly uncontroversial and most people will agree on the answer. Although they would probably use a quite different vocabulary to express it, almost everyone would agree that mobile phones, PCs, laptops and the Internet are now 'real', but that PDAs, Videophones and SmartCards are at present probably not real.

It is probably true to say that initially most new technologies are not considered to be real, and only become real after some time. People need a period in which to evaluate the innovation to see whether or not it might be of use to them and so become something they might think of as real. This raises the question of how something becomes real.

> "Real isn't how you are made," said the Skin Horse. "It's a thing that happens to you. When a child loves you for a long, long time, not just to play with, but REALLY loves you, then you become Real." (Williams 1922 :14)

Perhaps, like toys, an item of technology only becomes real when enough people really 'love' it, but love it not just to play with. Perhaps it becomes real when they find what they see as a significant use for it. When it is just fun to play with it is still a toy, but when we can use it for something significant that we want to do it is well on the way to becoming real. In actor-network terms (Callon 1986a; Law 1991; Latour 1996), things become real when they have gathered enough intermediaries, enrolled enough allies, and have made enough associations to be seen to be of use by lots of people.

Like most new technology, the innovative Parisian public transport project known as Aramis (Latour 1996) was not seen as being real at the beginning of its development. In common with other technological projects it could not possibly be real at the beginning as it did not then exist for people to see and to evaluate whether it might be something they could use. The problem was that Aramis never did succeed in becoming real and hence eventually died. Latour describes Aramis as "merely realizable" and "not yet real" (Latour 1996 :85) and notes that Aramis should have taken on reality by degrees.

> "But anything can become more real or less real, depending on the continuous chains of translation. It's essential to continue to generate interest, to seduce, to translate interests. You can never stop becoming more real." (Latour 1996 :85)

VAL, Aramis' predecessor, also began as a technological project but went on to be fully implemented in the French city of Lille. Unlike Aramis it did succeed in becoming real, and the people of Lille found it useful.

> "VAL, for the people of Lille, marks one extreme of reality: it has become invisible by virtue of its existence. Aramis, for Parisians, marks the other extreme: it has become invisible because of its nonexistence." (Latour 1996 :76)

Victor Frankenstein (Shelley 1818) never permitted his creation to become real. His revulsion at what he had created, and his refusal to accept the creature or even to give it a name, meant that the creature's quest to become real, and so to be accepted, was doomed to failure. But if Frankenstein's monster never succeeded in becoming real in the world of Shelley's novel, in many ways it has become real, even if only as a concept, in our world. We have found a use for the analogy of Frankenstein's monster to describe any 'unnatural creation' of modern technology. For instance, in an article on human cloning Weiss (1999) raises the spectre of Frankenstein's monster without any further explanation, confident that this concept is well known to his readers. The concept of creating something that seems to go against the natural order of things (Anderson 1999) is one that is closely linked in our minds with the monster of the novel, and Frankenstein's monster has become real in that sense. In using the concept of a monster like this, we have made it 'real' in much the same way that the term Luddite has become real as a concept used to refer to those people who oppose the increased use of technology. Of course the Luddites (Grint and Woolgar 1997) did actually exist whereas Frankenstein's monster is only a work of fiction, but in each case it is the *concept* that is real, and it is real because we have found a good use for it.

Mythology about computer companies has also come to be very 'real' to many computer users. The myth that IBM is a bureaucratic company that supplies over-priced hardware and conservative solutions to business problems; the myth that Apple is a small innovative company that produces simple-to-use computers and cares deeply about education; and the myth that all Microsoft is interested in is making money by writing quick-and-dirty software of low quality, probably all have some basis in reality but have been taken far beyond this in the popular imagination. To many people, these myths have become 'real' and an accepted part of the way they see the world. They have become real to the extent that they affect the way we relate to these companies and whether we willingly purchase and use their products. These concepts have shaped our view of the world of technology and computing in much the same way that concepts of Frankenstein's monster and the Luddites have shaped this view.

There are thus many different ways that something can be seen as real, and different ways that this can affect what we do, but once something becomes real it will remain real providing that the allies who made it real remain loyal.

> "The Boy's Uncle made me Real," the Skin Horse said. "That was a great many years ago; but once you are Real you can't become unreal again. It lasts for always." (Williams 1922 :15)

3   REAL PROGRAMMING LANGUAGES

One of the first tools by which computer professionals defined themselves was the use of programming languages. But to be considered a computer *professional* it could not be just any programming language that you used; you had to use a 'real' programming language (Maynard 1990; Juliff 1992) or else you were seen as just a hobbyist playing with a toy. In similar vein, the operating system you worked with was another way of determining whether you were a 'real' computer professional. Apple II DOS was definitely not considered real whereas CP/M and Unix were. At one extreme some would also not consider MS-DOS, Microsoft Windows or Mac OS as real either; to them it had to be something like MVS or OS/400. Franklin puts it this way:

> "The historical process of defining a group by their agreed practice and by their tools is a powerful one." (Franklin 1990 :16)

Whether or not a programming language is considered to be 'real' within the Information Systems community is generally related to its use in industry and in commerce. Cobol and Fortran are considered real because they have long been used, and indeed relied upon, in business and science respectively. Pascal, with its academic origins and quite small user-base in business has never been thought of as real (Juliff 1992). Basic, which was invented forty years ago as a simple teaching language, has had great difficulty shaking off its unstructured, 'quick-and-dirty' image, and its image as a language for beginners in programming. Although never seriously used as a mainframe programming language, the growth in respectability of the microcomputer in the 1980s contributed to making Basic, and later Visual Basic (VB), the 'real programming languages' they are seen as being today. Not all computer professionals *like* Visual Basic, but few would challenge its reality. In actor-network terms (Latour 1996), what matters is the length of the network, its allies, and the intermediaries it is able to marshal on its behalf. VB's network is now long; it has attracted many allies and has been able to make use of many intermediaries.

Pascal was seen only to be used in education, despite the fact that it did have some practical uses, and thus was often not considered real. While the traditional universities might take the view that although a given language was not used much in business, if it was a 'good teaching language' they would 'use it anyway' (Juliff 1992). This view was, however, much harder to sustain in the more practically-oriented Universities (or Institutes) of Technology where applied knowledge was considered much more important (Maynard 1990). Educational institutions have always had to suffer the criticism of being detached from the 'real world', and have attempted to address this criticism in two different ways. In relation to information systems, the traditional universities have often taken the line that it is their purpose to educate, not train, and so it does not matter if the programming languages they teach with are not those used in industry as long as they are appropriate for teaching programming. Institutions such as Universities of Technology, on the other hand, have generally attempted to make their educational offerings more relevant to commerce and industry and so be seen to cater for the 'real world' in this way. These institutions have defined their educational context as containing the real and relevant (Seddon 1995) but to do this they have considered it necessary to use only 'real' programming languages and other real 'industry standard' technology where this has been possible. In doing so they have defined Information Systems curriculum as necessarily practical and proceeded to use teaching practices to reinforce this definition. As Seddon says:

> "... this 'reality' is not only the tangible, obdurate, empirical world of everyday experience; it is also discursively constituted through practices that re-present and therefore, define, the 'real' and what is 'relevant'." (Seddon 1995 :401)

Can something, such as a programming language, be real in education only, even if it is not much used in commerce and industry? It may be possible to argue that this is the case in some situations, but with the definition accepted by computer professionals and by academics at institutions like Universities of Technology, there is only one version of real: it must be extensively used in business. Although conceding that at primary and secondary school the situation is different and that something might be seen as real in this context, arguing this in Australia at a University of Technology would be very difficult.

4   GAINING A 'REAL PLACE' IN THE INFORMATION SYSTEMS CURRICULUM

Programming languages like Visual Basic and Java are now quite real in the Information Systems curriculum of many universities, but this has not always been the case. In the mid to late-1990s neither had many allies and neither had yet managed to further its network of associations. How does something gain a 'real place' in the curriculum? My research (Tatnall 2000) suggests that a programming language, IS concept or technology becomes *real* in the Information Systems curriculum of a university when the consensus among academic staff is that it occupies a useful place and fits in well with the university's educational mission of preparing its students for the future. It becomes real when it has enrolled enough of the academic staff in its support, and mobilised (Callon 1986b) them to speak on its behalf.

When a technology has acquired an educational network that would be difficult to disassemble, it becomes real. A technology's progress towards becoming real in the curriculum could be pictured as follows:

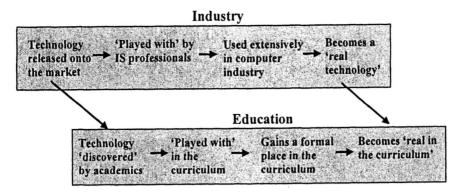

Figure 1: Becoming 'real' in the Information Systems curriculum

A 'real' place in the curriculum is however, not guaranteed forever and a technology needs the support of all its allies to keep this place, under challenge from other technologies.

"Nothing becomes real to the point of not needing a network in which to upkeep its existence." (Latour 1991 :118)

5   CONCLUSION

How important is it for information systems curriculum content to be seen as 'real'? The answer is that it all depends on the particular university involved. For some, more traditional, universities this is seen as an irrelevant concept, as all that matters is that something is considered 'academically worthwhile' – whatever they might mean by this. In other universities, especially in Universities (or Institutes) of Technology, there is felt to be a particular need to relate IS curriculum to the needs of the local industry and of students. It is in the latter case that issues of 'real' IS curriculum content will be debated.

6   REFERENCES

Anderson, A. (1999). Beware the F Word, Unless You Know What it Means. *New Scientist*. 20 March 1999: 3.

Callon, M. (1986a). The Sociology of an Actor-Network: The Case of the Electric Vehicle. *Mapping the Dynamics of Science and Technology*. Callon, M., Law, J. and Rip, A. London, Macmillan Press: 19-34.

Callon, M. (1986b). Some Elements of a Sociology of Translation: Domestication of the Scallops and the Fishermen of St Brieuc Bay. *Power, Action & Belief. A New Sociology of Knowledge?* Law, J. London, Routledge & Kegan Paul: 196-229.

Franklin, U. (1990). *The Real World of Technology*. Montreal, CNC.

Grint, K. and Woolgar, S. (1997). *The Machine at Work - Technology, Work and Organisation*. Cambridge, Polity Press.

Juliff, P. (1992). Personal communication. Melbourne.

Latour, B. (1991). Technology is society made durable. *A Sociology of Monsters. Essays on Power, Technology and Domination*. Law, J. London, Routledge: 103-131.

Latour, B. (1996). *Aramis or the Love of Technology*. Cambridge, Ma, Harvard University Press.

Law, J., Ed. (1991). *A Sociology of Monsters. Essays on power, technology and domination*. London, Routledge.

Maynard, G. (1990). Personal communication. Melbourne.

Sculley, J. and Byrne, J. A. (1989). *Odyssey: Pepsi to Apple*. UK, Fontana.

Seddon, T. (1995). "Defining the real: context and beyond." *Qualitative Studies in Education* 8(4): 393-405.

Shelley, M. (1818). *Frankenstein, or the Modern Prometheus*. London, this edition published by Penguin Classics in 1992.

Tatnall, A. (2000). Innovation and Change in the Information Systems Curriculum of an Australian University: a Socio-Technical Perspective. *PhD thesis*. Education. Rockhampton, Central Queensland University.

Weiss, R. (1999). Facing Frankenstein. *The Age*. Melbourne: 24.

Williams, M. (1922). *The Velveteen Rabbit; or How Toys Become Real*. London, Heinemann.

LEARNING FROM THE ICT INDUSTRY REAL-LIFE CONTEXT

Mikko J. Ruohonen
School of Economics and Business Administration, University of Tampere, Finland
Mikko.Ruohonen@uta.fi

Abstract: The ICT industry has faced many radical reorganisations and transformations during the last few years. This has pressured managers to renew their leadership cultures and practices. Action research driven results are interpreted in this paper to reflect the kind of learning challenges that are to be transferred in real-life learning situations. Different examples and potential solutions are discussed.

Key words: ICT Industry, real life learning, university-industry collaboration.

1   TURNAROUND EVOLUTION IN THE ICT INDUSTRY

After the ICT bubble period it seems that industry has moved to a new phase of evolution. Complexity and ambiguity have increased and the lucrative image of ICT has diminished (Earl 2003). Investors now understand more about the nature of the ICT industry and think more carefully of using their money. Information systems are now more integrated which demands not just nice multimedia properties: there are also difficult combinations of different age transaction systems. Internal systems renewal is just a start for whole industry-level changes (Kalakota & Robinson 2001).

The ICT industry is also growing towards a service business. In service business you need different leadership skills to face customers. Customization and bundling of service and product knowledge are needed (Pine 1993, Pine & Gilmore 1999, 2003) Companies need to upgrade their service processes as when crossing borders value chains, a help desk is not enough (Davenport & Beck 2001, Norris et al. 2003). The ICT industry needs to become a partner relationship: part of their customers' knowledge networks (Barney 1991, Dyer & Singh 1998, El Sawy et al. 1999).

Management and leadership need to change, too. Lucrative and open organisational culture was favoured some years ago. People were friends together and spent their free time together, maybe even in office parties. Sweet family culture is now very often broken and the grey reality of taking care of cash funds, thinking of your future with budgeting and keeping your staff in work, are dominating. Learning of qualitative work and leadership cultures needs close collaboration with ICT companies. Universities and other educational institutions need to build competencies to recognize and share these challenges. One way of doing this is to involve students in small field works and even action research projects. In this paper an attempt is made to discuss topics and learning areas in which this particular leadership culture is dominating.

2   LEADERSHIP CHANGES IN ICT COMPANIES

2.1   A Need for Contextual Understanding

The ICT industry went through a period of strong turnover of personnel which occasionally resulted in poor quality management, and productivity problems. Business know-how was too often sacrificed for Initial Public Offerings (IPOs) (Kühl 2002, 2003). Hence, growing importance is now on sensibility of the work, work community, organisational culture and management style. The proposed framework (Fig. 1) serves as a theoretical lens for exploration. Competitive requirements make companies aware of good quality and project deadlines. Personnel differences refer to differences in age, culture, job career, professional backgrounds, even gender, and race in some contextual settings. This framework serves as an eye-glass for reviewing each company's situation. The dimensions are i) external variety i.e. growing competition, more complex business models and even harder requirements for products and services, and ii) internal variety i.e. growing divergence of personnel which is emphasized in more difficult customer service situations and ICT industry convergence evolution.

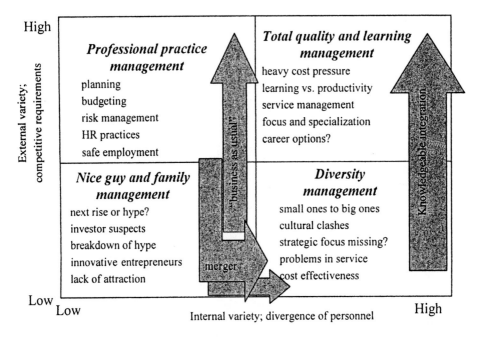

Figure 1. A framework for knowledge work & leadership management

The framework is proposed after a three-year action research project in three Finnish ICT companies with follow-up of the whole ICT industry evolution (Ruohonen et al. 2003, Ruohonen et al. 2004). Contextual dimensions describe four generic types of leadership cultures. They are introduced below and discussed from the learning challenge view.

3 REAL LIFE CONTEXTS AND LEARNING CHALLENGES

3.1 Nice Guy and Family Management

This context is represented in typical start-up ICT companies, such as the so-called new media companies of the 1990s. Customer intimacy might be very intensive and knowledge sharing is easy due to small company size. Knowledge workers participate in joint problem solving and meetings. However, recognition of complementary competencies is seldom done explicitly. Governance of projects might be poor, quality of project management low and timetables flexible. Quality management becomes a problem, although there might be high motivation for new projects. People management is based on "nice guy feelings", managerial structures are often neglected and systematic administrative processes do not exist. Management follows the values of friendship or even family culture.

Most of these companies from the 1990s have now gone through a major change. They have either been bought or merged to a larger company or they have been forced to create more organised business management. Many of the "happy family" values have now disappeared and ICT workers have aligned themselves within a larger and probably a more bureaucratic working environment. They might also have been competitive enough to stay independent in the markets but have reorganised their internal processes, such as planning and budgeting principles. Knowledge workers might feel loss of freedom or innovativeness under the stress of profitability and deadlines.

Contextual learning challenges. This kind of work context was, and is, still very tempting for young students, at least in those times when things were better. Nice cars, flexible working hours, positive publicity, young heroes of ICT business have now turned to cost-effectiveness, boring work, failures and burn-out professionals. It is a highly risky environment, where students need to recognize the reality of running a business. Many of these success stories have now failed and people have lost their money.

Therefore all business start-up's and incubation arrangements for entrepreneurially oriented students need to have good business knowledge/ know-how content. This content needs to be aligned with your curriculum in a way that integrates knowledge to the company context. For example exercising with real company data or running business games with real-life contents can reveal more about the operations and management of a small, growing company. Topics such as finance and accounting, quality management and running of projects combine these things together.

3.2 Diversity Management

This context is typical for some of the fast growing dotcom-companies. After having increased their size, acquired smaller firms and got Initial Public Listing (IPO) their rapid growth has caused communication problems and a clash of cultures. Many "family" companies have been "chopped in pieces". Relation-specific assets grow but they are fragmented. Customers are not instantly customers of the new merger-based company. Projects are more diverse in nature and demand variety of personnel competencies. Experts might dominate their own domains of knowledge and do not collaborate. Key people might leave and set up a new company to compete with the previous one. Knowledge sharing might grow problematic due to rapid growth and different learning styles of personnel. Governance can still be poor, affecting quality standards. The challenge is diversity management, both projects and human resources become more diverse and managers need to know more about different psychological, social and cultural phenomena. ICT projects are increasingly tying together many professional fields such as IT security and infrastructures, domain applications, communications networks, and even understanding of human behaviour. Diversity management is increasingly moving towards knowledgeable integration.

Contextual learning challenges. This context proposes many important topics for students. Fast growth and constant re-organisation of your business pressures you to understand better the inner movements of industry. In order to change companies need to have a long term view of the future. They need to activate strategic actions and not just react to the current situation. It means a follow-up of industry changes and interpretation of the news which might show weak signals for understanding change. Strategic planning exercises with a real-life company feedback will help. Making a merger or an IPO plan would also focus on issues which are relevant when growing. Diverse culture management can be improved by mixing managers and knowledge workers together with exchange and local students. This will also help in explaining the human resource management challenges in a diverse business context.

3.3   Professional Practice Management

This is the direction for rather homogenous company personnel in an increasing competitive situation. Companies can create systematic approaches, improve strategies, structures, and processes in line with customer demands. Especially project managers need to be aware of project deadlines, strong enough to resist "last minute changes" and "over-quality". The advantage of these companies is customer relationships. Professional rules, patterns, and even support systems can help sharing knowledge inside the company and within customers. Complementary competencies are identified and constant review of service quality is done. Governance is more systematic but enables freedom when necessary. In these companies world-class innovations are possible. Professional practice management develops the company further. Kühl (2003) confirms that diverging needs, personal plans and group egoism can inferiorate organisation, if it is not fast enough to renew its decision making.

However, companies are in danger of being bought by a larger player or a growing industry giant. Then they need to learn buying company's rules and procedures while unlearning all their own routines and processes. For professional companies it might be more difficult to adopt new rules than for a happy family type of company. The greatest risk is to loose key people due to this change. However, if the professional company is competitive enough it can stay independent and concentrate on its relation-specific assets in order to maintain financial health. On the other hand if they have no inimitable resources, they must accept the industry transformation.

Contextual learning challenges. One of the most important findings in this context is customer and service management. In order to be successful in your business you need to follow and even create your customer needs. For students this is one of the challenging areas, while you need both buyer and seller companies in order to understand the situation. Market research and customer surveys are useful but sometimes you need to contradict some of the assumptions made by seller companies.

Administrative rules, documentation and a more professional way of planning can be introduced by comparing and benchmarking different industry practices. It also provides some space for innovations. We can, for example, benchmark emergency health care and Internet service provision i.e. try to transfer contextual practices. We need also to understand organisational change and its implications to knowledge work management.

3.4   Total Quality and Learning Management

This context requires both the management of competitive forces and also different personnel management approaches. These companies are normally big players with diverse personnel also working abroad. They need to take care of both old legacy systems and emerging new e-business systems. Often these organisations take care of outsourcing and application service provision and also may hire people for customer companies. Relation-specific assets are usually managed by customer account managers. Projects and customers are categorized. Companies have initiated both formal and informal knowledge sharing practices. Complementary resources are gained through team building, task forces and evolving organisational arrangements. Governance uses total quality management.

These companies are in danger of becoming too bureaucratic, therefore active learning and innovation processes are needed. Constant quality and learning management means both keeping costs and schedules and enabling creativity and professional learning. It has been easy to recruit or even pick up ICT professionals from companies reviewed before. They are now attractive as "a safe company" in the new economic situation. However, innovation-oriented people do not necessarily stay in these companies if they are not actively motivated. People might leave or consider setting up or joining a smaller ICT company. The greatest risk of these established players is non-innovative culture. New competence building might stay hidden and the company become too mechanistic.

Contextual learning challenges. Management of innovations in the same time as quality demands a combination of project, process and human resource management. It also means development of career and other competence building programs. Learning by doing, incidentally or outside the workplace comes very important. For students this field is challenging while you need a quite long period of experiences in order to reflect professionally. One possibility could be a long term "godfather" type of collaboration with some selected companies in the ICT sector. This will enable long enough observation of the company . Students can continue their participation year after year and finally get a job from that company. Understanding of organisational culture and environmental change pressures demand tacit knowledge development. It is difficult to deeply simulate the organisational routines and embedded actions if you do not know the background and history of business.

4   CONCLUDING REMARKS

Real-life learning challenges were examined in the context of the ICT industry. One of the most challenging issues is leadership in emergent situations. Contextual changes can be due to competitive factors or evolution of the personnel variances. As start-up companies need IT competence and high level motivation of creating new artefacts in an inspiring atmosphere, a fast-growing IT company needs a more controlled and systematized way of doing business. "Clashes of culture" mean that knowledge is needed when companies outsource or merge together.

Strategic learning tasks in the changing ICT industry context are increasingly oriented towards human resource management. Service orientation demands learning of customer intimacy. A knowledge-intensive way of doing business relates to learning for sharing practices, reflection on past experiences and creating knowledge in communities of practice. Service and knowledge-based innovation are enabled through customer relationship intensity. A product and technology driven economy transforms to an experience economy which means that our learning systems need to be aware of industry changes and live together with real-life situations. However, there are no "quick-fix solutions" in the manner of: "just ask a company manager to give a lecture". Joint experience needs work assignments for students, reflection practices steered by senior teachers, sharing of problems in a discussion forum and mixing together company people and students. It is a systematic building of social infrastructure between universities and companies.

5   REFERENCES

Barney, J.B. (1991)"Firm resources and sustained competitive advantage" Journal of Management 17 (1) 99-120.

Davenport, T.H. and Beck, J.C. (2001): The attention economy: understanding the new currency of business. Accenture, Harvard Business School Press, Boston, Massachusetts.

Dyer, J.H. & Singh, H. (1998) "The relational view: Cooperative strategy and sources of inter-organisational competitive advantage". Academy of Management Review 23 (4) 660-679.

Earl, M. (2003). "IT: An Ambiguous Technology?", in: Sundgren, B., Mårtensson, P., Mähring, M. and Nilsson, K. (Eds.), Exploring Patterns in Information Management: Concepts and Perspectives for Understanding IT-Related Change., Stockholm School of Economics, Stockholm.

El Sawy, O.A., Malhotra, A., Gosain, S. & Young K.M. (1999) "IT-Intensive Value Innovation in the Electronic Economy: Insights from Marshall Industries" MIS Quarterly 23 (3).

Kalakota, R. & Robinson, M. (2001): E-Business 2.0. Addison Wesley Longman, Reading, Massachusetts.

Kühl, S. (2002) "Jenseits der Face-to-Face-Organisation Wachtumprozesse in kapitalorientierten Unternehmen". In Zeitschrift für Soziologie 31, 186-210.

Kühl, S. (2003) Exit – How Venture Capital Changes the Laws of Economics. Franfurt am Main.; New York: Campus.

Norris, D., Mason, J. & Lefrere, P. (2003) Transforming e-Knowledge – a revolution in the sharing knowledge. Society for College and University Planning.

Pine II, B. Joseph (1993): Mass Customization: The New Frontier in Business Competition, Harvard Business School Press, Boston, Massachusetts.

Pine II, B.J. and Gilmore J.B. (1999): The Experience Economy: Work is Theatre & Every Business a Stage, Harvard Business School Press, Boston, Massachusetts 1999.

Pine II, B.J. and Gilmore J.B. (2003): The Pine & Gilmore Body of Knowledge, www.customization.com, checked 28.7.2003.

Ruohonen, M., Kultanen, T., Lahtonen, M., Rytkönen, T. & Kasvio, A. (2003) Identity and Diversity Management for New Human Resource Approaches in the ICT Industry" in Avallone, F., Sinangil, H. & Caetano, A. (eds) (2003) Identity and Diversity in Organizations, Guerini Studios, Milan.

Ruohonen, M., Kasvio, A., Kultanen, T., Lahtonen, M., Lehtonen, J., Vanne, T. (2004) Tietoyritysten muuttuvat työkulttuurit. Tampere University Press.

PATHWAYS IN REAL-LIFE LEARNING
The road to expertise

Julia Walsh and John Cripps Clark
Faculty of Education, Deakin University, Burwood, Australia
jwalsh@deakin.edu.au and john.crippsclark@deakin.edu.au

Abstract: The pathway to expertise is a long journey, and few make it. Regardless of discipline, the journey is similar; what differentiates the journey is the knowledge that underpins the profession. This research explores expert teachers and the knowledge that underpins the teaching profession. Much research in teacher education has concentrated on individual elements of expert teaching. There has been less emphasis on understanding the complex real-life process of expert teaching in its entirety. The model presented here looks at an integrated approach to understanding the development of expert teachers through real-life learning experiences and related factors

Key words: Expertise, higher education, practicum.

1   INTRODUCTION

In teacher education, pathway planning enables pre-service teachers to situate themselves in the field, to monitor their progress, and to understand and organise their knowledge. This is only possible when understanding of what knowledge underpins the profession, the relationship between the knowledge domains, and how the different knowledge domains mature. This paper discusses an emerging evidence-based model of the 'expert teacher'. The model emphasises not only the usual elements of effective teaching – content knowledge, pedagogical knowledge and pedagogical content knowledge – but also takes into account the teacher's personal knowledge and knowledge of context, both of which are derived from real-life learning experiences. We suggest that it is not just this knowledge that teachers have in these domains but the way this knowledge overlaps and interacts both within the teacher and with the teacher's physical, social, intellectual and emotional environment. An examination of the expert teacher through the use of this model challenges us to rethink the way we educate both pre-service and in-service teachers and the way we assess, judge and reward teachers. It highlights the important role of real-life learning in the development of expertise and the need to accommodate it more robustly in Teacher Education programmes.

This study arose from our individual PhD research, which involved in depth interviews with primary science teachers (Cripps Clark) and elite sports coaches (Walsh). It emerged that these two very different groups of highly effective teachers – the coaches were overwhelmingly also teachers – were remarkably similar.

Common features that emerged, were:
- strong discipline content knowledge;
- pedagogical skills appropriate to the environment and discipline;
- personal knowledge which included: the ability to forge strong relationship with the students, a concern for individual students and a firm moral code.
- intimate knowledge of the context in which they were teaching.

We have used these components to develop a prototype model and then refined this model using observations and interviews with a more diverse sample of expert teachers.

2   WHAT IS AN EXPERT TEACHER?

The pathway to expertise is a slow process that few achieve. A number of lines of evidence have been used to identify expert teachers including: certification, results their students achieve, peer assessments, students or the community, the classrooms they establish, and their status in the profession. Shulman (1987) distinguishes between pragmatic effectiveness measured by correlation, usually with student academic achievement measures, and normative effectiveness measured by correspondence, usually with a model or conception of good teaching. Our study is inherently normative but builds on the data from pragmatic studies.

3   THE NEED FOR A MODEL

A model must simplify the representation of complex phenomena, making the abstract concrete, without masking essential elements that are needed to generate explanations and to interpret observations. This model is an attempt to create a coherent map of expert teachers so that our analysis can go beyond a mere checklist of attributes or behaviours. It attempts to provide a language for discussing not just the knowledge that expert teachers possess but also the way in which this knowledge interacts in formal and real-life learning, professional contexts, and pathway planning.

3.1   The Components of a Model

We have identified four clusters of knowledge domains: content (discipline) knowledge, pedagogical knowledge and skills, and knowledge of context and personal knowledge. Pedagogical content knowledge (PCK) is the intersection of discipline knowledge and pedagogical skills. The other intersections include such elements as: the teacher's personal epistemology; the teacher's knowledge of curriculum and their students; and the relationships that the teacher forges with colleagues and students.

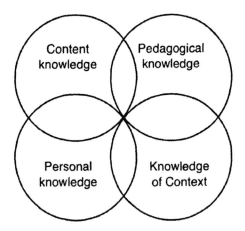

Figure 1. Foundation for a model of effective teachers

3.2   Discipline Knowledge

Often the public debate about teachers and teaching standards is reduced the claims of inadequate discipline knowledge. The question of the range and depth of discipline knowledge teachers need for students of differing maturity is accentuated by what is perceived as a time of rapid increase in knowledge in most disciplines. Discipline knowledge encompasses an understanding of the salient concepts, relations among concepts, ideas and skills of a subject (Shulman, 1987) and has always been acknowledged as the first prerequisite of ability to effectively teach a discipline. Teachers are often described in terms of a specific discipline knowledge.

Discipline knowledge is a necessary component of most theories of teaching whether they are traditional transmission models, constructivism or even behaviourist. This discipline knowledge is usually a significant part of a teacher's education. Research investigating discipline knowledge in teaching has examined the difference between novice and expert teachers in how they store, access and use specific discipline knowledge. The expert teacher is more likely to create mental models based on a problem solving approach and attach deeper meaning and extract more information from the environment in a more significant way. Discipline knowledge is also a crucial prerequisite in the development of teacher self-confidence. Understanding and being able to apply discipline knowledge builds self-confidence, and self-confidence is crucial in the development of an expert teacher.

Although discipline knowledge is an expectation, when it comes to choosing and judging teachers it is the combination of discipline knowledge, application, interpersonal skills and motivational style that is valued. There is also an increasing realisation that discipline knowledge and pedagogical skill are inextricably linked and cannot be taught independently.

3.3   Pedagogical Skills

With the rise of professional teachers – rather than the tradition of practitioners who apprenticed students, notably with the Sophists in classical Greece (Beck, 1996) – the distinction between the practice of a discipline and the teaching of the discipline gave rise to the notion of skills and knowledge independent of the discipline and particular to teaching. This art and science of teaching became known as pedagogy. Berliner (1991) defines pedagogical knowledge as consisting primarily of knowledge about classroom management, the organization of classrooms, assessment, methods for the motivation of students, personal knowledge about particular students and their families, and social-interactional skills. Research investigating expert teachers verifies that pedagogical expertise resembles expertise in other fields, is a very sophisticated form of knowledge that is not easily gained or mastered, and not available to everyone that seeks it (Berliner 1991)

There remains however a tension over the separation of the categories of discipline and pedagogical knowledge. Lusted (as cited in Tinning, MacDonald, Wright, & Hickey, 2001) proposed that how one teaches cannot be separated from how one learns and the nature of the subject matter. Therefore instruction cannot be separated from learning or curriculum.

Berliner (1991) postulates that to study pedagogy independent of discipline knowledge is to miss something of the intimacy of the relationship. He also draws attention to the question of low transfer of pedagogical skills across disciplines. Tytler (2002) has pointed out that the learning of new discipline knowledge is of itself a pedagogical exercise. Different subjects have different epistemologies, hence an expert physical education teacher is not automatically going to transfer their expertise into the teaching of English. In each field there are also specific and explicit and implicit prescriptions and proscriptions of behaviour for teacher and student.

The separation of pedagogical skills and personal qualities is also artificial. Taking a more people centred view, Van Manin (1994) describes pedagogy as the relational knowledge of children, that one understands children and youths: how young people experience things, what they think about, how they look at the world, and how each child is a unique person. He also notes that neither the European nor the North American scholarship of teaching seems to have fully explored the significance of the 'pedagogical relation' for the practice and teaching of learning. In this description the relationship between the teacher and the student is paramount. The teacher establishes the relationship with the student, cares for the student by caring for what they may become, and makes adjustments to their interactions based on the situation and experiences of the student. For the student the teacher provides opportunities for heightened experiences, a sense of self, and a real growth and personal development.

3.4 Knowledge of Context

The classroom, school culture, community, educational system and students can all significantly influence the effectiveness of a teacher. A teacher who may be an expert in one context may struggle in another. Any model of teaching expertise must be situationally contingent (Locke, 1991). Any theory of contingency will need to involve such factors as the volatility of the environment the discipline taught, the community, the school and departmental organisation and philosophy and the backgrounds of the students. As the context changes the weight or degree of importance accorded to the various components of teacher knowledge may vary rather than the components themselves. Thus in a highly academic environment discipline knowledge becomes more important while for marginalised students, personal qualities come more to the fore.

3.5   Personal Knowledge

Van Manin (1994) describing expert teachers, states that what we receive from a great teacher is less a particular body of knowledge or set of skills, than the way in which this subject matter was represented or embodied in the person of this teacher; his or her enthusiasm, self discipline, dedication, personal power, and commitment – characteristics which draw strongly on many aspects to the teacher's real-life learning experiences.

The teacher's personal qualities are recognized as being influential in the overall picture of an expert teacher. Two components of personal qualities are: a moral code of behaviour such as honesty, and integrity, and the teacher's personal philosophy and self-belief, which is best described within a motivational framework. Understanding the role personal qualities play and how they interact with other characteristics of effective teaching addresses and provides insight into the "who question" which Zembylas (2000) claims has been ignored in research on expert teachers. The behaviours most cited as reflecting expert teaching and leadership are honesty, and integrity (Locke, 1991). In combination these behaviours provide the foundation for a trusting relationship between the teacher and his or her students.

Expert teachers and leaders are driven by a strong and coherent philosophy, and influenced by their self-efficacy beliefs. Not unexpectedly these teachers reveal a holistic philosophy that centres on educating students for life. These teachers also have positive self-efficacy beliefs and are comfortable with innovation and risk taking (Gibbs, 1999). Self-efficacy beliefs are powerful predicators of behaviour and explain the choices people make, their aspirations and persistence in difficult situations (Bandura 1977, 1982). Developing positive self-efficacy beliefs is a slow process built up over time through experience, exposure and a deeper understanding of self.

4   THE EMBEDDED NATURE OF KNOWLEDGE

Teachers' knowledge does not exist in isolation—it is part of a greater shared knowledge and practice with which they have a continuing dialogue. Fig. 2 is an attempt to locate it within teachers' physical, social, intellectual and emotional environments. Thus the content knowledge is but a subset of the whole discipline knowledge and forms (albeit a small) part of it. The pedagogical knowledge is intrinsically bound to the community of practice that the teacher contributes to. Context knowledge exists in a continual dialogue with the actual context: classroom, school and community. Their personal knowledge is bound into their relationship with those they relate to.

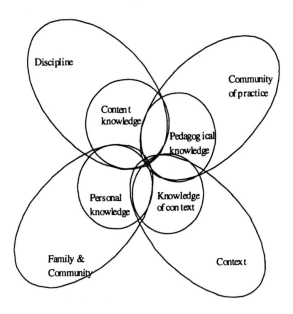

Figure 2. Embedded knowledge model

5 DYNAMICS

This model is not just a way of conceptually organising the checklists that are normally given to describe expert teachers. Knowledge and skills exists in real human beings not in isolation and thus interacts both within the teacher and with the teacher's intellectual, social, emotional and physical environment. This model provides a basis for discussing and analysing these interactions in specific teachers.

6 CONCLUSION

Real-life learning is dependent on opportunities for engaging with knowledge, the manipulation and the application of knowledge, and the capacity to deal with complexity. Developing teaching expertise is about real-life learning. In teaching, the pathway to expertise, as identified by this research, is a slow developmental process. Four knowledge domains underpin teaching expertise, with each knowledge domain maturing at a different rate. During the early stages of teacher education students engage with the theory, have opportunities to apply their knowledge in the field, and with deliberate experience develop the capacity to deal with complexity. The evidence-based model presented in this research provides a way of thinking about the development of teacher expertise. There is a tendency to expect pre-service teachers to make sense of their education. This model provides a pathway or road map to assist pre-service students in understanding their journey with a pathway, and course architecture designed to develop appropriate domain knowledge.

7   REFERENCES

Bandura, A. (1977). Self-efficacy: toward a unifying theory of behavioural change. *Psychological Review 84*, 91-215.

Bandura, A. (1982). Self efficacy mechanisms in human agency. *American Psychologist 37*(2), 122-147.

Berliner, D. (1991). Educational psychology and pedagogical expertise: New findings and new opportunities for thinking and training. *Educational Psychologist 2*: 145-155.

Garrison, J. (1997). *Dewey and eros: Wisdom and desire in the art of teaching.* New York, Teachers College Press.

Gibbs, C. (1999). *Believing, thinking and feeling: Putting the teacher back into effectiveness.* Joint Conference of the New Zealand Association for Research in Education and Australian Association for Research in Education, Melbourne.

Justi, R. & J. Gilbert (2002). Modelling, teachers' views on the nature of modelling and implications for the education of modellers. *International Journal of Science Education 24*(4): 369-387.

Locke, E. A. (1991). *The essence of leadership.* New York, Macmillan.

Loughran, J. (2001). *A methodological maze: Attempting to capture pedagogical content knowledge.* Contemporary Approaches to Research in Mathematics, Science, Health and Environmental Education 2001, Deakin University, Burwood: CSMEE.

Raban, R. (2002). *Work based learning partnerships.* Experiential learning workshop, 5-6/3/02, Deakin University, Geelong.

Shulman, L. S. (1987). Knowledge and teaching: Foundations of the new reform. *Harvard Educational Review 57*(1): 1-22.

Tinning, R., D. MacDonald, et al. (2001). *Becoming a physical education teacher: Contemporary and enduring issues.* Sydney, Prentice Hall.

Tytler, R. (2002). personal communication, Melbourne.

Van Manin, M. (1994). Pedagogy, virtue and narrative identity in teaching. *Curriculum Inquiry 24*(2), 135-170.

Zembylas, M. (2000). Emotions and elementary school teaching. University of Illinois.

REAL-LIFE LEARNING IN VIRTUAL COMMUNITIES OF TECHNOLOGY

Luiz A. M. Palazzo, Antônio C. R. Costa, Graçaliz P. Dimuro, and Fernando Schirmbeck
School of Informatics – Catholic University of Pelotas, Pelotas RS Brazil
lpalazzo@ucpel.tche.br rocha@ucpel.tche.br liz@ucpel.tche.br
Center for Educational Informatics – Serviço Nacional de Aprendizagem Industrial (SENAI),
Porto Alegre RS Brazil fernando@dr.rs.senai.br

Abstract: This paper introduces an approach to building virtual communities for Real-life technology learning. The aim is to keep technicians and technologists updated with new advances in their specific technology area. The learning strategy is based on a 'skills and competences' pedagogy and the community is built in an adaptive and collaborative information system environment which provides tools for collective knowledge management with adaptive distribution. A methodology for building Virtual Communities for Technology Learning is presented, and the ongoing experience of implementing such a community in a countrywide institution of technology learning in Brazil is also reported.

Key words: Virtual learning communities; knowledge management, real-life learning.

1 INTRODUCTION

Technology learning is nowadays a central issue, especially in developing countries, where it is often the target of strategic policies in education and professional fields. Three major problems can be found related to technology learning: (1) The volatile nature of most technologies, which can become obsolete in a very short time, (2) The growing complexity of technologic concepts, which can make it very difficult or even prevent further learning in certain cases, and (3) The lack of effective communication and collaborative behavior among technologists or teams aware of the novel concepts being introduced in labor activities, even when the WWW and full networking support is available.

To deal with these problems, Virtual Communities for Technology Learning (VCTL) seems to be an attractive idea, as they could provide students and professionals (technologists) with the necessary resources to keep their knowledge up-to-date and share it in a very flexible way. In a VCTL, the learning goal is to share not only information but also the technologic *knowledge* and *practice (know-how)*. Sharing of practice is essential for the correct understanding and use of tools and technologic processes of any kind. The usual pedagogy for technology learning, based on skills and competences, is well suited to organize the information flow in a VCTL, according to the evolution of the user model of each member of the VCTL, in relation to a desired profile. In addition, the pedagogic approach based on skills and competences suits the goal of supporting VCTL interactions directed to update the knowledge and skills of active professionals in areas suffering major technological innovations.

The research presented here aims to develop VCTL software environments endowed with three main features: (1) *adaptive interface*, so that each VCTL member can access specific contents to improve his/her learning process, according to his/her own user *model*, (2) *ontology-oriented tools* for supporting the VCTL goals, shared by all members, that will be building and keeping updated an ontology for representing and sharing knowledge related to the technologies focused by the VCTL, and (3) *collaborative tools* enhancing synchronous and asynchronous communication among VCTL members, so that goals can be assigned to groups and collaboratively solved (Palazzo et al, 2001).

VCTLs are intended to engage for life, not only for a short or medium-sized period of online technology courses. While collaboratively building the technology ontologies and keeping them updated, the technologists gather and share knowledge using their adaptive interfaces. These interfaces are dynamically framed in login time, with content matching the technologists' user models. The system tries to make available, for each one, adequate content and pointers that will help him/her to acquire the skills and competences of a desired referential professional profile, as well as to interact with fellows interested in the same subjects. We have designed a methodology and architecture for VCTL development. A prototype is being tested by SENAI (National Service for Industrial Learning), a countrywide traditional institution for technology learning in Brazil. The prototype implements the three features commented above and new studies are being developed to introduce additional functionalities to the system.

Created in 1942, SENAI (National Service for Industrial Learning) is one of the most important Brazilian poles of professional grade, as well a generator and diffuser of applied knowledge to industrial development. Rendering services in all country, SENAI has a more detached area of development in Southern Brazil, comprising the Paraná, Santa Catarina and Rio Grande do Sul states, where it includes 111 units.

2 AN APPROACH TO VIRTUAL LEARNING COMMUNITIES

Virtual Communities (VC) are associations of individuals (members of the community, participants or users) sharing information, knowledge and objectives in some domain through the Internet. Examples of Virtual Communities include the groups constituted of the members of any organization in corporative, surrounding on-line spaces, intranets for collaborative action, distance Real-life educational systems, and so on (Rheingold, 1993; Kollock, 1997).

Virtual *Learning* Communities (VLC) are VCs where the main goal is to *learn*. All members of a VLC are *learners*, but this does not mean that the learning process must be the same for everyone. Instead, each learner can be *modeled* by the system and learning is made to fit the needs of each one. VLC interfaces can also be constructed to be *adaptive* (Brusilovski 1997, 2001), as structures based on personalized interfaces, dynamically constructed from the user models.

In our approach to VCL, data about users are automatically collected and stored in databases which are kept updated, reflecting the evolution of user skills and competences in a specific domain. A large amount of information about the user, such as cognitive profile, previous formation, objectives and main interests, are also made available to the system through the *user model*. With this information the system will then construct personalized interfaces, with adaptively selected contents to fit the needs of each user.

New knowledge can be automatically produced, stored and distributed for the community through a set of knowledge management tools. These includes a search engine, tools for validating and describing resources, support for groups to participate in collaborative problem solving activities and collaborative project execution tasks, etc.

The main features designed to support VLC, briefly described below, are:
- Adaptive Hypermedia Interface

- Ontology-oriented Tools
- Collaborative Tools

2.1 Adaptive Hypermedia Interface

Currently, one of the main branches in Adaptive Systems research is Adaptive Hypermedia Interfaces (AHI) and its related technologies, as User Modelling (UM) and Intelligent Interfaces (II). One of the most critical features in an AHI is the *user model*, a representation of the goals, knowledge, preferences, needs and desires of its users. The underlying idea is that users with different profiles will be interested in different pieces of information presented on a hypermedia page and may also want to use different links for navigation.

AHI attempts to use the knowledge about a particular user, represented in the user model, to adapt the information and links being presented to that. User models can also be viewed as constraint sets imposed on the available hypermedia. The adaptation task performed by an AHI is oriented to assist users with personal-tailored hypermedia information and navigational help.

A major difficulty in producing AHI or indeed user-adaptive systems in general, lies in structuring information in such a way that it will be possible to do adaptations. The representation must include user profilers that allow for useful adaptations, and the interface must be designed to allow the underlying system to infer the required patterns from user actions at the hypermedia interface (Palazzo and Costa, 2001). This problem is most apparent in domains where the information is rapidly changing or highly unstructured. How could one, for example, analyze and represent the widespread needs of users of the Web in such a way that it would be possible to filter information or adapt navigation to an individual user? And even if it is possible how one could infer those needs from just observing the user's navigation through the Web?

2.2 Knowledge Management with Ontology-oriented Tools

Interaction in VLC informally produces a Shared Knowledge Web (SKW) that is indexed by the community learning domain *ontology*. This ontology is a conceptual network with *annotations* that can be of any format (text, video, audio, links, etc.), but are always about the learning domain. Community SKW can then be viewed as being its own ontology which is dynamically built by its members in a learning process.

VLC dynamics produces intensive communication among learners that share the knowledge individually gathered through SKW. New *discoveries* about any domain topic can be made available to all by anyone, stimulating knowledge interchanging and sharing. The SKW is then a dynamic collective knowledge body, a concrete product of a VLC and should be portable and reusable in other contexts. To make this possible, a document standard is needed as RDF (*Resource Description Framework*, W3C/RDF 2002) or XML Schema (W3C/XML 2002).

2.3 Collaborative Tools

Collaborative action is very important in modern learning environments and can enhance the interaction among the members of a community. Problems and challenges can be set to adaptively selected groups and collaborative action is supported by tools that, for instance, allow two or more participants to navigate together or present to the group a common blackboard or agenda, where they can share ideas, annotations, assignments, etc. In Figure 1 these three features are shown in its relation with the VLC learning domain

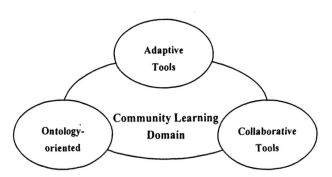

Figure 1: Key features in a VLC conception.

3 VIRTUAL COMMUNITIES FOR TECHNOLOGY LEARNING (VCTL)

3.1 Pedagogical Framework

Technologic learning has a special trait related to what is technology and how someone can learn about it. Virtual Communities for Technology

Learning (VCTL) are a specialization of VCL that incorporate information about *professional profiles*, so that the learning can be directed to such profiles.

Skills and Competences have been considered the two main concepts around which to organize technology learning. At SENAI, professional profiles are defined, based on an analysis of the competences and skills needed for the corresponding professionals, in their daily work in industry. Figure 2 shows the *profile ontology* around which SENAI's professional profiles are defined. Such profile ontology, when integrated to a VCTL, can usefully index documents and activities in the community, helping the users to find information relevant for their corresponding professional profiles.

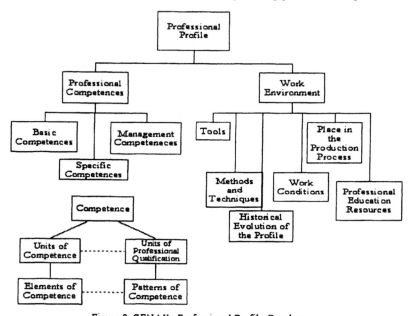

Figure 2: SENAI's Professional Profile Ontology

4   A METHODOLOGY FOR BUILDING VCTL

The construction of a VCTL is a gradual process, introducing one by one the competences associated with the desired technologic profile. A natural sequence for the VCTL evolution until its consolidation is shown in Table 1.

In the first stage the participants will learn the use of New Technologies of Information and Communication (NTIC). At the same time they *live* in VCTL, they learn about it and help in its construction. This is an adaptive stage where basic competences for belonging to and acting in a VCTL are introduced to all. At the end of this stage, all participants must be able to produce new content, express themselves, communicate in several vehicles, search for and locate information and act collaboratively sharing common challenges.

In the second stage, the participants are introduced to the concepts of *skills and competences pedagogy*, working in groups for analyzing and designing reference profiles for their corresponding learning objectives. Activities here aim to stimulate work with the NTIC instruments from Stage 1 for modelling contents, relationships and tasks related to the skills and competences of any desired reference profile. At the end of this stage, all community members must have clearly understood the proposition of technology learning by means of the skills and competences pedagogic framework and how such framework is modelled in VCTLs.

In the third, participants are grouped by interest area for building specific VCTLs. These VCTLs should be designed to support a specific professional profile. In this stage the participants should acquire the necessary competence to conceive, model, design and implement VCTLs in practice. Different interest groups establish an initial state for the area underlying professional profile ontology. This ontology is collaboratively built as the SKW of the group. The challenge is to establish an ontological ground able to support the autonomy and evolution of the VCTL.

Finally, in the fourth stage, the several groups implement their own VCTLs. The four stages are shown in Table 1.

Table 1: Stages in Building a VCTL

Stage	Key Activity	Description
1	Instrumental: NTIC	Participants learn to use NTIC and how to apply it in VCTL.
2	Instrumental: Skills and Competences	Participants learn about skills and competences for technology learning in VCTL.
3	Content Design and Community Evolution Plans	Participants are grouped by specialty to learn how and to design contents for specific topics in the SKW. They will also define and develop reference profiles for matching desired skills and competences for each considered domain subset.
4	Open Community	The CVTL is open for new participants that will learn from the contents already provided by older members that will also keep related SKW updating.

4.1   Implementation

The subsystems that support VCTLs are:

(i)   *Dynamic Interface*: changes at any new access in response to the evolution of the users profile.

(ii)   *User Model Base*: stores and updates each user profile.

(iii)   *Resources Description Base*: describes in *RDF/XML* each resource existing in the web that may be of community interest.

(iv)   *Shared Knowledge Web*: it is organized as an ontology, covering the focus of the community where concepts and their relations can be noted and enriched with text, media, links added by any participant.

(v)   *Adaptation Mechanism*: comprehend a base of rules and an algorithm for the appliances in entries of the items (ii), (iii) and (iv).

As users interact with the community their profiles become more precise, allowing the system to create more effective feed-back in selection and resources. Besides, the *RCC* of the community develops in relation to notes about their concepts and their relations.

As a result, the interaction with the community presents more fluidity and objectivity in the prosecution of the themes that compose its focus. This strategy allows that the participant receives contents and resources in a customized way making the interaction process more effective and productive.

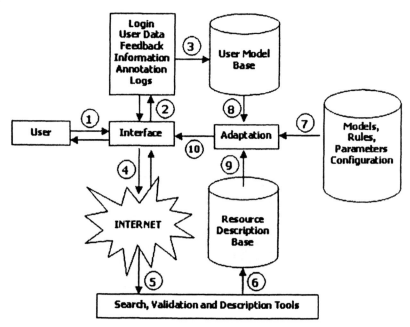

Figure 3: Functional Diagram of a VCTL

Figure 3 shows a simplified functional diagram of the VCTL/SENAI representing in the blocks the main components of the system. The numbers in the black circles represent the relations between the components, through which is described the general function of the system.

1. *User - Interface*: the relation of the user with the system always occurs through the interface. This is an adaptive hyper document that can be visualized through a *navigator*. As there is the prospect of a large number of users in the future it may be interesting to invest in the development of a client module, installed to accomplish several tasks such as, for example, optimize the communication with the server, the temporary information stock, etc. It is required that the interface has the presentation and functions of good quality.

2. *Interface – User's Entries*: the user's information are continually captured to update their profile and to add descriptions, opinions, links, etc, in the *RCC* of the system.

3. *User's Entries – User Model Base*: an agent mechanism must transform the captured information in significant expressions of the profile of each user to subsequent application in adaptation processes.

4. *Interface - Internet*: Most resources described here and made available and distributed on the Internet. The system interface presence must be guaranteed during navigation. It can be achieved, for example, by opening every external site on a new browser window.

5. *Web Search - Internet*: An agent is permanently searching the Web for resources related to the community interests. To do so, it applies the specific ontology for the community knowledge domain and keywords associates with each concept. It is possible to use available indexes and web search engines. This process creates a file containing the initial information about each specified resource.

6. *Describe and Classify - Resource Description Base*: Information about resources found on the Web is refined and classified using a description pattern (i.e. RDF/XML) that provide portability and allow future reuse.

7. *Models, Tables and Configuration - Adaptation*: The system must be constructed in a way that allows that all parameters of all processes can be revised and updated collectively. This is extremely important to make maintenance easier and guarantee generality. "Parameters" are not only values, but also images, texts and other objects that will dynamically compose the user interface at every new login. Ideally, every object in the system is an item in a database.

8. *User Models Base - Adaptation*: To make Adaptations, the user model (UM) must be available to the system. The UM is, therefore, loaded at every login. Among the UM information there are interface

presentation parameters, resources to be presented in a certain order, research results, specific contents e-services etc.

9. *Resource Description Base - Adaptation*: The RBD completes the set of databases necessary to the system. All resource descriptions are stored in the RBD, classified by keywords and containing meta-information (RDF/XML). The database will be continuously verified to check URLs validity and modifications that may have occurred in the resources referred.

10. *Adaptation - Interface*: Interface is generated by an adaptive action the uses the information contained in the user model to aggregate the elements at the description base and the different models, tables and configurations of the system, producing an interface adapted to the user, that is renewed at every login. This is the nucleus of the system, to which all other components converge. At the end, all the system processes result on this interface, that must be unique to each user, providing easy access to all the resources that, in thesis, will contribute for his/her learning.

5   CONCLUDING REMARKS

This article presented a definition for the concept of *Virtual Communities for Technology Learning* (VCTL). It has also presented a possible pedagogical definition for this kind of virtual community, based on the idea of competence based teaching. This pedagogical approach is justified, in VCTL context, by its practical character and by a strong connection with the market that teaching must have on these communities. Furthermore, this article presented a methodology propose for creating and developing VCTL.

The ideas presented were elaborated for the creation of VCTL/SENAI, a virtual community for technological learning that is being built at SENAI. This is a partnership work between SENAI/RS and the School of Informatics at Catholic University of Pelotas, through its Artificial Intelligence (GPIA) and Web Programming (WPG) research groups.

These ideas are an adaptation of the concepts and the methodology adopted for the construction of the Virtual Learning Community at ESIN/UCPel that those groups are working on in the context of technological learning.

VCLT/SENAI will be fully operational by the end of 2004, with at least three thematic communities and a support community.

The planning experience of VCLT/SENAI itself has been productive from a conceptual point of view, because it has been confronted researchers with concrete problems and practical demands, brought by the professionalizing teaching institution, which the construction of a VC in an academic environment cannot provide.

6 REFERENCES

Brusilovski, P. (1997). "Efficient techniques for Adaptive Hypermedia, in *Intelligent Hypertext: Advanced techniques for the World Wide Web*, C. Nicholas and J. Mayfield, Eds., Berlin, pp. 12-30, Springer-Verlag, Lecture Notes in Computer Science 1326.

Brusilovski, P., (2001). "Adaptive Hypermedia", in *User Modeling and User Adapted Interaction*, v. 11, n. 1, pp. 87-110.

Kollock, P. (1997). "Design Principles for Online Communities", in: *The Internet and Society: Harvard Conference Proceedings*, O'Reilly and Associates, Cambridge.

Palazzo L. and Costa, A.(2001). "Towards Proactive Hypermedia Systems", in *Encontro Nacional de Inteligência Artificial*, Fortaleza, SBC.

Palazzo L. and Ulysséa, M. and Porto, P. (2001). "Comunidades Virtuais de Aprendizado Adaptativo", *Conferência Nacional em Ciência, Tecnologia e Inovação*, Florianópolis, Ministério da Ciência e Tecnologia.

Rheingold, H. (1993). "The Virtual Community: Homesteading at the Electronic Frontier", available at http://www.rheingold.com/vc/book, accessed in December, 2001.

SENAI, Brasília, (2002). *Metodologia para a Elaboração de Perfis Profissionais, Fase 2*, second edition.

W3C World Wide Web Consortium (2002). "Resource Description Framework (RDF)", available at http://www.w3.org/RDF/, accessed in May, 2002.

W3C World Wide Web Consortium (2002) "Extensible Markup Language (XML)", available at http://www.w3.org/XML/, accessed in May, 2002.

ACKNOWLEDGEMENT

This research is partially supported by CNPq, UCPel, SENAI and Fapergs (Brazil).

TEACHER TRAINING ON THE JOB
A generic metadata modeling approach for personalised learning and learner support

Dekeyser H.M., Van Rijn F.H.M and Jansen, D.
Open University of the Netherlands, Ruud de Moor Centre RdMC@ou.nl

Abstract: Since mid 2000 in the Netherlands full teacher qualification can be obtained in real life training trajectories 'on the job', by means of a tri-partite contract between a teacher (trainee), the school where the teacher/trainee will be working/learning and a teacher training institute. The Ruud de Moor Centre (RdMC, Open University of the Netherlands) was established to support these trajectories on the job, especially by means of ICT based distance learning and support. Like all real life learners these teacher trainees form a heterogeneous group, which requires a highly tailored approach for learning and support. Such a tailored approach not only has to take into account personal characteristics of the trainees, but also the working/learning contexts that differ from school to school. Tailoring includes (but is not limited to) personalisation and contextualisation of content delivery, adapting presentation modes and individualising user support. This imposes severe constraints on the organisation and management of the learning materials and on delivery modes. Adequate metadata, conceptual structures for organisation and processing of knowledge, proper search tools and engines for information retrieval are requested. The RdMC is developing a flexible and modular system architecture as well as a data model, with emphasis on didactic potency, enabling design and delivery of tailored learning and learner support on the job.

Key words: Personalisation, teacher training, in service training, knowledge databases, user perspectives

1   INTRODUCTION

The Ruud de Moor Centre (RdMC) of the Open University of the Netherlands (OUNL) is supporting a typical category of real life learners: career switchers who enter a teaching job in a school (in this paper we will address these learners as "new teachers"). While working as a teacher they have to acquire their formal qualification in one or two years, for which the new teacher, the school and the teacher training institute enter a tri-partite contract. This on the job training, i.e. in the school, is becoming increasingly important in the solution of the problems caused by the shortage of teachers, especially in primary and secondary education.

In general the actual knowledge and the experience of these new teachers do not fit too well with respect to the subject to teach and/or with respect to pedagogic and didactic competences.

Like all real life learners these teacher trainees form a heterogeneous group, differing in characteristics such as prior knowledge, competencies or cognitive style. Also working/learning circumstances, contexts and facilities differ from school to school. Schools, mentors and training institutes work with different didactic models, are confronted with cultural differences, differ from school type, ...

Most often the schools lack the expertise in training trajectories on the job. Support by the school, by new colleagues or by mentors on site is not developed to its full extent yet. This requires new organisation processes from the schools where these new teachers learn while working, as well as from the supporting organisations (e.g., teacher training institutes).

For new teachers this situation means coping with the challenges of learning and working in a rapidly changing context from an organisation that in its turn is also learning while doing. These developments and the needs (expressed by all parties) were the guiding principle for the Open University of the Netherlands in the establishment of the Ruud de Moor Centre. The Centre is now developing a "toolbox" of learning materials, tools and services to support the new teachers, their schools and the teacher training institutes involved as well as the interactions within the tripartite. End-users of the products are not only the new teachers but also trainers, mentors and institutes. The elements of the toolbox are chosen and constructed in an ongoing process of supply and demand. All users could have the role of content provider, adding their input to that provided by experts at the RdMC and external authors.

In these conditions a highly tailored (multipurpose, multi-actor and flexible) approach is a conditio sine qua non. Personal differences (prior knowledge and expertise, learning or teaching style) are taken into account, delivery systems memorise user settings, learning tracks, address the user in a personal way (personalisation).

Learning takes place in contexts, and preferably, these contexts fit the learning objectives. Contextualisation varies the contexts to the particular target group, even if the basic information remains the same for all target groups. For new teachers the most important context will be the school in which they are learning while working. For their trainers this might be the teaching institute. Adequate tailoring will take these differences into account.

Tailoring requires a flexible, multi-purpose environment for learning and learner support, accessible by all actors according to their needs, preferences and contexts, from the workplace as well as from the distance (i.e. by IT-tools and/or consultancy). Developing such an environment is about creating an open, complex working environment, embodied by three major functionalities: authoring, repository and delivery.

This working paper focuses on one of the key factors to create, maintain and use well structured, interrelated repositories: an accurate metadata model. It elaborates the discussion of tailoring an environment to support the multiple and heterogeneous groups of real life learners, their schools and their trainers, and then proposes a generic metadata model. Finally the preliminary test results of two pilot studies are presented and discussed.

2   CONSTRAINTS FOR METADATA MODELLING

Tailoring is conditional to offer adequate products, provide requested information, limit or reduce the amount of information to what is really relevant for the user. It is alleviating the risk of the "lost in hyperspace syndrome" (Foss, 1989), it offers timesaving benefits by pointing immediately to the information that is specifically needed, opens opportunities to consult related information in order to explore a subject as deeply as needed, etcetera.

For example a teacher at the eve of his first class activity in a new school does not expect an overwhelming amount of eventually interesting information but might prefer an immediate, relevant and limited range of information. In a later stage the same teacher might be willing to go deeper into a specific theoretical topic, a good practice, new didactic method... In the first situation the new teacher will appreciate a restricted (or filtered) version of the learning and materials, while in the later version he might be willing to browse through additional materials, to search specific topics ...

The situation of a highly tailored approach imposes demanding conditions to an adequate Virtual Working and Learning (VWL) environment. This VWL environment should function as an extension of the real working environment of real life learners, as a working process aid. It should function as an open, modular architecture that allows for different authoring systems, a flexible repository (cf. a number of interrelated repositories) and delivery to a variety of learning/working environments by a wide range of media (web, dvd/cd-rom, paper, mobile devices).

Creating and maintaining a multi-functional and flexible repository especially puts severe constraints on the metadata model. Metadata are key elements in tailoring mechanisms such as information retrieval, sorting, filtering, presenting the same content in a different mode, in different didactic approaches, combine content units fit for all with tailored content, … Content entities have to be isolated from their presentation mode or medium, from the didactic and instructional meanings of these entities, and from the information on the relations between content is of absolute importance, in order to be able to reassemble the same content with other content entities, present it in different modes, in different didactic settings. From a logistic point of view, tailoring is based on a "Assemble to order system" (ATO) in which units of content are assembled according to needs and demands. ATO systems are based on accurate labelling by means of parameters and classes of parameters (metadata). Robust metadata models are key factors for ATO systems (Hegge, 1990).

Theoretically a lot of the problems might be solved rather easily if all elements of the system architecture were compliant to international standards as described for Dublin Core, SCORM, LOM, IMS Learning Design etcetera. However, in practice it appears to be very difficult to develop an all-inclusive holistic metadata model that covers all functional dimensions (domain, user, instruction/didactics, authoring) of storage, retrieval, reusing and sharing of learning material. Even when such a model might be created, it is hardly possible to get it accepted by all actors. In many cases different terminology is used for the same types of metadata. The VWL environment needs to support different metadata "dialects" and different sets of metadata types. And even if a common model might be accepted, it should be able to face frequent revisions, in reaction to the rapidly changing reality.

3   A GENERIC APPROACH FOR METADATA MODELLING

Therefore we propose a generic approach for functional metadata modelling of (learning) material that can lead to many metadata profiles. This generic model consists of a set of sub-models for separated dimensions and sets of rules to define the relations between them. We propose four (sub) models with their own organising principles: the content domain model, the authoring model, the instructional and the user model. The model contains metadata and metadata-types, values of metadata, and relations between metadata (or their specific values). These models reflect the different perspectives or dimensions of the generic model. The models should be orthogonal: metadata should apply for one model only. 'Combined' metadata will be generated by the management and authoring tools.

3.1 Critical characteristics of the model

- Metadata are descriptors of content units: content fragments (or assets, information objects), content objects, learning objects, ...
- Allow labelling of content elements with metadata on all levels of aggregation - even the smallest resource types (i.e. content fragments) when useful
- Units of content can be related to many meta-data
- The metadata model allows usage of dialects for different actors (different actors use different terminology to find or use equal information objects; Metadata used to support the development of the content are different from those used by the end-users)
- The model is robust enough to withstand changing situations and conditions, changing user groups and user needs
- Changes in one subset of the model does not lead to changes in other subsets: they are orthogonal
- The model supports maintainability: content objects are unique in the repository, even if it is delivered many times in different didactic situations, for different user groups, used by many authors
- Discern "what" from "how". i.e. discern domain metadata from didactic metadata: (in order to allow reusability of content in several didactic setting or to allow that equal didactic settings can contain different content for different user groups.)

3.2 The four basic orthogonal dimensions

3.2.1 Domain model

Knowledge, skills, attitudes and meta-cognition relevant in this domain
- Structuring and organisational metadata: content entity or aggregation level (asset, paragraph, document, chapter, module, ...) and domain structure (reflected in concept maps, tables of content - hierarchical tree model or network model). (A lot of this meta-information will be

generated automatically by the system and will be supported by the metaphoric structure of the authoring and management tool "create a paragraph, a document, a chapter,..." Other information will be author-generated, e.g. titles, document names, ...)

- Semantic metadata (domain classification): descriptions of the knowledge, skills, attitudes and meta-cognition for the content domain (e.g. economics, mathematics, communication, ...)

3.2.2 Authoring model

- Managerial and lifecycle metadata (date, author, version, status, rights, roles...)
- Collective authoring metadata (to allow exchange)

3.2.3 Instructional model

- Didactic metadata
  - o type of didactic material component with values such as: learning goal, assignment, source, illustration, case, advance organiser...),
  - o didactic method (case-based, competency based, problem-oriented, thematic, question-based,...),
  - o support device (tip, feedback, cognitive stimulus,)
- Navigational model: sequence, relations ("is conditional for", "requests prior knowledge of "),
- Target group metadata

3.2.4 User model

- New teachers:
  - o prior knowledge and expertise
  - o cognitive style
  - o ambitions
  - o social interactions skills and style
  - o deficiencies
  - o preferred didactic method
- School
  - o type
  - o didactic method used
  - o size
  - o culture
  - o organisation type
  - o organisational expertise in teacher training on the job

- Training institute:
  o didactic methods
  o Level of experience with mentoring new teachers
  o Learning environment
  o Preferred delivery mode (Word, pdf, Scorm package, interactive reader, Bb-course content, …)

3.3 Sets of rules

A second essential part of the model is the set of relations between the values of the metadata, which form the basis for pre-tailoring while authoring. This leads to sets of rules such as:
- If the value of user type Training Institute is "No experience with mentoring new teachers" than the module "Supporting new teachers on the job" will be presented.
- If the value of user characteristic "Deficiency" for user type "new teacher" is "No experience with eventual misconceptions of pupils in sciences" than the didactic support device "Eventual misconceptions" is added to all science concepts.
- If the "preferred didactic method" of the new teacher is case-based then the module will start with case description and assignment.

These types of rules are a helpful mechanism to tailor the learning and support to the characteristics and/or the context of the user.

The definition of accurate right sets of rules is based on thorough knowledge of the user, gathered by the RdMC in in-depth interviews with representatives of the field.

4 TESTING OF THE MODEL IN THE PROJECTS OF THE RDMC

The model was tested in two ways during the period of August-September 2004. In these tests two sets of interrelated repositories were built, by means of an open authoring tool and Learning Content management system "Content-e" and delivered in common delivery environments (several-browser based web-players, Blackboard) and media channels such as internet, Pdf, Word and Zip-file.

The model was discussed in a national and international expert group during the period of October-November.

In the pilot project "Palet: the Crash course for new teachers and their mentors" an instantiation of the generic model was tested against the criteria of consistency and practical value for the developers (and will be tested for the added value of tailoring for multiple user groups). The generic capacities of the model are tested. One of the major issues is to observe whether (or at what cost) existing models fit into the generic model. Another concern of the pilot is to confirm the assumed added value of tailored approach for multiple user groups with rapidly changing needs and contexts. A basic assumption of the tailored learning principle is that in a tailored environment the questions of users are answered quickly, easy and accurate, and that the user does not get lost in unwanted, superfluous information (objective benefit). A second and related assumption is that users also appreciate these benefits (subjective benefit).

In a mock-up prototype the model is used to create a multifunctional and tailored repository "The Bach therapy knowledge base", created to reflect in a nutshell the complexity of the conditions of real life learners. In the mock-up prototype the model is tested against the criteria internal consistency, robustness in changing situations and practical value for developers and authors.

In both test situations the following aspects are investigated: "How intuitive or contra-intuitive is it for authors to respect the orthogonality of the dimension and to express relations between metadata in sets of rules?"

"Are the four dimensions sufficient or would it be necessary to add one or more extra dimensions?"

5   INTERMEDIATE RESULTS

Results available at the moment for both tests are mainly based on evaluation of the value of the model for *developers and authors,* and some intermediate results from *end-users.* The data are mainly written or verbal feedback, spontaneous reactions, formal evaluation results and reports from in depth discussions.

Using the model to create the mock-up prototype confirms the consistency and robustness of the generic model for *developing and maintaining* a multipurpose knowledge database, learning environment, support environment and course for multiple heterogeneous target groups,.

In both test groups developers report finding it rather hard to respect the orthogonality, especially when it comes to unravel instructional and authoring issues from the domain structure. Initial concept maps, concepts of tables of content, project plans show mixed models containing instructional and even authoring or user information unsystematically interwoven in the domain model. Separation of content, presentation, instruction, and didactics appears to be conflicting with teacher's tradition of developing integrated learning materials.

However, for the Mock-up group, which is starting from scratch with the model, it seems to be easier to get used to this systematic way of developing materials. In both groups the developers report that the process goes much easier, quicker, and that the results are more flexible and reusable, once they get familiar with the orthogonality and with its authoring consequences.

The pilot test reveals that the generic metadata-model does allow using metadata-dialects for different groups of authors/developers as well as for different user groups. The generic metadata model proves to be generic enough indeed to incorporate the original metadata-model of the pilot project group.

Developers report that the development process might be supported by intuitive metadata management tools, such as automation of application of metadata (where possible), generating reports and overviews of the metadata (values) and how they are interrelated.

Intermediate results of *user evaluation* within the threefold user group confirm the appreciation of tailored materials. (Exclamations as: "This is exactly what I was looking for!" express a user's feeling that the information he received was not more and not less than what he needed. The tailoring seemed to be successful...)

6   DISCUSSION

Although the evaluation process is still ongoing, the results of working with the generic model are promising. Using the generic model requires a shift in development procedures, a demanding process for authors and developers. The question remains whether the model will be able to correspond well enough with the procedural aspects of content development and behaviour of authors and developers, whether it will prove to be facilitating the content development process rather than hindering it. Further analysis as well as testing will show whether these four dimensions will be sufficient for this complex and changing situation or whether more dimensions should be added.

7   REFERENCES

Brusilovsky P. (2003) Developing adaptive educational hypermedia systems: From design models to authoring tools. In: T. Murray, S. Blessing and S. Ainsworth (eds.): Authoring

Tools for Advanced Technology Learning Environment, Dordrecht: Kluwer Academic Publishers.

Dekeyser, H.M. (2003) Surf Meeting on LCMS 2003, LCMS and Educational Quality: the conditions (June 25, 2003). Surf. [http://elearning.surf.nl/docs/e-learning/dekeyser.pdf]

Foss, Carolyn L. (1989), Tools for Reading and Browsing Hypertext. Information Processing and Management, Volume 25, Number 4, 1989, pp. 407-418.

Goldiamond, J. (2003), Aspects, Challenges and Repositioning of Distance Learning, EADL Conference 2003: Annual conference of the European Association for Distance Learning, 2003, Hamburg, 14-16 May.

Hegge, H., (1009), Intelligent Product Family Descriptions For Business Applications. PhD-thesis. Eindhoven University of Technology.

Open Universiteit Nederland (2002), Plan van aanpak Project lerarenopleiding, http://www.ou.nl/rdmc

Straub, R. (2003), The Learning Society on its way, EADL Conference 2003: Annual conference of the European Association.

EXPLORING THE ROLE OF INFORMAL LEARNING IN REAL-LIFE LEARNING

Mike Kendall
East Midlands Broadband Consortium, Northampton, UK
mkendall@embc.org.uk

Abstract: When we refer to real-life learning we can readily image learning taking place in our everyday lives, at work, rest and play, with and without information and communications technology (ICT). The new competencies of young and old peoples to create their own learning communities, using ICT, is one that can provide powerful informal learning situations. The paper will ask questions about the impact of informal learning on attitudes to learning; about the demands placed upon real-life learning provided in professional and vocational education; and upon the role of ICT in building capacity for communities and economies.

Key words: Informal learning, learning communities, citizens, social impact, competencies.

1   INTRODUCTION

This paper takes the position that real-life learning and lifelong learning are, in effect, the same activity with different names. However, the author acknowledges that it can also be defined with an emphasis on vocational and professional education. Hence, the paper will explore the increasing prominence of lifelong learning, its relationship to community based and informal learning styles as well as its role in vocational and professional education.

Lifelong learning, and hence real-life learning, is a prominent public policy theme for many countries and non-governmental organisations for education, economic, political, social and cultural purposes. The increasing prominence of lifelong learning has taken place alongside the increasingly dominant role that ICT has in all public policy considerations. With this is mind IFIP TC3 established the Lifelong Learning Taskforce in 2001 to consider the role of ICT in lifelong learning. The taskforce was responsible for the development of an *IFIP TC3 Position Paper on Lifelong Learning* (Kendall, et al, 2004) initially published in 2002 and revised in 2004. At the IFIP TC3 e-Train conference in Pori, Finland, 2003, invited participants contributed to the further development of the IFIP TC3 position paper and the subsequent book, *Lifelong Learning in the Digital Age: sustainable learning for all in a changing world.* (Weert and Kendall, 2004). In this book Kendall (2004) argues that community based learning provides a key interface for the learner and society between informal and formal learning, between learning directed from within and learning directed by others.

2   THE QUEST FOR LEARNING

People are natural learners; they seek to explore the world in which they live and work, in which they become social and economic beings. Learning from the cradle whereby a child learns to survive, nurtured by the mother and the immediate family, and as they grow older involves more people and contexts. The informal learning of survival becomes more formal as the child and the family meets the formal educational demands of society. The quest for learning that was initially driven by internal survival instincts becomes formalised and defined by the society in which they are living. This is real-life learning, providing learning for life. The concept of lifelong learning has evolved slowly with the changing requirements of employment and the need for employees to increasingly acquire new competences within the same or new employment. The early definitions of lifelong learning tended to focus on giving adults access to formal courses, generally at educational institutions. Lifelong learning is now a major political issue, one that is being tackled by all governments in the developing and developed world, although not always for the same reasons. The quest for definition often seeks to differentiate the definitions of learning from lifelong or real-life, to draw out new and refined definitions of learning as well as the changing purposes of learning as one progresses through life – it may be learning from the cradle to the grave, but the impact and intent of such learning may not be constant.

In seeking to define the purposes and processes of learning, the Delors Commission (UNESCO, 1996) proposed the four pillars for learning, applicable across nations, in different and evolving social, economic and technological contexts. They are: learn to know, learn to do, learn to live together, and learn to be. The French Commission for UNESCO and the Council for Europe, in responding to the Delors Commission, focussed on The *Winds of Change in the Teaching Profession* (UNESCO 2002) in 2001 recognising that "teaching is changing and becoming more complex, this profession is becoming more diversified." Noting that, "Teaching doesn't only take place in classes or in institutions, but in a larger and more complex system. Teachers no longer simply teach a group of students in a class but do so in a system: an education system, a country, a society and an international education system which makes the teachers of the world." Whilst this relates to the teaching profession, it can readily be applied to the whole of education and training. Real-life learning is no longer simple, if it ever was, it is no longer about simple inputs and outputs defined in narrow competences or closed processes, the demands of the modern world mean that educators are operating in a complex, often global system, with new professions emerging that support the real-life learning of people as citizens, as students, and as employees throughout their lives where change is taking place at an accelerating rate.

The changing purposes and processes for education are evidenced across the globe. In Latin America:

"Education has become increasingly important within governmental policy, and particularly social policy... We need to imagine the building of an education system that is flexible, open to all, independent of age or life conditions: a system that guarantees education as a right for life... We need to think of an open system that incorporates all educational resources in the society, including the media and new communication technologies." (Machado, 2000)

The need to redefine learning to take account of the "...scale of current economic and social change, the rapid transition to a knowledge-based society and demographic pressures resulting from an ageing population in the industrialised countries are all challenges which demand political attention and a new approach to education and training" lead to the Feira European Council to *A Memorandum of Lifelong Learning* (European Commission 2000). The memorandum defines Lifelong Learning as "...all learning activity undertaken throughout life, with the aim of improving knowledge, skills and competence, within a personal, civic, social and/or employment-related perspective." The challenge is to support and extend learning activity, making it relevant to the social and economic well-being of citizens and employees, seeking to extend access and opportunity through ICT.

3   THE QUEST TO EXTEND ACCESS TO LEARNING

The way people engage with real-life learning is changing as a result of their experience and opportunity to exploit information and communication technologies in an ever growing range of contexts, socially and informally, as well as professionally and formally. For example, Veen (2002) suggests we have a media generation, the 'Homo Zappiens', with new competencies for multi-dimensional scanning, multi-tasking and existing in virtual environments, where school is a meeting place, not a learning place. The public policy drive for lifelong learning leads to a range of considerations. In considering the role of the school, Carnoy (2001) comments that "... the central organising point in our society at the neighbourhood level is the school – elementary and secondary, as well as child development centres. Children could thus act as the fulcrum around which family, community, and the future worker (the child) are brought together in a system of interaction, blending instrumental goals (child-care, development and education) with expressive, emotional, and social interactions". With a strengthened community based role that extends beyond what is often seen as the traditional role of the school, the school is no longer isolated, but "Through the school, other social networks organised at the municipal level could come into contact with each other [and] the development of electronic communications also offers the possibility of creating virtual communities, in a new form of spatial organisation ...".

To extend the range of opportunities to access ICT, the UK government has connected all libraries to broadband networks, with free computers and internet access, supported by newly trained librarians and community tutors. The provision of support to people to develop new competencies and opportunities to use ICT for formal and informal learning, supporting people and their communities to utilise new media, complementing existing roles of the libraries in the provision of services through traditional media, has been a clear public policy goal. Additionally, the UK government has sponsored a programme to provide 7,000 UK online centres across the country in a wide variety of community settings, generally in communities that would not have access to ICT and other online services, such that no citizen is more than one mile from online access in an urban area. The centres' role is to "bridge the gap between those in society who have access to and are able to use information and communications technologies competently, and those who do not. The key success criteria are the extent to which the centres increase ICT awareness, ICT skills and people's participation in local communities." (DfES 2002) The DfES report sought to evaluate the impact of the online centres on informal learners and their subsequent progression into formal learning or into work. The reported findings indicate that 21% of the users surveyed felt that the centre could help them get a job and that 31% felt it would help them to progress into further or higher education.

In identifying such learning communities, often characterised as communities of self and shared interest, it is possible to envisage social, economic, residential, knowledge and educational as well as familial communities, all of which are undergoing change, often as a result of the opportunities offered by new information and communications technology. "Visions of learning have been evolving, and informal learning communities and communities of practice have become important concepts that highlight the fact that learning is no longer happening in classrooms or through formal e-learning mechanisms. The 'Knowledge Economy' implies a far reaching transformation of the learning process" (Tremblay, 2002). The way we visualise learning communities has also changed, as the Archbishop of Canterbury noted in 2000, "Increasingly we are not only citizens of the world but also citizens of the World Wide Web". Hence our experience of learning communities, whether formal, non-formal or informal has changed, hence the spaces and times in which community based learning can take place are also changing. Perhaps one of the advantages of informal learning is that activities are not mapped to a formal learning process or qualifications, and are often motivated by fun, or the sense of achievement that comes from completing a project.

4   THE QUEST TO FORMALISE INFORMAL LEARNING

Employers and training organisations are recognising the growth of informal learning which they are witnessing in the workplace and in the personal experiences of their staff. Increasingly employers and training organisations are observing this energy and commitment that staff and students exercise when engaged in informal learning activities. Cross (2002) argues that "Informal learning is effective because it is personal. The individual calls the shots. The learner is responsible. It's real. How different from formal learning, which is imposed by someone else. Workers are pulled into informal learning: formal learning is pushed at them." Cross further argues that that "Most training is built on the pessimistic assumption that trainees are deficient... rather than make what's good better." The capacity within real-life learning to build on the achievements and enthusiasm to improve economic benefits of learning is acting as a counterbalance to prescribed, or as Cross referred to deficit models of training.

The providers of information and communications systems and services are very aware of the changing marketplace for learning, and are seeking to develop tools and understanding that can be used formally and informally. For example, Bob Mosher (2004) from Microsoft acknowledges that as the role of the traditional classroom is declining and e-learning becomes more popular that industry needs to "...harness the more informal technologies that our students are utilising." Stating that, "If you ask many advanced learners today, they will tell you they are gravitating toward these more informal learning methods and away from traditional ones. Understanding, tracking, creating and encouraging these informal methods of learning can reach a growing population of students you may currently be ignoring or losing touch with altogether." He further argues that these methods are becoming more popular is due to their immediacy and relevance, as well as a lack time or budget for formal learning. "With the maturation of our learners and the advent of collaboration technologies, informal learning can become a powerful part of a company's robust learning offering." The recognition of a clear business case from the technology industry means that increased levels of investment and promotion of supporting tools will increase. The ready access to the internet, with the ubiquitous use of the browser, means that further tools will be made available and exploited by the formal and informal training communities.

The Campaign for Learning, a UK based lobby group, carried out a survey in Summer 2000 about attitudes to eLearning in the workplace. The survey found that the majority of eLearning occurred in the workplace, with nearly a third of learners doing most of their eLearning at home. The formal eLearning tended to be work related and required by employers, whereas informal eLearning was most frequently surfing the web. The survey found that "The quality of the learning experience is rated more highly for informal learning (58% excellent or good) than for formal methods (45%).

The increased availability of the internet, supported by communities of practice and interest, where self-determined learning goals are developed, implicitly and explicitly in the actions and desires of citizens, the impact of real-life learning is having a broadly based impact. In the UK where local government is promoting increased access to and the use of the internet, "...new types of internet-based community are more visible, and where people have engaged online around local issues, there has been a tendency to by-pass traditional democratic institutions." (NLGN, 2004) A US study suggested that the internet can be a force for local and non-local community, specifically that "The internet helps many people find others who share their interests no matter how distant they are, and it also helps them increase their contact with groups and people they already know and it helps them feel more connected to them." (Horrigan 2002) Suggesting that the internet connects people regardless of the distance. The internet supports people to belong to communities through social software which allows groups of people to communicate, and importantly collaborate and begin to develop a collective memory, actions and goals, whether this is through email, chat or more formal web sites such as the BCC's ICAN web site www.bbc.co.uk/ican which supports people to form communities of interest, launch public campaigns, taking the first step in addressing issues that face them. In this context the internet is not just providing information, it is providing social contact, perhaps a different digital divide. As I have argued elsewhere (Kendall, 2000) lifelong, real-life learning requires active participation in learning teams and communities and that citizenship is lifelong learning, and hence real-life learning.

5   CONCLUSION

Informal learning has always been a part of real-life learning. Its role is gaining increasing recognition as employers' and governments' seek to mobilise people to exploit ICT to increase economic and social well-being, for all. However, the opportunities to exploit the growing confidence and competence of citizens is not yet being utilised effectively in vocational and professional education; it is not yet changing the premise on which work based training is provided, moving from a deficit model of provision to one building on the achievements and enthusiasm of people.

6   REFERENCES

Campaign for Learning (2000), *Attitudes to eLearning in the Workplace*, London

Carnoy, M. (2001) *Work, Society Family and Learning for the Future*. In: What Schools for the Future, OECD, Paris

Cross, J. (2003) Informal Learning: A Sound Investment, CLO Magazine October 2003, CLOmedia.com

DfES (2002) *Evaluation of Pioneer and Pathfinder UK online centres: follow up study*, Hall Aitken Associates, DfES

European Commission (2000) *A Memorandum on Lifelong Learning*. Brussels, 30.10.2000, SEC (2000) 1832.

Horrigan, J (2002) *Online communities: Networks that nurture long distance relationships and local ties*, PEW Internet and American Life Project

Kendall, M. (2000) *Citizenship is lifelong learning: the challenge of information and communications technology*. In: Benzie D. and D. Passey (Eds.), Proceedings of Conference on Educational Uses of ICT, Publishing House of Electronics Industry, Beijing, 2000

Kendall, M (2004A) *Community Based Learning: Developing the interface between formal and informal learning communities* In: Weert, Tom J. van and Kendall, Mike (Eds.) Lifelong Learning in the Digital Age, Kluwer, Boston

Kendall, M., Samways, B., Weert, T J van and Wibe, J (2004) *IFIP TC3 Position Paper on Lifelong Learning* In: Weert, Tom J. van and Kendall, Mike (Eds.) Lifelong Learning in the Digital Age, Kluwer, Boston

Machado, A.L. (2000) *Current status and perspectives for education in Latin America* In: Taylor, H. and Hogenbirk, P. (Eds.) The Schools of the Future, Kluwer, Boston

Mosher, B. (2004) The Power of Informal Learning, CLO Magazine July 2004, CLOmedia.com

NLGN, 2004, *invisible villages: techno-localism and the enabling council*, New Local Government Network, London

Tremblay, D.G. (2002) *Informal learning communities in the knowledge economy: informal knowledge development in the multimedia sector.* In: Passey, D & M. Kendall (Eds.) TelE-LEARNING: The Challenge of the Third Millennium. Kluwer, Boston.

UNESCO (1996) *Education Holds a Treasure* Prepared by Jacques Delors on behalf of the International Commission on Education for the Twenty First Century.

UNESCO (2002) *Winds of change in the teaching profession*, French National Commission for UNESCO, Paris

Veen, W. (2002) *Students of the media generation, Coping with homo zappiens.* Voordracht op de SURF Onderwijsdagen 2002, SURF, Utrecht. http://www.surf.nl/onderwijsdagen2002/video/veen/index.htm

Weert, Tom J. van and Kendall, Mike (Eds.) (2004) *Lifelong Learning in the Digital Age: Sustainable learning for all in a changing world* Kluwer Academic Publishers, Boston

SIMULATING REAL-LIFE PROBLEMS
Use of Problem-Based Learning in Information Systems

John Bentley
Victoria University of Technology, Melbourne, Australia
John.Bentley@vu.edu.au

Abstract: This paper explores use of problem-based learning (PBL) in an introductory first-year undergraduate course in systems analysis and design. Problem-based learning is a pedagogical approach that encourages students to become active learners and to take responsibility for their learning within the setting of their intended profession. Learning is initiated by problems that are sourced from actual situations in the profession. The fundamental principle is that the problem is always introduced first and must precede any teacher-supported learning such as a lecture. This paper describes how problems are used to initiate learning. The problems in this course initially simulate real-life systems development situations that information systems professionals may face, followed by problems that involve a real client. Students are required to plan and reflect on their learning weekly. In the use of PBL a number of issues arose for both staff and students. The issues were derived from student's perceptions, weekly planning sheets, diary submissions, and staff observations. For students, major issues include: dealing with a new approach to learning, workload, the requirements of group work, class and meeting attendance, and group communication. For staff major issues are: using facilitation rather than lecturing, design of appropriate teaching environments, assessment of process skills, and developing problems to match curriculum. Feedback from students indicates that PBL challenges and motivates them. However, they perceive the course requires more work and time than the lecture-based courses.

Key words: Information systems education, problem-based learning, real-life learning.

1 INTRODUCTION

Problem-based learning (PBL) is an approach that encourages students to become active learners and to take responsibility for their learning. Some researchers such as Fogarty (1998 p.1) see PBL as "learning in its most authentic state." PBL contextualizes learning towards the real world. An objective of PBL according to Biggs (1999, p.71) is "to get students to solve problems they will meet in their professional careers – the teaching method is to present them with problems to solve; the assessment is based on how well they solve them." The learning begins by presenting a problem scenario to the student before any relevant theory or practice is given. Engaging in a problem scenario within the discipline context drives motivation to learn and apply appropriate theory. Students work in small learning groups and, through a process of inquiry, have to develop their skill at acquiring, communicating, and integrating information to solve a problem (Woods, 1994; Savery & Duffy, 1995; Delisle, 1997; Fogarty, 1998; Savin-Baden, 2000).

PBL has been used successfully in disciplines such as medicine since the mid 1970s (Savery & Duffy, 1995; Boud & Feletti, 1997). The use of PBL is being adopted in computing education as is evidenced at sources such as the ACM Digital Library, by the increasing number of papers since 2000.

PBL is seen by Bentley et al. (1999) as a better way to develop graduates who are more suited to the practice-based and project-oriented world of the information systems professional. Also McCracken and Waters (1999) using PBL for software engineering suggest that PBL is an approach to overcome the "instructional gap" between what is taught, and what needs to be taught. By simulating real-world scenarios PBL should lead to a closer alignment between the teaching and learning approach used in undergraduate education and the work of an information system professional, with the outcome of an IS graduate better equipped to work in professional practice (Bentley et al., 1999).

Savin-Baden (2000, p.15) identifies from the PBL literature four key reasons to adopt PBL: 1. develop student's reasoning skills; 2. enable learning to take place within a context that is relevant to the students; 3. ensure that learning is attuned to the world of work; and 4. promote student's self-directed learning abilities.

This paper discusses problem-based learning in an introductory first-year undergraduate systems analysis and design course.

2   METHODOLOGY

The study used a qualitative approach to understanding PBL and employed action research in refining the approach to PBL. A phenomenological research approach was used to gain student's perceptions of PBL. Student perceptions were obtained from face-to-face interviews, focus groups, tutor observations, student emails, course evaluation forms, and examination of diaries and planning sheets. Individual interviews were conducted with PBL students. Email feedback was sought from course graduates. The data collected was analyzed for shared themes, experiences, key words, and phrases.

3 TEACHING USING PBL

The first-year compulsory course "Introduction to Business Systems Development" has used PBL as the teaching method since 1999. The teaching structure and PBL resources are summarized in Table 1.

Table 1. Teaching structure and PBL resources

Timetabled classes	Learning aids and information sources
2-hour tutorial/workshop	PBL handouts and video.
1-hour lecture	Course and student expectations.
1-hour group meeting	Internet, intranet, self-assessment tests, discussion server and e-mail, textbooks and libraries.
	Weekly planning sheets and diary entries.
	KNDA Planning sheet.
	Mini-lectures
	Workshop exercises

Small class sizes and the delivery format have allowed some freedom to experiment with PBL. Class times are scheduled to provide an opportunity for students to meet regularly and spread their contact across the week. In an attempt to achieve an academic balance within groups, students are placed into groups based on their prior academic performance. Groups generally consist of five members. To foster a strong working relationship and team commitment, groups are together for the whole semester.

The IS professional activities of planning and reflection are simulated by students completing weekly planning sheets to guide their learning and weekly reflective learning diaries where they record their reflections on their learning and activities for the past week. The ITiCSE Working Papers (Ellis et al., 1998, p52b) state, "A key issue in professional development is to have the skills of self-evaluation and the ability to steer one's activities." Students are encouraged to see themselves as junior IS professionals.

To aid in the understanding and tackling of a problem a KNDA planning sheet is used. The KNDA has columns headed: What we already Know, What we Need to know, What tasks we need to Do, and Who the task is Assigned to. The KNDA is an adaptation of KWL (Know, Want, Learned) in Barell (1998, p.35) and a KND (Know, Need, Do) in Fogarty (1997, p.6)).

Using the completed KNDA planning sheet students develop their own individual learning plan for the week(s).

The PBL problems are sourced or adapted from real situations, though structured to provide clues and "scaffolding" to guide the students in their learning. The use of tiered problems (parts a, b, c etc) provide students with an example of what an IS professional is likely to do. This allows students to reflect on their solution and provide direction for tackling the next part of the problem.

Table 2 shows the schedule of problems over a 12-week semester. The early problems simulate real-life systems development situations, followed by problems that involve a real client. Large problems, termed "assignments", involve a number of weeks. In smaller problems each part is completed over one week. The smaller problems early in the course assist students in understanding the PBL approach. Student feedback indicates they see the problems as realistic and relevant to the work of an information system professional.

Table 2. Schedule of problems

Problem	Nature of the problem
Problem 1 Parts a, b & c	Understanding systems and roles and incorporates EAI. Feasibility and project selection.
Problem 2 Assignment 1	SDLC, project planning, analysis modelling techniques, data gathering.
Assignment 2 Parts a & b	Methodology, requirements specification, design and prototyping.

After reflection and discussion of the solution to a problem, a "mini" lecture is often given. The timetabled lecture is sometimes used to present material related to the student questions or comments from the previous week's planning sheets and diaries. Assessment includes the process of learning, as well as the content learning and deliverables.

The benefits perceived by both staff and students include: increased motivation and enthusiasm; improved problem solving; improved time management; improved self-directed learning skills; improved research skills; improved self-evaluation skills; and improved group work skills.

4   MAJOR ISSUES AND CHALLENGES

Major issues in the course include: a new approach to learning; design of the physical teaching environment; group work; assessment of process skills; attendance; facilitation and small group teaching; and, problem design. Some challenges include: a focus on factual knowledge; problems with group work participation; weaker students requiring more direction; and, preparation and motivation for PBL. Some of these are now discussed.

4.1 New Approach

PBL is often a new approach to learning for students, as is the role of a PBL facilitator for many teaching staff. The first three weeks emphasize the techniques of the PBL approach, however, only about 4 hours is spent specifically on PBL. It is observed that students have to unlearn their prior conceptions of learning. Some students, especially the weaker ones, find responsibility for self-learning difficult. In feedback this year on PBL, Student A wrote: "Has been a very difficult subject. Learning new topics and learning approach."

Students require reassurance that they are learning content as well as acquiring process skills. Students report they are uncertain as to whether they are learning anything. Self-evaluation content-based tests are given on a regular basis. Students report these tests help confirm their knowledge or lack of, and provide pointers for follow-up learning if they identify a knowledge gap.

The role for tutors in PBL is to be a facilitator to empower students. Russell et al. (1994, p.59) suggests "educators are therefore required to implement strategies which promote self-directed learning skills, are conducive to students' construction of knowledge, and promote reasoning skills". The challenge for lecturers in Information Systems is to adopt a philosophy of using active learning strategies from traditional passive teaching approaches. Lecturers' skills in PBL for this course were gained by attending PBL workshops, reading (especially the work of Woods (1994), subscribing to PBL and education list servers, visiting lecturers at educational institutions using PBL, and through team teaching.

4.2 Group Work

Issues regarding group work include: leadership, composition, contribution and meeting attendance. Acquiring group leadership skills is addressed by having each student act as team leader during the semester, so that everyone in the group has at least two weeks as leader. The leader chairs meetings, acts as a communication facilitator and monitors team member's progress during the week.

The knowledge that groups are together for the whole semester seems to engender a greater sense of group commitment and motivation. A positive comment by graduate Student B reflecting on their PBL experience from a few years ago wrote: "Considering that all components of the PBL subject were done in teams, my ability to work successfully within a team environment improved. Working within a team environment has also improved my social skills and has enabled me to become a pro-active team member within the working environment." Having a coherent semester group fosters a stronger team environment.

4.3 Physical Environment

Consideration has to be given to the design of the teaching environment to support PBL. Group work in computer laboratories causes difficulty, as the room arrangement does not allow students to interact well as a group. Computer laboratories often lack tables where students can sit around to have meaningful face-to-face discussions. An effective meeting environment that encourages interaction needs to be available. Fortunately students have been able to utilize vacant classrooms near the computer laboratory. Extra classrooms are not a resource that universities can usually sustain. If PBL is to be adopted as the major teaching approach, the teaching environment and arrangements to support PBL group work should be provided.

4.4 Attendance and Time Management

Attendance at classes and group meetings is crucial in this format of PBL. As an incentive to maintain attendance and participation, marks are awarded. An unsupervised laboratory hour is timetabled for students to meet; this provides a common time and little excuse not to attend group meetings.

Students are concerned about the time they spend on preparation, meeting time, reading and completion of plans and diaries. The completion of these tasks is often seen as encroachment on their time. Student C commented, "administration takes more time than the learning." The tools to aid and reflect on learning are seen by some students as a burden that is not encountered in other courses. Student D wrote "Another problem I am having is time management as PBL requires a lot of time to work with which I am finding hard to spare with other subjects as well."

4.5 Problem Design and Development

Setting and developing the PBL problem is a challenge. There was uncertainty about the nature of problems set, and whether the problems were authentic PBL problems. McCracken and Waters (1999) compare PBL problems in software engineering with medical school problems suggesting there is a potentially significant difference between problems in the two fields. Medical problems tend to be shorter, with solutions consisting of a diagnosis and proposed treatment, the students then move onto the next problem. In software engineering, however there are deliverables developed over a longer period of time and the assessment of these is a substantial part of a student's grade.

Problems need to be authentic and presented as such, rather than being task-based or project-based. Explicitly setting learning objectives for each problem is required to assist in scoping problems, so solutions and learning are achieved within the time limitations imposed by courses. Problems should be fully written up as a PBL case for tutors to understand the learning objectives of the problem and assist them in guiding students' learning. Wider discussion and sharing of PBL cases in the computing education community may help to develop a norm of applicable IS problems.

4.6 Academically Weak Students

There is a danger that academically weak students can be left behind and likely to achieve only surface learning. The challenge for tutors is to identify and support weak students. Tutors need to provide them with encouragement and feedback as they require more direction and structure to direct their learning, whereas Conrick (1994, p.250) suggests "deep learners may be intrinsically motivated." Graduate Student E who when doing the course a few years ago would have been considered a weak student, recently wrote: "I found with the PBL is that at the time as a student, it was such a diversion from the normal course for me that I didn't fully appreciate the skills I was learning and didn't like it as much. However in hindsight I can see that it was a useful way of placing us in that kind of self-learn environment as if we are in the workforce." This graduate also stated "My other studies were influenced through having gained a better ability to research and utilise the tools available. Additionally it provided me with valuable teamwork skills that have already come in useful in the working environment."

5 CONCLUSION

This paper has presented the approach, benefits, challenges and issues of PBL in an Introductory Systems Analysis and Design course including a snapshot of typical student responses. Outcomes of PBL indicate improved active student learning leading eventually to better graduate outcomes. Students perceive the course presents them with real-life learning situations. Typical of student responses is this statement from a graduate Student F now in an IT position: "From my experience with PBL I found it had the advantage of placing the student in a more realistic (i.e. work-like) environment when considering a task. Rather than the normal procedure at university it placed more emphasis on yourself researching and learning rather than being fed the information to take in through osmosis it was a more interactive approach."

6   REFERENCES

Barell, J. (1998) *PBL: An inquiry approach*. Australia: Hawker Brownlow Education.

Bentley, J. F., Lowry, G. R., and Sandy, G. (1999) Towards the compleat information systems graduate: a problem based learning approach. In *Proceedings of the 10th Australasian Conference on Information Systems (ACIS)*, vol. 1, B. Hope and P. Yoong, Eds. Victoria University, Wellington, New Zealand: School of Communications and Information Management, 65-75.

Biggs, J. (1999) What the student does: teaching for enhanced learning, *Higher Education Research & Development*, 18, 1, 57-75.

Boud, D. and Feletti, G. (1997) *The challenge of problem-based learning*. 2nd Edition. London: Kogan Page.

Conrick, M. (1994) Problem based learning - managing students transistions. In S. E. Chen, R. M. Cowdroy, A. J. Kingsland, and M. J. Ostwald (Eds.), *Reflections on problem based learning*, Sydney, Australia: Australian Problem Based Learning Network, 237-255.

Delisle, R. (1997) *How to use problem based learning in the classroom*, Association for Supervision and Curriculum Development, USA.

Ellis, A., Carswell, L., Bernat, A., Deveaux, D., Frison, P., Meisalo, V., Meyer, J., Nulden, U., Rigelj, J., and Tarhio, J. (1998) Resources, tools, and techniques for problem based learning in computing: report of ITiCSE'98 working group on problem based learning. In *The Working Group reports of the 3rd annual SIGCSE/SIGCUE ITiCSEC Conference on Integrating Technology into Computer Science Education*, (30), Dublin, Ireland, 45b-60b.

Fogarty, R. (1997) *Problem-based learning and other curriculum models for the multiple intelligences classroom*. Australia: Hawker Brownlow Education.

Fogarty, R. (ed.) (1998) *Problem-Based Learning: A Collection of Articles*, Skylight-Hawker Brownlow, Frenchs Forest, Australia.

McCracken, M. and Waters, R. (1999) Why? When an otherwise successful intervention fails. In the *Proceedings of the 4th annual SIGCSE/SIGCUE conference on innovation and technology in computer science education*. Krakow, Poland, 9-12.

Russell, A. L., Creedy, D., and Davis, J. (1994) The use of contract learning in PBL. In S. E. Chen, R. M. Cowdroy, A. J. Kingsland, and M. J. Ostwald (Eds.), *Reflections on problem based learning*, Sydney, Australia: Australian Problem Based Learning Network, 57-72.

Savery, J. R. and Duffy, T. M. (1995) Problem based learning: An instructional model and its constructivist framework. *Educational Technology*, (35), 31-38.

Savin-Baden, M. (2000) *Problem-based learning in Higher Education*. Buckingham, UK: Open University Press.

Woods, D. R. (1994) *Problem-based learning: how to gain the most from PBL*. 2nd ed. Waterdown, Canada: Donald R. Woods.

A MODEL FOR UNIVERSITY SEMINARS HELD IN COMPANIES
A case study

Peeter Normak
Tallinn Pedagogical University, Tallinn, Estonia
pnormak@tpu.ee, http://www.tpu.ee/~pnormak

Abstract: The paper discusses a model for university seminars that take place in ICT companies or IT departments of companies. The presentation examines the main implications in the light of three years of experience in running such seminars.

Keywords: Enterprise-based seminar, curriculum development, work preparedness.

1 INTRODUCTION

Although there seems to be a consensus among the main actors that experts from companies should be invited to take part in development and running of study programs, no big progress can be observed. Therefore, new forms of university-enterprise cooperation should be introduced tuned to local conditions. For example, in a small country like Estonia, the following important observations can be made:

1. The universities running ICT-curricula are preparing specialists for different ICT-sectors (Tallinn Pedagogical University (TPU) mainly for the educational sector).
2. The student intake in ICT specialties in universities was recently considerably increased and new curricula were started. Most of the students are already employed before university graduation.
3. The interest of companies in producing software for different sectors varies considerably. For example, because of the small market and lack

of finance there is almost no interest in producing educational software for schools.

4. Most ICT companies are working in a project-based mode. This means that they do not have far-reaching professional development plans and clear visions about personnel needs in the future.

All this has the consequence that without any special effort the companies are interested in universities only occasionally. In the following we will discuss a model of university-enterprise joint seminars that turned out to be extremely successful from the point of view of all the main actors: students, university teachers and the participating industry people.

2   BACKGROUND

Students must make an important decision when they choose the company for practical placement. The feedback information from students and graduates indicated that their expectations toward the company's profile they started to work in, as well as the expectations of companies towards the competence of graduates were in many cases only partly/partially met. A small empirical study performed in 1999 and 2000 with a sample size of about thirty persons – interviews with the graduates as well with some students – revealed some difficulties they had in starting their professional activities:

- University graduates do not have an adequate overview of different ICT companies, their profiles, priorities, needs, salary levels etc. Consequently, their first job is determined more or less opportunistically; in many cases a recent graduate moves after a relatively short period of work to another company.
- Graduates are uncertain in applying to a company; they do not know how to behave, what professional competencies and personality properties are preferable, and most importantly whether the organizational culture corresponds to the applicants' wishes and habits.
- The work in a company will in most cases start with a relatively long study period, which is sometimes devoted to topics completely missing in university curricula.

3   THE MODEL

The aim was to develop a model for seminars taking place in different companies that will give the students a possibility to understand and assess basic activities of the companies: institutional management, ICT production, marketing, strategic planning and innovation, personnel policy etc. Organizational details of these seminars can be found in Normak (2003). Here, only the main features of these seminars are described:

- The academic tutor compose a list of companies and makes arrangements with them. The seminars take place once a week during one semester and last for 90 minutes.
- The seminars are planned during a preparatory meeting with the students. For each seminar, a *discussion group* of at least three students is formed. The main task of discussion groups is to study the company before the seminar and to prepare discussions for the seminar.
- Before each seminar, the academic tutor informs the receiving officers of the company about the aims of the seminar; the company should be sent the syllabus for the seminar (containing the possible list of problems that could be discussed), and the university curriculum.
- The students are accompanied by their academic tutor and/or by the head of the curriculum.
- The seminar should be led from the company side by a key person (- in fact in about 80% of cases the students were met by the heads of the companies/ICT departments).
- At the end of semester, every student writes an analytical report. The reports should contain, in addition to a general analysis of the ICT domain in Estonia, a discussion of the companies visited during the seminars and recommendations for changes for seminars in subsequent years.
- Based on the quality of preparation for the seminars, the level of participation in discussions, and on the quality of the analytical report, every student will be assigned a mark (0-5, with 0 indicating not qualified).
- Every qualified student is awarded three ECTS credits.

4 EVALUATION

During the last three years, three student groups (consisting in average of 16 students) had seminars in ICT companies (35 seminars) and ICT departments of companies (9 seminars). For determining a long-term impact of the seminars the former students were asked to fill in a questionnaire one to three years after graduation. As the university does not keep regular contacts with the graduates only about 50% of them did receive the questionnaires; 16 were returned. The questions were divided into two groups, eight questions each.

In the first group questions and answers were the following:
1. *Did you have a permanent job during the period of time the seminars took place?*
   Two third of the students did have a permanent job.
2. *Did the seminars help you to find a company for practical placement?* Only one student found a placement in a company that was visited.
3. *Did the seminars motivate you to change the company you worked in?*
   In two cases the students moved to a company visited during the seminars.
4. *What could be changed in the format of the seminars?*
   There were only few suggestions like *"Companies should not use the seminars for promotion of their products"* or *"There should be more discussions about work conditions and work content, and less about the company's history."*
5. *What were the most valuable outcomes from the seminars for you?*
   The outcomes most frequently mentioned were as follows:
   - Understanding what are the main problems of ICT-companies.Generalized view about the ICT market and its development trends.
   - Motivation to analyze personal career possibilities.
   - Overview of working conditions and needs in personnel.Understanding that for success permanent, learning is necessary.Information on how companies evaluate their people.The visions company people had concerning future developments in the IT sector.Understanding that performance of different companies can differ enormously. *What kind of knowledge obtained from the seminars turned out to be useful for you?*
   Most frequent answers were the following:
   - Knowledge of which companies are trustful and which not.Ability to recognize advanced as well as weak companies.Understanding that employment interviews should be prepared.Knowledge of competences mostly needed in companies.Personal contacts with company people.Understanding the value systems of company people.Possibility to compare work conditions in different companies with those in the company I am working in.Understanding that the image and the actual level of a company should not necessarily be positively correlated.*Did the seminars change your attitude towards the university studies?*

About half of the students indicated that the seminars helped them to perform their studies in a more focused manner.

8. *How you rate the necessity of the seminars on the scale from 1 (absolutely not necessary) to 10 (absolutely necessary).*
   The average score was 8,8. The average score could even be higher if some students did not score every single company separately.

The questions in the second group asked students to assess the level of knowledge on certain aspects of ICT-companies before and after the seminars, on the scale from 1 (absolutely no knowledge) to 10 (excellent knowledge). The questions and average marks were the following:

1. General knowledge about the activities of Estonian ICT-companies (4,2 and 7,3, respectively).
2. Areas of activities (4,7 and 7,2).
3. Knowledge and skills expected from the employees (4,1 and 6,5).
4. Work methods and tools (3,4 and 5,9).
5. Organizational and work culture (3,3 and 6,5).
6. Personnel policy, employment possibilities (3,4 and 5,8).
7. Salary levels (4,2 and 5,1).
8. Difficulties and problems (3,6 and 6,2).

As we see the biggest differences in average marks are by questions 1 and 5, the smallest difference by question 7. This is quite understandable as the company people were relatively reluctant to discuss the salary levels, even in a relatively general manner. In personal advancement of students (measured by difference of total score after and before the seminars) the students formed two groups of an equal size: one consisting of those having total advancement between 23 and 31 and another of those with total advancement between 7 and 16.

5   IMPLICATIONS AND CONCLUSIONS

The experience obtained from planning and running the seminars, and from analytical reports and post-seminar activities allow us to formulate some general conclusions.

1. The companies are interested in this kind of seminars; only in two cases were the initially planned companies replaced because the companies were not cooperative enough (no company refused directly). Very often the company people were surprised about the amount of information the students found out about the company.

2.   The level of preparation for the seminar and actual running from the company side varied considerably, from very good presentations and tours, distribution of information materials and souvenirs, refreshments etc. to companies that did not do any preparation at all.

3.   The companies usually did not keep to the proposed topics for discussion, and discussions evolved in a natural way (this was appreciated by students). Some presenters did pay more attention to the general problems – how to start a successful company, the role of education and personal qualities etc. – some did stick to problems of the company currently under discussion.

4.   The company people are not interested in analyzing the university curricula: a fact that was disliked by many students. The main recommendations from company people were that university curricula should: a) develop team-working and social skills; b) teach fundamental ideas as concrete knowledge about specific problems can be taught at the working place; c) ensure foreign language skills (English and sometimes Russian).

5.   The students identified in their analytical reports the main problems in ICT development in Estonia at the moment as the following: a) lack of skilled ICT specialists and project managers; b) too big a percentage of very small ICT companies who push the prices down and provide insufficient quality level; c) the Estonian market is too small for effective development of ICT companies.

6.   The students considered the seminars extremely useful and interesting. There was no consensus about recommendations for the future (example: whether to visit for comparison purposes some weak companies as well).

7.   The students are interested to meet with mid-level and lower-level employees of companies as well; this would give a broader view about the company rather than discussions solely with top managers.

8.   The seminar should be kept within a time limit; very often there were some students interested in a particular company and eager to hold long discussions.

9.   For comparison purposes, quality indicators should be set so that students could evaluate the companies.

10. The seminars deepened the involvement of companies in the university's academic life. For example, the IT department of the second biggest bank of Estonia became a strategic partner in running the IT-management master's program; highly qualified professionals were included in university graduation committees and invited to present lectures devoted to the case studies arising from their activities.

11. The seminars in many cases influenced the topics for graduation papers.

12. The seminars allow some generalizations concerning the main processes used in the companies. For example, only very few companies are using some software development models or taking into account maturity models.
13. A discrepancy between beliefs and real practice was observed. In many cases the company people were very positive about different practices but did not use these themselves (for example, usage of pair programming).

6   REFERENCES

Normak, P. (2003) University-enterprise joint seminars as tools for preparing students for the world of work: a case study from Estonia, *Industry and Higher Education* Vol 17, Number 2, April 2003, pp. 103-109.

CUSTOMIZATION OF INDUSTRIAL TRAINING
Benefits and Problems

Timo Lainema and Sami Nurmi
Turku School of Economics and Business Administration, Turku, Finland
timo.lainema@tukkk.fi
Educational Technology Unit, University of Turku, Finland sami.nurmi@utu.fi

Abstract: The main focus of this paper describes how authenticity can be applied to computer-based learning environments through customization. We argue for using learning tools, which not only provide realistic and complex models of reality, but are also authentic, facilitate continuous problem solving and meaningful learning, and embed learning in social experience. We describe a continuously processed business simulation game, which differs from the majority of business games in the way it is processed. Two company in-house training sessions are then described. In these sessions the learning environment was customized to describe the real-world environment of the case company. We conclude that customization of a business learning environment increases the learners' motivation and meaningful experiences. Furthermore, customization includes potential in facilitating transfer of learned knowledge and skills to a real world working environment.

Key words: Industrial Training, customized learning environments, business training.

1   INTRODUCTION

Realgame (the argumentation behind *Realgame* is presented in Lainema 2004a and 2004b) is a computer-based simulation game, which creates a complex and authentic-like environment for learning business studies. *Realgame* models the environment of up to 8 manufacturing companies that compete against each other in a virtual computer network environment. Each participating company consists of optimally three participants. The company decision-making application (used by a student group) includes the main decision-making functions of a manufacturing company.

Traditionally, business games have been batch-processed. The game participants create plans for their companies for a certain period (typically a few months or a year). These plans are then entered to the simulation model. The simulation model calculates the results from the plans and generates a historic report. Thus, the simulation model is a black box within which the game participants have no internal view. The decisions and the results from them have no explicit cause-relationship as the black-box structure of the simulation prevents any direct interaction with the simulation processes. In this process there is no guarantee that the learner creates a valid presentation of the cause-relationships.

Realgame, however, is operated in real-time – continuously. *Realgame* includes a clock-driven market engine on the server of a computer network, creating demand and supply. The groups constantly exchange information with the market server over the network. This interactivity brings along some advantages not met in batch-processed games. Decision-making and feedback from the decisions takes place in an interactive on-line mode. Decisions are made as soon as they are needed or at least as soon as the decision-maker notices that the situation needs actions from them. This is radically different from traditional business gaming which presents a static view of business operations at a specific time between game periods and where decisions can be entered only when the simulation is halted.

Continuous processing means that the game clock and game events keep on taking place continuously when the game clock is turned on. This resembles, e.g., modern production management information systems. In *Realgame* the game market application triggers the game internal clock in one-hour cycles and the participant game applications follow the market time. The participants see the game clock (hour, day, and month) on their computer screens. One game hour may take from 30 seconds (in the beginning of the game) to one real world second (in the end of the game). The process described above is much like real-time video games – for example, SimCity (see http://simcity.ea.com/).

The participant decision-making application includes the major business functions of a manufacturing company. Although we refer here to business functions, this does not mean that we regard the game as being a mechanistic view of a business entity with high differentiation of different functions, but rather as an open system of interrelated subsystems, with tasks and individuals belonging to a larger whole (Morgan, 1997). Furthermore, these game companies are able to play an active role in shaping their future by making decisions on which products to sell and which markets to function within. Morgan stresses that organizations are open systems best understood as ongoing processes rather than a collection of parts. This, we feel, describes quite well the functioning of *Realgame*. On the other hand, we feel that the traditional batch processing in business games represents the mechanistic, Taylorian view of business organizations with its budget making process, where the top management makes decisions on behalf of the whole organization. *Realgame* starts by introducing the floor level business operations and then – as the participants develop their skills and knowledge about the business environment – proceeds step by step towards more holistic decisions.

Realgame's environment can be customized according to the case company's real world environment. This configurability concerns, for example, the market structure, the structure of the companies' internal materials process, the supply market structure, and so on. Through manipulating these parameters either before or during the training sessions, the game operator is able to radically change the game environment.

2   OVERVIEW OF THE CASE STUDY

Our research questions were the following:
1. How does the continuous processing element of *Realgame* affect participants' experiences and working processes?
2. What are the effects of configuring *Realgame* on participants' experiences and working processes?
3. Is working with *Realgame* beneficial to learning?

Alpha (a pseudonym) develops, manufactures and markets analytical systems, instruments, reagents and computer software for clinical diagnostics and biotechnology. It has a worldwide sales organization. Alpha products are highly technical and research and development has a central role in their operations. Alpha has more than 500 employees and its turnover is more than 100 M€.

2.1   The Configured Realgame Model

In the Alpha case the *Realgame* model was configured to substantially resemble the Alpha real-world environment. The process aiming at an authentic configuration included meeting Alpha key managers and game environment configuration. The configuration included the following customization:
- The manufacturing process was configured for two production lines.
- The markets and customers within the markets and their volumes and purchase behaviour.
- The general cost structure of the company.
- Raw material prices, terms of delivery, and terms of payment.

- The available delivery methods.
- External environment: loan interest, workers' terms of notice, the time from the machine investment decision to the point of time when the machine was in use, and so on.

This Alpha configuration is quite complex and being able to manage the configuration requires perquisite knowledge about the Alpha real-world environment.

2.2   The Participants

The 43 participants were well-educated managers or scientific experts from the Alpha main site. 38 participants answered our pre-game questionnaire (response rate 88.4 %), and these had an average work experience of 14.3 years and an average work experience of 8.7 years in Alpha.

26 (68.4%) of the participants had a master's degree, mostly in chemistry/biochemistry/ biotechnology/physics (N=12/31.6%), in some business subject (N=7/18.4%), or engineering (N=4/10.5%), but also some in sociology, languages, or computer science. Two had a PhD (5.3%), and 10 (26.3%) a BSc or equivalent. 23 (60.5%) stated that they had played business games before.

2.3   The Structure of the Game Sessions

The training sessions took place on 16th and 23rd of October 2002 (sessions A and B). In session A there were 21 participants (seven groups of three participants) and in session B, 22 participant forming eight groups (six groups of three, two groups of two participants). The training sessions lasted approximately 10 hours, breaks included.

There was one clear distinction between the two sessions. In session A the market volume was erroneously high, 10-fold compared to the total manufacturing capacity of the companies in the beginning of the game. This situation led to extensive capacity investments, resulting in two very different training sessions, as this error was corrected in session B. As there was excessive demand in session A there was no need for tight price competition and the most important thing to take care of was to try to deliver the orders in time, and, thus, avoid a drop in the company's image because of late deliveries. In session B the market demand was balanced with the total manufacturing capacity. In the results section we will analyze how this discrepancy between these sessions affected the participants' experiences.

3   COLLECTION OF EMPIRICAL DATA

The questionnaire used was delivered to the participants at the end of the training sessions. The first part of the questionnaire consists of 15 questions on a seven-point Likert scale and one Yes/No question. The structured questions of the first part measure the participant opinions on how well they thought the game represented different business phenomenon. The second part of the questionnaire consisted of five open-ended questions (introduced later).

4   RESULTS

4.1   Findings on the Statistical Data

When comparing the mean responses of participants in the two Alpha game sessions A and B (N=14 and 18) with T-tests, we can find three questions out of 15 questions in which these groups differed statistically significantly. These questions dealt with *the game ability to represent a holistic view of a company* ($p < 0.01$), *how realistic was the uncertainty in the game* ($p < 0.05$), and *the game was too complex* ($p < 0.05$).

The significant differences in the first two questions in Table 1 can be explained with the production-focused nature of session A. The abundant customer demand in session A led to a situation where the problem was to fulfil all the incoming orders. This means that the participants concentrated heavily on the materials process. There was no need to pay that much attention to other functions like sales. This explains why in session B the participants had to deal with a more holistic view of the business operations. This same explanation applies also to differences in question 2 in Table 1.

The difference in the third question in Table 1 indicates that the abundant customer demand with excessive incoming orders created a situation where the participants where not equal to the requirements of the order management process and the order back-log piled up uncontrollable. However, the mean of the answers is still only 2.93 implicating a not too complex model.

Table 1. Comparison of the responses between Alpha training sessions A and B on selected questions.

Question	Sess.	N	Mean	Std.dev.	t	df	Sig.
(1) Game ability to represent a holistic view of a company (grades from 1/Poor to 7/Excellent)	A	14	4.57	0.938	-3.152	30	0.004
	B	18	5.61	0.916			
(2) How realistic was the uncertainty in the game (grades from 1/Poor to 7/Excellent)	A	14	3.50	1.225	-2.430	30	0.021
	B	18	4.50	1.098			
(3) Game was too complex (grades from 1/Disagree to 7/Agree)	A	14	2.93	1.269	2.133	30	0.041
	B	18	2.11	0.900			

The last question in the closed part was: *Did the game help you to get a holistic view of business processes (Yes/No)?* Here 93.7 % (N= 30) of the answers were positive. This implies that *Realgame* represents potential especially as a business process-training tool.

4.2 Findings on Open Ended Answers

Next we will go through the answers to the open part of the questionnaire. The participants were first asked: **Did the game reveal something new about the flow of business processes?** The answers were again mostly very positive. The only critical comments came from session A where the participants complained about the abundant market demand. One of the most accurate answers representing the general attitude of the participants to the question is this one: *"Best game (of three) that I have played, reflecting reality. The insights were to experience in a limited timeframe cause-effect relationships from a large number of functions/areas."*

The second question concerned tailoring: **Did tailoring enhance the learning experience?** The vast majority of the answers were positive towards game tailoring. Several responses mentioned that it was easier to adopt the game environment as it was familiar to them: *"Tailoring was an excellent way to get the player into a familiar environment and have a better understanding of how everything goes in our own company. It also helped a lot in communicating with other team members."* Some were also more critical, the next one representing possibly the most critical opinion (session

A): "*This tailor-made case was also confusing because the volumes were too high and people did not believe the figures.*"

Next the participants were asked: **What do you feel you have learned during the training?** The following answer comes from a person with a background in natural sciences: "*For me this was the first contact with running a business, so I suppose there were many important things. Maybe the most interesting thing was that within the group there was an old veteran, who made us to follow key figures (I myself would not have understood...).*" Mostly the answers concern the learning of some larger context and the complexity of the business entity: "*I learned about sequential dependencies and how long it really takes to affect production. In real-life, time can be multiplied by a factor of 10. I learned to think in a broader way – or should think in a broader way.*" Another answer describing the complexity in the game: "*The game made it very clear that the business itself is complex – it really opened my eyes and will hopefully remind me in the future to always take different points of view into account before decision-making.*"

Other learning topics that were mentioned were the sequential dependencies in production, financial key figures, management of the production process and purchases, timing in sales operations, pricing, and so on. Some respondents put nicely how impossible it was to make perfect decisions in an environment continually evolving: "*Act although there is not enough time to grasp all the possible factors. The importance to decide which factors to emphasize.*"

The next question proved to be difficult to answer: **How do you transfer these learned things to your current work?** Here the participants clearly had difficulties in explicating what they felt they had learned. The following examples give a good idea of typical answers: "*Maybe as an ability to take a bit more distance to decision making and try to view the whole picture before making decisions.*"

The following question deals with continuous processing: **Do you feel that the continuous surveillance was an important feature of the game from the point of view of learning and understanding?** The answers to this question were without exception very positive and almost all regarded continuous processing as a clearly important feature of the game: "*This feature was an important factor. It gives a possibility to see the whole process and not only to concentrate on inventories or sales or other functions.*" Several answers made reference to the real-world resemblance: "*Yes, I think it was, because that is realistic, you can't make just one decision and trust that it will work.*" Some also stated that continuous processing makes the game experience more engaging: "*Real-time playing makes learning more interesting.*"

The last question dealt with team working: *Was the playing interesting, did you negotiate your decisions inside the group intensively?* Again, the answers revealed that the participants' experiences about their team working were very positive and comparisons were made to other learning experiences: *"It was very enjoyable game, far better than the table board game I have earlier played."* One respondent describes gaming as visual: *"More interesting and visual than other methods I have experienced. Decisions were negotiated which at the same time gives atmosphere of team-working."* Here we cannot be sure whether the word visual means the game interface or the game processing method. However, continuous processing could also be described as visual as the processes evolve on-line on the computer screen. Therefore *Realgame* can be regarded as a shared frame of reference that could support and inspire collaboration and interaction between the participants: *"Playing was extremely interesting; we did a lot of negotiating during the game, even though we had slightly divided responsibilities."* The following answer describes well the nature of decision-making: *"Very interesting & intensive day with continuous negotiation and decision making."*

4.3   Summary of Findings

We will next answer the research questions. **Research question 1.** *How does the continuous processing element of Realgame affect on participants' experiences and working processes?* Based on the questionnaire answers the working in small groups proved to be very intense and engaging. *Realgame* seemed to maintain the task-orientation of the participants well over the long training day. The continuous processing element of *Realgame* helped the participants to see how the different business processes elaborated, emerged and linked together. Continuous processing represents authentically business processes and real world complexity. The participants thought that the game represented very well information flows and demands, sequential dependencies in operations and a holistic view of a company.

Research question 2. *What are the effects of configuring Realgame on participants' experiences and working processes?* The configuration of *Realgame* resulted in both positive and negative outcomes. On the one hand, the configuration shortened the time required for familiarization with the game and made it easier to understand the functioning of the game environment. On the other hand configuration caused some troubles, because the game model didn't resemble Alpha's real world environment with 100 % precision. Still we feel that we can claim that the game configurability increased the acceptability from the part of the participants. The answers to the open part of the questionnaire give strong support for this. Besides its acceptability, configurability shortened the time the participants needed to get into the game model.

However, whether the game configurability increases the authenticity of the learning environment or not (resulting in meaningful working) is problematic to assess. Our questions were probably not perfect regarding this issue. For example, the next answer can be interpreted to both support and oppose this: *"It was good to have a realistic set of products and if this seemed complex, you can only imagine how it is in real life."* In other words the respondent argues that the model included reality, but then again she makes a comparison to the more complex real world. Other comments give support for authenticity on a general level stating that it is easier to adapt to a game if it was tailored for a specific company. Some were very critical, especially in session A.

We believe that when we try to imitate the real world and make this aim explicit to the participants, they start to expect very accurate real world representations. In the Alpha case the deficit in the (possibly) expected authenticity did not spoil the learning experience but the general attitude towards gaming was still very positive.

Research question 3. *Is working with Realgame beneficial for learning?* We have noticed that what is learned through playing *Realgame* is not easy to recognize. The game participants clearly regard the gaming experience as useful, but they have difficulties in expressing what the concrete benefit was. However, according to the questionnaire answers *Realgame* helped them to construct a holistic view of the functioning of a manufacturing company, and to see the interdependencies between different business operations.

It seems to be the case that the Alpha participants faced problems when they tried to express the potential learning. There are several explanations for this: a) there was no learning; b) the learning that took place had not yet crystallized when they answered the questionnaire a week after the training; c) the learning that took place was by its very nature difficult to explain. We are referring to tacit knowledge, which involves both technical and cognitive elements, like mental models (individual's images of reality and visions for the future) and know-how, crafts and skills (as opposed to explicit knowledge that can be expressed in words and numbers; Nonaka, 1994). Our belief is that the true explanation is c), and partly also b). Unfortunately our research instruments were not quite capable to answer this proposition, but it is also true that the nature of learning from simulation working is very hard to tap with traditional test questions (Swaak, Joolingen & de Jong, 1998).

This leads us to the following comment regarding tailoring and authenticity. Configurability is probably useful for the learning outcomes if one is to carefully plan how configurability will be presented and argued. Both the teacher and the learner have to understand that the real world resemblance is not a means to an end but an opportunity to increase participant motivation. A computer model can never accurately represent the real world. What is essential is that the participants experience meaningful decision-making problems and regard them as relevant to the real world.

5   CONCLUSIONS AND FUTURE RESEARCH

As a concluding comment we state that *Realgame* was found to be a very useful tool to be used in these in-house trainings. Participants regarded *Realgame* training as a very rewarding and interesting experience. But game customization is like a double-edged sword. On the one hand game configurability increases the participants' motivation, meaningful experiences and the possible transfer of learned knowledge and skills to real world working environment. On the other hand – since 100 percent precision in configurability is not possible – configurability can also cause misunderstandings and concentration on the not-realistic issues of a game which are irrelevant learning-wise.

6   REFERENCES

Jonassen, D., K. Peck, & B. Wilson. (1999). *Learning with technology. A constructivist perspective*. New Jersey: Prentice Hall.

Lainema, T. (2004a, Forthcoming). Building Technology-Based Training on Relevant Learning Perspectives. In Thompson, Barry (ed.), *E-Training Practices for Professional Organisations*. Kluwer Academic Publishers.

Lainema, T. (2004b, Forthcoming). Introducing Organizational Characteristics in Learning Environments. In Thompson, Barry (ed.), *E-Training Practices for Professional Organisations*. Kluwer Academic Publishers.

Morgan, G. (1997). *Images of Organization*. Sage Publications.

Nonaka, I. (1994). A Dynamic Theory of Organizational Knowledge Creation. *Organization Science*, Vol. 5, No. 1, pp. 14-37.

Swaak, J., W. R. van Joolingen & T. de Jong (1998). Supporting simulation-based learning; The effects of model progression and assignments on definitional and intuitive knowledge. *Learning and instruction*, Vol. 8, No. 3, pp. 235-252

WORK INTEGRATED LEARNING IN INFORMATION TECHNOLOGY EDUCATION

Patrick Poppins and Mohini Singh
School of Business Information Technology, RMIT University, Australia
patrick.poppins@rmit.edu.au and Mohini.Singh@rmit.edu.au

Abstract: Work integrated learning, generally referred to internship programs in university undergraduate degrees provides graduates with real-life learning before they face the real world as an Information Technology graduate. This paper presents and discusses the process of managing work integrated learning in the IT undergraduate program at RMIT University. It also highlights the benefits and challenges to students, coordinators and the industry.

Key words: Work integrated learning, internship programs, cooperative education.

1   INTRODUCTION

This paper discusses real-life learning with WIL (work integrated learning) in the Information Technology undergraduate program at RMIT University in Melbourne. It discusses the role of WIL, the process of managing WIL, advantages, challenges and its future.

Incorporating mandatory Work Integrated Learning into an academic course is becoming popular with many tertiary institutions to provide IT students with real-life learning. RMIT University's Business Portfolio incorporates a year-long work integrated learning in the undergraduate program by placing students in industry, in the areas of Economics, Marketing, Accounting, Management and Information Technology. This unit of study is generally called co-operative employment. The university has employed this model of learning for the last 20 years, forming strong links with industry and with formal methods of assessment and monitoring student learning while they are with industry. This includes rigorous training in preparing students prior to placement using a process similar to a real, competitive job search process. The process of training students, monitoring their progress with industry, benefits of WIL and challenges is discussed.

2   LITERATURE REVIEW

Work Integrated Learning is the current term for what has been known in education for the last forty years as internship, sandwich year or cooperative education (Edmunds, 1999 and McLuskie and Zipf, 2003). It is a period (or periods) of time in a tertiary degree program curriculum where the student becomes immersed in the pursuit of professional work in industry. Providing students with real-world experiences is one of the best methods to prepare them to be successful in their careers (Fox, 2002). Carpenter (2003) refers to work integrated learning as 'internship', and describes it as on-the-job experience prior to graduation. He further explains that meaningful internships are based on formal learning objectives and these learning objectives should be part of a complete curriculum. Practical internship programs described by Carpenter entail formal partnerships between businesses and educational institutes where expectations and responsibilities of all parties are precisely defined. Fields (1996) emphasized that internships give students an employment edge, resulting in a job offer. It helps the students to 'test out' and gain experience in their chosen career field as well as networking and employment opportunities (Centre for Career Development, 2004) Fields (1996) further supports this by emphasising that with an internship a company has an opportunity to look at the student and vice versa. Fang, Lee and Huang (2004) also advocate that new employees with internship experience received greater entry-level compensation than non-interns and time to obtain their first positions was significantly shorter.

Edmunds (1999) suggests that by placing students in industry there is a presumption that employers, universities and students learn from the experience. Students especially are able to integrate theory with practice, mature, become more self confident and gain experience of the world of work. Smithers (1976), cited in Edmunds (1999) emphasised that the period of time spent in industry also increases student motivation and helps them acquire greater skills in human relations. Fang, Lee and Huang (2004) are of the opinion that in the current job market for IT graduates, which is not as favourable as it used to be five years ago, an internship program experience becomes more important than other factors in obtaining a position.

Although literature highlights several advantages of the internship program to the students and the employers, universities managing and monitoring student internships face several challenges. In the next section we will present the internship system for Business Information Technology students at RMIT University and discuss process, advantages and challenges.

3   WORK INTEGRATED LEARNING (WIL) FOR BACHELOR OF BUSINESS IT

The School of Business Information Technology at RMIT has used WIL for the last 20 years in a four year degree program with a one year industry placement in the third year. The WIL is placed in the later part of the degree program to ensure that students have sufficient professional skills to undertake work in industry. At the end of WIL students are able to complete the final part of their studies by undertaking some capstone subjects, as well as choosing electives. The industry experience has a marked influence on what students choose to study in their electives in final year. Figure 1 below presents the structure of the Bachelor of Business in Information Technology program that is discussed in this paper.

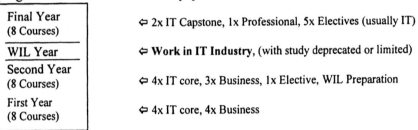

Final Year (8 Courses)	⇐ 2x IT Capstone, 1x Professional, 5x Electives (usually IT)
WIL Year	⇐ **Work in IT Industry**, (with study deprecated or limited)
Second Year (8 Courses)	⇐ 4x IT core, 3x Business, 1x Elective, WIL Preparation
First Year (8 Courses)	⇐ 4x IT core, 4x Business

Figure 1: Structure of the Undergraduate Course in Business IT at RMIT

In the first two years the courses provides knowledge of three IT streams: operating systems, hardware & communications; applications development; and systems analysis and design. The core business subjects of accounting, economics, management, marketing and law also have to be successfully completed. Integral to the second year is a subject that prepares the students for WIL in their third year. The year students spend in industry is equivalent to one subject. In the final year, the focus is on capstone subjects addressing issues of systems implementation, professional practice & IT specialisations.

3.1   WIL Management Process

The school has appointed a coordinator for WIL; an academic to manage the process of placing and assessing students in industry. At the beginning of the second year of their studies students are expected to register for WIL and are asked to indicate their IT preference. To assist students at the decision making stage the coordinator sends an email pointing them to www.gradlink. edu.au/content/view/full/238. Built by the Australian Computer Society, this site lists and describes careers in IT. The real preparation for WIL commences with a second year subject, delivered weekly with lectures on:

- The role of WIL in the course and how it works;
- Resume writing;
- Covering Letter writing;
- Interview techniques;
- Job search techniques – emphasis is on students tackling the real world in search of jobs via the visible and hidden job markets; and
- Ethics in the workplace.

Although most of the students have some previous work experience it is rarely in the area of IT. The WIL preparation classes are designed primarily to prepare students for job search within their profession, and implore them to be fastidious in their paper documents, honest in their claims, neither understating nor overstating their skills. Interview techniques sessions prepare students to respond to common questions from their own experiences and to a variety of interviewers. During the preparation lectures, students are taught how to apply for jobs. At the end of second year students apply for places in companies that offered jobs through RMIT. They are allowed to seek their own job placements. This process is described in detail in the next section. To manage student responses, the University has designed a number of forms to capture the necessary information. These are:

The Registration Form. This captures student data and is used in advising employers about a prospective applicant. A section of this form is devoted to initiate students thinking about fields of employment in their WIL year. It begins with subjects they have enjoyed or done well at, introduces professional titles, and gets them to select a ranking from a list. URLs with Graduate Career details of titles and occupations within ICT Industry are given to students to help them understand positions and job descriptions.

Employment Record. Once a student has found a position, this form is used to capture information on the student's employment details: name of company that they are working with, position they have been offered, their contact and salary level. They are also asked to provide details of their supervisors so that the School has an up to date record of where students are, what level positions they hold and who their supervisors are.

The Job Search Statistics. Because all jobs are won on a competitive, real world basis, this form collects data on the methods students used to find a job, number of applications made, and sources of job vacancies eg, newspapers, the Internet, other networks or the University. The analysis of this data enables the coordinator to target employers and to prepare students for industry placements in the following year.

Review of Job Search. This form gets students to review what was learnt in the process of seeking a job placement and what were the highlights. It reviews the effectiveness of preparatory classes. Most of the data captured are collated on a database and analysed for improvements in the process of placing students, following their assessments while they are on the job and to keep updated records in the School of as many as 150 students each year.

For the last 20 years RMIT University has employed this system of WIL in most Business undergraduate programs. In the process it has developed a very good rapport with a large number of employers who continue to support RMIT to fulfil the WIL requirement for their students and also depend on these students for positions in their organisations. The employers generally appreciate early graduate recruitment (try before you buy) or they have need for emerging IT skills. It is also cost effective for these organizations. These companies contact the School with their requests which are disseminated to students via email, asking them to respond within five days. Applications are briefly scanned for quality, and student activity noted. At this point control is handed over to the employer to follow through with their normal selection process. Students are also allowed to seek their own placement.

3.2 Nature of Work in Industry

The nature of work that graduates of program generally get involved in are that of business analysts, software support, network analysts and programmers. Therefore it is important that work integrated learning during their course of studies is geared to give them experience in these roles. To ensure this the WIL coordinator provides simple rules for industry placement based on the following criteria:

1. That approximately 90% of the student's time with the business in which they are placed will be spent with software and computer systems. It is most desirable that hardware management, computer operating, data entry or basic clerical duties are below 10% of a student's productive time. Working with software can include software development, maintenance, support, teaching, training, designing, documenting, configuring, testing, metrication, auditing and selling.
2. A student must have either an IT trained or qualified supervisor.

3.3 How Students are Selected

The School plays no part in the selection process beyond confirming the students' academic record to the employer if requested. Students are interviewed by the organisations based on employers selection criteria which can include the modes of telephone interviews, aptitude tests, comprehension tests, panel and interviews.

3.3.1   Employer Description

Employers tend to be from SMEs but there are a few of the large employers such as Ernst and Young, KPMG and Coles-Myer that assist the University with student work integrated learning. These employers are sought from various avenues both in the IT industry itself and from IT departments in other industries. A number of business organisations with which students are placed are shown on a web site www.rmitbit.net/co-op to show prospective employers and encourage students. A small but growing category of employers who have been sought out by students, are those that have an IT department. Additionally some employers have been found through student networks, family, friends, neighbours and acquaintances.

3.3.2   Feedback

The students complete four assignments during the year while they are in industry. These assessment requirements cover different aspects of business IT issues requiring them to be able to describe the organization they are working with, note taking and record keeping of events, problems, other technical and non-technical issues as well as equipment use. The final assignment is to author a professional business report – 5000 words.

3.3.3   Remuneration

While the students are with industry they earn as much as $A22K to $A28K. Some large organizations may pay up to $A30K and sometimes more. Each year there a few students (5%-10%) who are not able to find a job placement and for who the school has developed a course titled 'professional skills development'. This is done in-house with a simulated work environment. However, since this is without any payment most students make a great effort to be placed in industry.

3.3.4   Benefits of WIL in IT Education

Students attain job seeking techniques as they prepare for a job placement in their course of studies. The students learn to prepare good application documents, interview skills and job search techniques which make them aware and ready for a job later in life.

Students graduate a year later with twelve months work experience in the area of IT. This enables them to find employment in a very short period of time after they graduate. Thirty percent of these students get a job with the employer they were placed with and ninety percent find a job within a month after graduation(graduates with IT work experience and Job search skills don't wait around for jobs). Organisations that employ the graduates who had done their WIL with them obviously had a chance to try these students before offering them ongoing positions. Students also get a chance to know the organization before they accept positions with them.

The impact of WIL on IT graduates also includes a high level of understanding of technology, it increases the standard of their work, provides experience that fosters maturity in approach to life, the disciplined environment of work focuses students to more diligently apply theory learnt. It also gives them a career direction. Graduates are able to combine theory with practice and gain a greater depth of knowledge and understanding.

Starting salaries for these graduates were usually higher than a graduate with no job experience giving them a competitive edge over other applicants for the same jobs. The employers get input from highly motivated pre-professionals who bring with them new perspectives to old problems. They also benefit from flexible cost-effective work force not requiring long term employment commitment. They get to evaluate potential employees before they recruit as they enhance their image in the community by developing strong links with the University. The WIL program in the undergraduate program is not a common practice at many other universities therefore this attracts many excellent students with high scores to choose the program for their tertiary education.

4   PROBLEMS

Although work integrated learning has many benefits in an undergraduate program and to students it is faced with some of the following problems. WIL management process entails extensive paperwork at the time of placing students, monitoring their progress and assessment. In one year as many 150 students undertake WIL, the management of which is a lot of work for the coordinator. At present an academic who has to spend a lot of time doing clerical work manages WIL in the school.

The students who are placed in industry sometimes take time adjusting to a full time job. Some find nine to five, five days a week on the job to be very demanding. At the same time they have four assessment requirements to complete and submit, therefore experience a heavy workload. Some students find it difficult to become a student again after being in the corporate environment for a year. The dress code, reduced income, relationship with peers and academics and the university system is a major change some of them have to cope with. At the end of WIL many students continue working with the organization and thus complete their degrees on a part time bases. This leads to low numbers in the final year of the degree.

5   DISCUSSION AND CONCLUSION

The perceived feedback from participants of the program has indicated what many authors have been saying for some time, and that is realizing, focusing and tackling the job market with WIL incorporated in the IT undergraduate program has many benefits. The work based reflective learning attained from WIL is valued by all IT graduates of the school. These graduates gain professional knowledge with academic and practical skills once they complete their qualifications. Therefore work integrated learning in IT education is a valuable and important part of the curriculum providing students with real-life learning before they enter the workforce.

WIL in the undergraduate program has also led to a close and strong relationship between the university and industry. Although this scheme is not available in many other universities and future government funding for WIL is in question, RMIT University will continue incorporating WIL in the IT curriculum due to its enormous advantages.

6   REFERENCES

Carpenter, D. A., 2003, 'Meaningful Information Systems Internships', *Journal of Information Systems Education*, Vol 14, Iss 2, pp 201- 210.

Centre for Career Development, 2004. http://www.city.ac.uk/careers/

Edmunds, M., 1999, 'Quality in sandwich year', Quality Assurance in Education, Volume 7 Number 2, pp 101-112.

Fang, X., Lee, S., Lee, T. and Huang, W., 2004, 'Critical Factors Affecting Job Offers for New MIS Graduates', Journal of Information Systems Education, West Lafayette, Summer, Vol 15, Iss 2, page 189 – 204.

Fields, C. D., 1996, 'Business Schools and Employment', Black Issues in Higher Education', Reston, Volume 13, Iss 21, pp 16 – 17.

Fox, Michael, 'E-Learning', *Duluth*: Mar 2002.Volume 3, Iss 3; pg. 26, 4 pgs

Gerrand, J. Saunderson, H. 'Compulsory Versus Optional Co-operative Programs, The *Journal of Cooperative Education,* 1, pp 46-56.

McLuskie, L. and Zipf, R.,2003, 'Collegiality: the foundation of a successful internship program', Working Paper, Central Queensland University, Australia.

PROVIDING MASTERS LEVEL COMPUTING STUDENTS WITH REAL-LIFE LEARNING EXPERIENCES VIA CAPSTONE PROJECTS

J. Barrie Thompson, Helen M. Edwards, and Colin J. Hardy
School of Computing and Technology, Informatics Centre, University of Sunderland, UK.
barrie.thompson@sunderland.ac

Abstract: Within academic programmes real-life learning experiences can be provided in a number of ways: internships/placements, group projects and individual projects. A comparison is made between the mechanisms that can be employed in programmes with a duration of several years compared with intensive taught masters programmes which have a total duration of 12 to 14 months. Details are presented of the range of taught masters programmes in computing that are offered at the University of Sunderland with emphasis on practical parameters and assessment. Actual problems and challenges that have had to be addressed in a changing academic climate are detailed. Finally some overall conclusions and outstanding questions are presented.

Key words: Higher Education, Curriculum, Computing, Projects, Industry.

1   INTRODUCTION

It is of the greatest importance that the graduates who enter the Information and Communication Technologies (ICT) sector, whether from undergraduate or postgraduate programmes, have appropriate real-life leaning experiences during their programmes so that they can immediately operate in an effective and professional manner. Within 3 and 4 year undergraduate computing programmes that lead to B.Sc. B.Eng. and B.A. degrees, and 4 and 5 year programmes that lead to computing qualifications such as M.Eng., real-life learning experiences can be achieved in a number of ways, for example:

- *By individual placements/internships within industry itself. These may be classed as short term (3 to 6 months duration) or long term. often occupying most of an academic year or even longer (9 to 15 months duration).*
- *By industry-related team/group projects within the body of programmes.*
- *By industry-related individual student projects that frequently occur in the final year of programmes and which may be a continuation of work which a student has begun during a placement in industry but with a more academic emphasis.*

Information on different approaches can be found in the Springer text edited by Holcombe et al. (1998). Of the three listed above, an actual placement within industry is probably the most effective and can bring clear benefits to both the student and the placement organisation (Thompson, 1990). However, experience at our own University has shown, that in the UK at least, the number of students wishing to undertake a long term (one year) placement has fallen dramatically over the last ten years. A driving force behind this trend is clearly student debt. Students want to complete their degree programmes as soon as possible and enter full time employment (hopefully well paid). A clear alternative (and complement) to industrial placements/internships is for academic programmes to incorporate industry-related projects within the body of their programmes. Many of these are group-based because it is recognised that real-life learning experiences ideally involve working with others. The role and operation of such group projects have been discussed in depth in the papers by Stein (2002 and 2003). However, there can be significant problems in running such group projects as has been made clear by Umpress et al. (2002). Also, as highlighted by Wilde et al. (2003) it is difficult to reproduce all the pressures and constraints of an industrial setting within an academic environment. Many academic programmes include an individual industry-based project in the final year of study as has been described by Beasley (2003) whilst others provide the opportunity for a much more academic orientated research type investigations with an associated dissertation. There is also the possibility of very clear individual assessment within a large group-orientated project - a topic that is addressed in depth by Hayes et al. (2003).

Within the types of computing programmes where students are undertaking their studies over a period of several years it is normally possible to address real-life learning experiences without too much difficulty by adopting one or more of the approaches outlined above. The situation within intensive taught masters programmes that have a total duration of typically 12 to 14 months full-time study (or equivalent part-time) is somewhat different. Although many of the issues which need to be addressed are similar to those found in longer programmes, and which are raised in papers such as those by Clear et al. (2001) and Williams et al. (2003), there is nonetheless the facts that these projects:

- need to be at a higher academic level,
- are much more likely to represent an individual piece of work rather than group work,
- tend to involve work that is very intensive, and
- have timescales that are likely to be quite constrained.

In the remainder of this paper we discuss the experiences and lessons that been gained from running capstone projects within intensive taught masters programmes during the last 15 years at the University of Sunderland. In the following section we provide what is essentially contextual information on the range of programmes concerned, their structure, development and the modes of operation. Following that, in the next two sections we provide what may be regarded as idealised views of the project stage within these programs and the assessment of projects. Then in the section headed "If it was only that simple" we look at some of the problems and challenges that we have had to address in a changing academic climate. Finally we present some overall conclusions and outstanding questions.

2 SUNDERLAND'S MASTERS LEVEL PROGRAMMES IN COMPUTING

Within the School of Computing and Technology at the University of Sunderland we currently offer a wide range of taught programmes at masters level in both computing and engineering management. The current masters level programmes in computing are: MSc. Computer Based Information Systems, MSc. Information Technology Management, MSc. Electronic Commerce, MSc Software Engineering, MSc. Health Information Management, MSc. Electronic Commerce Applications, MSc. Intelligent Systems, MSc. Network Systems, and MSc Internet Engineering

All the above are offered on-campus and the first three are also available off-campus at distance leaning centres both in the UK and across the globe from Nairobi to Hong Kong. The majority of on-campus students undertake the programmes in full-time mode while the majority of off-campus students study in part-time mode. Each of the programmes consists of three stages: a taught certificate stage that involves the students undertaking four taught modules, a diploma stage that involves the students undertaking a further four taught modules, and finally, a masters stage that consists of an individual capstone project for a real-world client. Each of these stages represents 15 weeks of full time study (15 x 40 hours of student learning). All of the programmes operate within a standard university wide Credit Accumulation and Transfer Scheme (CATS) within which each programme has a value of 180 M (Masters) level points. Full time students can complete the programme within a calendar year though typically they will take 14 months with a break of several weeks between the diploma and masters stages. Part-time students usually take 30 weeks to complete each stage within an overall three-year time span.

The development of the above suite of computing programmes can be traced back to 1989 when the UK Department of Employment, through its Training Agency, was running an initiative known as "High Technology National Training". Through this initiative, funding was awarded (to the then Sunderland Polytechnic) to mount a full-time masters programme in Computer Based Information Systems. The MSc. Information Technology Management programme was introduced in 1992 and then nothing more until the MSc Software Engineering in 1999. Since then there has been a rapid expansion in provision. Over the years different sources of funding have been available to support students on either selected or all the MSc programmes. For example, in the current academic year (2004/2005) some 200 funded places are available to European Union Nationals via the European Social Fund for study on MSc programmes within the School. It is unlikely that without this type of funding it would have been possible to develop such a wide range of programmes. However, programme development has also been driven by opportunities to meet a perceived (and actual) demand for MSc computing programmes by full-fee paying students from the Far East (mainly Mainland China) and the Indian Sub-continent (mainly Pakistan). Further details of the development of the MSc. Computer Based Information Systems programme and the MSc. Software Engineering programme can be found in papers by Thompson and Edwards (1996 and 2003 respectively).

In addition, to offering masters programmes on-campus in both full-time and part-time attendance modes selected programmes have been available in distance learning at approved centres both within the UK and across the world starting with the MSc. Computer Based Information Systems in 1994. The current operational form for distance learning programmes is that teaching materials and assignments are produced by staff at Sunderland. The delivery is face to face at a distance leaning centre by local tutor(s) with support from Sunderland where necessary (often via a video conference link). However, all the students' assignments are assessed by staff at Sunderland. These on-campus and off-campus developments mean that currently we have some 500 to 600 students studying masters level computing programmes each year.

3   PROJECT STAGE

The overall aim for the project stage in the School's computing programmes is that each student will demonstrate his/her ability to devise and plan, control and execute a substantial project and undertake effective research in the domain. The individual learning outcomes of a typical project with regard to knowledge and abilities are (University of Sunderland, 2004):

- Knowledge of a new area of the programmes discipline (practical and theoretical).
- Ability to effectively scope a project and meet stated objectives.
- Ability to assimilate and disseminate research relevant to the specific project area.
- Ability to use effective time management skills to meet objectives.
- Ability to present the results of a project both verbally and in written form.
- Ability to critically evaluate the work undertaken and the products delivered.

All these represent real-world skills that will support the graduates in their future careers. The practical parameters that are set for each project are (University of Sunderland, 2004):

- The project must have an explicit, identified client.
- The project should take approximately 600 working hours to complete (15 weeks full time work).
- The practical aspect of the project must have a clear link with the subject matter of the specific masters programme being undertaken.
- The practical work must result in a clearly defined product for the client.
- The student must endeavour to ensure that the client carries out a suitable evaluation of the product.
- The project must individual in nature: if it is part of a larger project each student's contribution must be coherent, discrete and well-defined.
- The project must offer sufficient scope for the student to conduct a critical review of current and relevant literature.
- This literature must feed into the practical aspect of the project in some defined manner.

In all cases the School's main concern is to ensure that the chosen project is of an appropriate standard to warrant the award of an M.Sc. and of a suitable size for it to be completed in the timescale specified.

The important actors involved in each project are:
- The Student
- The Client
- The Project Tutor(s) for the programme who will take overall responsibility for the particular project module
- The Student's Academic Supervisor
- The Second Marker for the project who will be a supervisor for one of the other students.

The client must to be able to identify a product (be it software artefact, strategic study, etc) that is needed by them and is of worth and which represents some 300 hours of practical work (i.e. half the total time for the project). Student and client must consult over the aim, objectives & procedures for the practical work and this should result in a formal agreement that is "signed off" in the student's project Terms of Reference and product requirements. The client needs to be able to support the student by providing sufficient contact time, any specific facilities (e.g. particular software or hardware), access to relevant documents, and /or personnel as required for the particular project. Also, the client (or his/her organisation) needs be involved in the evaluation of the eventual product.

Each student has an academic supervisor allocated from within the School who will provide regular support and guidance during the project in addition to acting as the fist marker for the project. For distance students, regular communication with their supervisor is through email and where appropriate, by post and video conferencing. There is also support sessions for students at Distance Learning centres via local tutors who can provide face to face discussions on the project work. However, such discussions would be in terms of general support rather than specific direction as this is the role of the supervisor.

The majority of part-time students both on and off campus are in employment and most are able to find a project and sponsor from within their employer's organisation. In fact in many cases their employer may have very specific projects lined up for them prior to starting the final year of their programme. In cases where a part-time student is unable to find such a project the University can offer help as it does for full-time students. The School is particularly proud that in all the years we have been engaged in MSc projects at a distance there has not been an instance where a student has failed to obtain a client. Many full-time students are also able to find their own projects, in consultation with the project tutors. This is often via links with previous employers, current part-time employers, family contacts, or through their own particular spheres of interest. The members of the academic staff are also able to identify projects either though their external contacts or research projects. For on-campus students the School is also able to identify some projects via its placement unit for undergraduate students. Also, the University itself provides assistance with projects via its Business Development Unit and its careers service.

4   ASSESSMENT OF PROJECTS

The assessment of the projects involves evaluation in five areas: research, success, dissertation, control, and viva. The balance between the assessment areas and the staff involved are detailed in the table below. Very clear guidelines have been published (University of Sunderland, 2004) with regard to the criteria which staff are to use when assessing each of the areas listed in the table. As is made clear in the documentation it is primarily the research element that identifies the project as being of postgraduate standard. Hence it is insufficient for a student to simply achieve a total numerical pass mark for the project. The Research element must also receive at least a pass mark. The research element provides the theoretical underpinning for the project and therefore must be treated in earnest. The research area is assessed according to the extent to which the completed project demonstrates achievement in research and includes an evaluation of the student's ability to:

- Assimilate and disseminate research relevant to the specific project area,
- Critically assess and present this research both verbally and in a written form,
- Relate and apply this review and assessment to the practical elements of the project, and
- Attain a level of expertise beyond that which is achieved in the taught course.

Success of a project is measured with regard to:
- The degree to which the objectives given in the terms of reference have been achieved, and
- The extent to which the deliverables satisfy the project client.

In the assessment of the dissertation, staff are directed to consider:
- The presentation of the initial problem and the results in a well-structured and logical fashion,

- How the research literature review has been related to the practical outcome, and
- The student's ability to critically assess the conduct and outcome of the project.

Project Assessment (University of Sunderland, 2004)

Assessors / Areas (% of mark)	Project Review Panel	Supervisor	Second Marker
Research (30%)		✓	✓
Success (20%)		✓	✓
Dissertation (20%)		✓	✓
Control (15%)	✓	✓	
Viva (15%)		✓	✓

When they are assessing the control element, the staff are directed to consider the student's capability, motivation, perseverance, resolution, and skill in managing the project. In particular they should focus on the student's ability to plan, schedule, and control the work. It is expected that students will produce and maintain formal Terms of Reference, Schedule and Gantt chart and that these will be included as an appendix in the student's dissertation. Two formal review sessions are held during the project to monitor progress. Wherever feasible these are face to face with School staff (possibly via videoconferencing), though where this is not possible paper-based submissions can be used instead.

Finally, the viva sessions provide a formal opportunity for the students to demonstrate the grasp (or otherwise) they have of their subject to assessors. The viva thus provides a means of ensuring that the student had undertaken the work and had produced the submitted dissertation. It normally consists of a short, focused, presentation followed by a detailed question and answer session. It also provides an opportunity for assessors to resolve any differences they have in their evaluations of the submitted work.

5   IF IT WAS ONLY THAT SIMPLE

Until the late 1990s the School was offering only two major MSc. programmes: MSc. Computer Based Information Systems, and MSc. Information Technology Management. These were being offered on and off campus and in both part-time and full-time modes of study. On-campus, the part-time students were nearly all in employment and most found projects with their employer. The same was normally true for part-time students who were studying off-campus. On-campus the full-time programmes had reasonable, but not too high, numbers (typically 30/60 per intake), the majority of the students were from the UK, and many had existing links with the immediate geographical area. Finding projects for such students did not present too much of a problem. Many students through their own contacts were able to identify suitable sponsors and the School was able to assist via its placement unit, which at that time was still assisting a fair number of undergraduates with year-long industrial placements. A relatively small number of key staff were involved in the overall management of both on and off campus projects which ensured compatibility of approach and reasonably accurate tracking of each student's progress even when they took breaks, changed modes of study, or had referred work to undertake.

During the last four years (and in particular during the last two years) there have been a significant number of events and situations that have impinged on the project stage of our MSc programmes:

1. The overall number of students undertaking MSc programmes has increased enormously to some 500 to 600 each year (on and off campus total) and these are spread across many programmes.

2. There has been a significant increase in the number of programmes.

3. There has been a significant increase in the number of staff involved in teaching at masters level.

4. The majority of the students are no longer from the UK and hence do not have the same links that will assist them in finding projects local to the University. Students are allowed to take up projects in other parts of the UK or even back in their home countries but this raises extra problems with regard to supervision, control, and tracking.

5. The senior project tutor (with overall responsibility for projects within MSc. Computer Based Information Systems, and MSc. Information Technology Management) with some 13 years of experience with such projects has retired.

6. Relatively few undergraduate students were undertaking placements, the number of staff in the placement unit was reduced, and the number of links with industry via the unit was reduced. Other links with industry have been made via the University's Business Development Unit, the careers service, and the various research groups within the institution. However, these not all these have proved to be as effective in finding projects despite significant expenditure in monetary and staff terms by the Business Development Unit.

7. Differences in approach to obtaining, approving, and managing projects had become apparent across the programmes.

8. More projects are being undertaken which directly support the research groups within the School. In previous years there had been an insistence that all projects had sponsors from outside the School and ideally from outside the University.
9. Many more staff became involved with MSc. project supervisions (several with little experience of such, or a detailed knowledge of the particular programme which their supervisee was undertaking).
10. Providing and timetabling rooms for reviews and vivas became a major problem. This was for two main reasons: the number of students had increased, and the University was trying to make more efficient use of its buildings by moving part of the School of Education into the building previously occupied only by the School of Computing and Technology.

At the start of the 2003/2004 academic year the first two authors of this paper formally took responsibility for projects for on-campus instances of the MSc. Computer Based Information Systems, the MSc. Information Technology Management, and the MSc Software Engineering. Both had previous extensive experience of programme leadership at masters level and wished to improve external links with industry as they saw this as a means of advancing the University's reach-out and research in Software Engineering. They were subsequently asked to take on overall responsibility for all masters computing projects. This situation lasted for about 4 months and resulted in the production of a single set of documentation for the relevant programmes (University of Sunderland, 2004). Unfortunately, it proved impossible to reach consensus agreement with all the staff involved in the management and running of the various programmes and hence there was a return to the original responsibilities. However, several of the other programme teams have subsequently adopted the procedures that were laid down during those 4 months and are using the assessment and control documents that had been developed. So despite the problems there have been benefits. A clear attempt is being made to introduce more structure into the processes and more formal documentation is generally being used.

6   CONCLUSIONS

In this paper we have attempted to provide not only contextual information on a range of masters capstone projects but also details of what could be regarded as good practice with regard to: practical parameters, assessment, and operation across widely distributed centres. We have also provided details of the actual problems that can occur when there is a rapidly changing academic climate. It would appear that to run a successful set of projects it is not sufficient to simply address the purely academic issues such as assessment. It is just as important to ensure that the wider issues concerned with obtaining, approving, and managing projects plus providing appropriate academic support are not neglected. Our experiences during the last year have made it clear that to successfully run a large number of these projects there needs to be very clearly documented procedures and support documentation and that intermediate deadlines, as provided by our two interim formal project reviews are essential. However there are still many managerial issues that still need to be resolved such as:

- How should supervisors be chosen and allocated to programmes/projects?
- Should a member of staff act as both sponsor and supervisor for the same project?
- What should happen if a student wishes to change from full-time study to part-time study during the project?
- How should student claims for mitigation be handled? During the project time or after?
- How should late starting projects be handled when there is no reason for the delay?
- How should late starting projects be handled when there is a good reason for the delay?
- How should we handle students who are out of synchronisation with the others due to referrals etc?
- Which staff should be involved in interim reviews?
- What is the best way to manage and support student reviews and vivas?

7   REFERENCES

Beasley, R.E. (2003) *Conducting a Successful Senior Capstone Course in Computing*, Journal of Computing Sciences in Colleges, Vol. 19, Issue 1, October, pp. 122-131.

Clear, T., Goldweber, M., Young, F.H., Leidig P.M., and Scott, K. (2001) *ITiCSE 2001 working group reports: Resourcses for Instructors of Capstone Courses in Computing*, ACM SIGCSE Bulletin, Vol. 33, Issue 4, December, pp. 93-113

Hayes, J.H., Lethbridge, T.C., and Port, D., (2003) *Evaluating Individual Contribution Toward Group Software Engineering Projects*, Proceedings of the 25th International Conference on Software Engineering, May, pp. 622-627.

Holcombe, M., Stratton, A., Fincher S., and Griggiths, G. (eds) (1998) *Projects in the Computing Curriculum: Proceedings of the Project '98 Workshop*, Springer, London.

Stein, M.V. (2002) *Using large vs. Small Group Projects in Capstone and Software Engineering Courses*, Journal of Computing Sciences in Colleges, Vol. 17, Issue 4, march, pp. 1-6.

Stein, M.V. (2003) *Student Effort in Semester-Long and Condensed Capstone Project Courses*, Journal of Computing Sciences in Colleges, Vol. 18, Issue 4, June, pp. 200-212.

Thompson J. B. (1990) *Preparation for Placement and the Benefits to Employers: A Case Study of Business Computing Students*, WCCE/90: Fifth World Conference on Computers in Education, Sydney, Australia, July, pp. 599-604.

Thompson J. B. and Edwards H. M (1996), The Hybrid Manager: Achievement within a World-Wide Dimension, IFIP WG3.4 International Working Conference on Information Technology in Management and Business Education, Melbourne, July, (Proceedings edited by Ben-Zion Barta, Arthur Tatnall and Peter Juliff published by Chapman & Hall, London 1997, ISBN 0-412-79960-X, " The Place of Information Technology in Management and Business Education, pp. 199-206).

Thompson J. B. and Edwards H. M. (2003), *Reflections on a UK Masters Level Software Engineering Programme Intended for the Home and International Market*, Sixteenth Conference on Software Engineering Education and Training (CSEE&T 2003), 20-23 March, Madrid, Spain, Proceedings published by the IEEE Computer Society, pp.166-173.

University of Sunderland (2004), Computing Masters Projects Handbook, v1.f/t on-campus, School of Computing and Technology, Jan 2004, http://osiris.sunderland.ac.uk/~mcproj/ , accessed 25 May 2004.

Umpress, D., Hendrix, T.D., Cross J.C., (2002) *Software Process in the Classroom: The Capstone Project Experience*, IEEE Software, September, pp. 78-85.

Wilde, N., White, L.J., Kerr, L.B., Ewing, D.D. and Krueger E.A., (2003) Some Experiences with Evolution and Process-Focused Projects, 16th Conference on Software Engineering Education and training (CSEE&T 2003). March 2003, pp. 242-250.

Williams, J.C., Bair, B., Borstler, J., Lethbridge, T.C., Surendran, K., (2003) Client Sponsored Projects in Software Engineering Courses, ACM SIGSE Bulletin, Proceedings of the 34th SIGCSE Technical Symposium on Computer Science Education, Vol. 35, Issue 1, January, pp. 401-402.

A STRUCTURAL MODEL OF THE INFORMATION SYSTEMS PROFESSIONAL
Comparing practitioners, employers, students, and academics

Rodney Turner, Glenn Lowry and Julie Fisher
Victoria University, Australia; College of Business and Economics, United Arab Emirates University; and Monash University, Australia.
Rod.Turner@vu.edu.au g.lowry@uaeu.ac.ae julie.fisher@sims.monash.edu.au

Abstract: This paper reports the identification and modelling of four latent variables in the makeup of the professional repertoire of information systems professionals. The relative importance of work experience, soft skills, IS education, and non-IS education to four stakeholder groups, IS employers, professionals, students, and academics, is graphically and quantitatively represented through a second-order structural equation model. The model is simultaneously tested against the four stakeholder groups, the fit measures are the same for each of them, providing a commensurate basis for comparison. The fit measure values indicate an excellent fit, within accepted limits. The model provides a quantitative basis for identification of the relative importance of the respective variables to the education and career development of IS professionals. The model also includes features of the working environment which may influence the career choices and progress of IS graduates. Analysis of the shifts in importance attached to latent variables between groups may provide improved understanding of changing values and perceptions of IS professionals as careers develop and as individuals change stakeholder group membership.

Key words: Information Systems, IS professional, IS graduates, technical skills, soft skills, hard skills, structural model.

1   INTRODUCTION

The preparation, quality, and expectations of new information systems (IS) graduates continues to be the focus of many discussions, conferences, workshops, and publications by IS practitioners, employers, students, and academics.

Employers and experienced practitioners are often critical of a lack of practical experience or unrealistic views and expectations perceived to be held by some new graduates. Students and new graduates necessarily lack real world work experience, yet they sometimes have unrealistically high expectations about their immediate value. Academics continually revise curricula to accommodate change and growth in the body of knowledge and the skills that they believe are needed by students preparing for entry into professional IS roles.

How do the perceptions and needs of stakeholders change as careers develop and mature? What are the "essential" bodies of knowledge, skills, and personal characteristics that are essential for successful IS professional work? How do the relative importance of *work experience, soft skills, IS education, and non-IS education* differ across different groups.

2   PREVIOUS STUDIES

Numerous studies of the skill requirements of IS graduates, including soft skills, hard skills, and job features that help motivate IS professionals are available. (Van Slyke, Kittner *et al*, 1997; Young (1996).

Some compare various stakeholders such as academics and industry, or student perceptions. In the main, these studies are descriptive in nature covering curriculum emphasis, importance of skills rated in order of importance (Williams, 1998; Wong, 1996; Orr, 2000; Lee & Koh, 2002; Goles, 2001; Farwell, Lee *et al*, 1993, 1995).

Interpersonal skills and technical skills are recognised as possessing equal importance for IS professionals. (Young & Keen, 1997) IS students must develop "soft" skills and abilities in various areas including teamwork, creativity and communication.

Determining those skills employers of new IS graduates seek is important for educators in designing curricula and advising students. Van Slyke (1997) found that specific technical skills were less important than basic technical skills and non-academic skills.

Doke and Williams (1999), in a study across various IS job classifications, found that systems development skills and interpersonal skills were common across classifications but programming skills were more important for entry level IS positions.

Core curriculum requirements have been set in association with professional bodies in Australia (Underwood, 1997) and the USA (Gorgone, Feinstein *et al,* 1997). However, it has been suggested that course requirements surrounding the IS 2002 model curriculum (ACM-AIS, 2002) as it stands probably contains more technical material than can be covered in an undergraduate degree program (Beachboard & Parker, 2003).

Yet as Ross & Ruhleder (1993) note IS education often is seen as concentrating too much on a narrow set of technical skills and suggest that the IS curriculum should concentrate on developing technical & business skills. Others (Ashley & Padgett, 1997; Turner & Lowry, 2001) have shown that despite the call from IS employers for more business orientated skills in graduating IS students, core business subjects do not rate highly.

Technical skills are not the total answer in preparing IS professional (Ross & Ruhleder, 1993). They suggest that programs aimed at developing IS professionals of the future must cover a wide range of skills and assist the integration of these skills in complex environments. Little, Granger *et al,* (1999) suggest that it is not sufficient for IS graduates to just possess technical capabilities but should be aware of the need for professionals to take responsibility for their work and the importance of appropriate ethical behaviours. They further suggest a need to include these aspects in the curriculum of current IS programmes. They identify an "industry-academic gap" that leads to dissatisfaction amongst employer groups with IS graduates (Little, Granger *et al,* 1999).

It is indicated above that there is an interaction between the competing aspects in the development and education of IS graduates. How can these interactions be measured? The purpose of this paper is to present the results of a study utilising structural equation modelling methods to develop and validate a model that illustrates the possible relationships between these areas and the emphasis that students and IS decision makers place on them.

3   METHOD

A multipart questionnaire was developed to solicit the views of four different groups of stakeholders regarding the importance of academic and useful adjunct skills and abilities areas included in information systems degree programs. Drawing on previous surveys (Cheney, 1988; Cappel, 2001/2002; Farwell, Lee *et al,* 1995; Leitheiser, 1992; Leonard, 1999; Snoke & Underwood, 1998a, 1998b; Tang, Lee *et al,* 2001; Van Slyke, Kittner *et al,* 1997; Trauth, Farwell *et al,* 1993) the instrument developed for this study included some additional items in the area of job features and conditions. Items were organised into several sections: demographic data, IS and business computing related skills, non-IS academic subjects, soft skills and personal characteristics, and workplace conditions and incentives.

Four variations of the instrument were developed and administered to the four stakeholder groups as follows:

1. Students were senior undergraduate information systems students in three universities in Victoria, Australia. Of a total of 300 surveys distributed to students during regular classes, 254 usable responses were received, a response rate of 84.6 percent.

2. Academics were those teaching IS subjects at Australasian universities were invited to participate by email containing a hotlink to the on-line form. A total of 396 emails were sent and 195 responded with usable replies, a response rate of 49.2 percent.

3. IS Practitioners were employed in an IS/IT capacity in Australia. One thousand two hundred questionnaires were delivered by email. A total of 136 usable responses were returned, a response rate of 11.3 percent.

4. IS managers and decision makers were those in a supervisory or managerial role responsible. One thousand seven hundred and eighty questionnaires were distributed by email. The response for this survey resulted in 153 returns with 138 usable, a 7.7 percent response rate.

4   ANALYSIS

4.1   Factor Analysis

Nine different factors were identified through exploratory factor analysis using PCA analysis with Varimax rotation. Two items were concerned with the IS job and its features, two were concerned with soft skills and personal qualities and five were concerned with educational matters from IS technical areas (three items) and non-IS academic areas (two items).

Questions that did not clearly load onto a single factor or did not have a value of at least 0.5 were excised from analysis. Item reliability was tested using Cronbach's α. Item reliability was good with the overall value for each subscale exceeding recognised benchmark value of 0.7 (Cronbach, 1951).

Summated scales were computed using a weighted mean approach (Holmes-Smith & Rowe , 1994; Hair, Anderson *et al,* 1998) where the mean scores are multiplied by their respective factor loadings, summed, and divided by the sum of the factor loadings. This procedure ensures that the factor loadings are properly and fully taken into account when computing the summated scales.

As a result, nine separate factors in four separate areas of interest were identified. Two factors SF1W and SF2W were identified as soft skills and these were measured by eight questions. Two factors WF1W and WF2W concerned work related incentives and these were measured by seven questions. Two factors OAF1W and OAF2W measured by eight questions were identified as non-IS academic subject areas and three factors F1W, F2W and F3W were identified as IS academic subjects, measured by eight questions. An interpretation of these factors is given in Table 1 below.

Factor	Interpretation	Emphasis
F1W	IS academic subjects	High level applications
F2W	IS academic subjects	Design and development
F3W	IS academic subjects	Web related applications
OAF1W	Non-IS academic subjects	Inwardly focussed core non-IS business subjects
OAF2W	Non-IS academic subjects	Outwardly orientated non-IS subjects
SF1W	Soft skills	Get on with people, communicate or stand-out
SF2W	Soft skills	Skills acquisition and able to do job
WF1W	Work related incentive	Environmental and comfort
WF2W	Work related incentive	Reward related (hygiene) factors

Table 1: Factor Interpretations

4.2 Structural Modelling

The model was developed using AMOS R5. The structural model has four latent variables. These are *soft skills* referring to soft skills such as interpersonal skills and team work; *IS ed* referring to the IS education skills outcomes and technical skills such as web development, analysis and design; *non-IS ed* referring to non-academic subjects such as accounting, economics and commercial law, and finally *work aspects* referring to aspects of the IS/IT work environment that may influence the professional. The dependent variable, *IS Professional*, is the combination of soft skills, education and work environment.

Appropriateness of the model structure has been discussed elsewhere (Turner, Fisher & Lowry, 2004) and validated against independent groups. A group model was tested against sets of independent data from four stakeholder groups: students, academics IS decision makers and IS managers. The values of the relative importance between latent variables expressed by the four stakeholder groups are shown below.

The fit parameters for the model in Figure 1 indicate an excellent fit and are within the acceptable levels (Schumaker 2004). As the model is being simultaneously tested against four groups, the fit measures are the same. The model fit values for the four stakeholder groups are: GFI=0.964, AGFI=0.934, TLI=0.974, RMSEA=0.018 (range LO90=0.00, HI90=0.028), RMR=0.027, p=0.051 and CMIN (discrep) =1.24. These values all indicate the model fit is sound. Standardized residual covariance values between indicators are each below the critical value suggest by Hair, Anderson *et al,* (1998) of 2.58 supporting the fit of the model to the data.

With the exception of the path WF1W<---work_aspects which is not significant, each of the regression weights is significant at p<0.001. Table 2 shows the standardised regression coefficients determined for the model. These standardized regression coefficients are significant at p<0.001 with critical ratios great than 2.

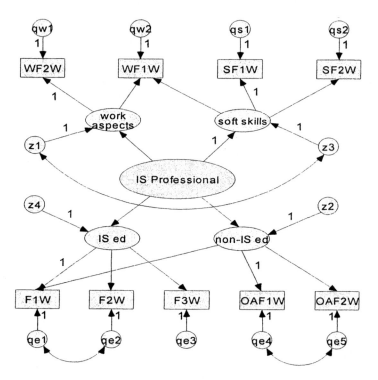

Figure 1: Model Path Diagram

Standardized Regression Weights

Path			Students	Academics	IS Practitioner	IS Decision Makers
non-IS ed	<---	IS Professional	0.96	0.76	0.96	0.72
IS ed	<---	IS Professional	0.85	0.82	0.32	0.70
soft skills	<---	IS Professional	0.88	0.82	0.85	0.76
work_aspects	<---	IS Professional	0.87	0.57	0.42	0.61
SF2W	<---	soft skills	0.63	0.55	0.61	0.54
F1W	<---	IS ed	0.32	0.38	0.48	0.43
F3W	<---	IS ed	0.56	0.67	0.70	0.73
OAF2W	<---	non-IS ed	0.63	0.60	0.57	0.78
SF1W	<---	soft skills	0.72	0.65	0.76	0.62
F2W	<---	IS ed	0.53	0.54	0.66	0.64
OAF1W	<---	non-IS ed	0.46	0.48	0.42	0.62
WF1W	<---	work_aspects	0.02	0.08	0.08	0.10
WF2W	<---	work_aspects	0.61	0.84	0.75	0.98
F1W	<---	non-IS ed	0.33	0.33	0.32	0.38
WF1W	<---	soft skills	0.57	0.40	0.49	0.43

Table 2: Standardized Regression Weights

Regression weight values below 0.3 are weak, between 0.3 and 0.5 as mild and above these values as strong (Holmes-Smith, 2000). From Table 2 below it can be seen that most regression weights are mild to strong and above 0.3. Those below 0.3 include the path WF1W←work_aspects which suggests that this is not regarded as a work related feature but as a soft skill. Squared multiple correlations presented in Table 3 are generally above the recommended minimum value of 0.3 suggested for good item reliability (Holmes-Smith, 2000).

Squared Multiple Correlations

Variable	Students	Academics	IS Practitioner	IS Decision Makers
work_aspects	0.41	0.32	0.17	0.37
non-IS ed	0.87	0.57	0.93	0.51
IS ed	0.71	0.67	0.10	0.50
soft skills	0.80	0.67	0.73	0.58
OAF1W	0.24	0.23	0.18	0.39
F1W	0.41	0.41	0.42	0.49
F2W	0.28	0.29	0.44	0.41
F3W	0.31	0.45	0.49	0.53
OAF2W	0.40	0.36	0.32	0.60
SF2W	0.38	0.31	0.37	0.29
SF1W	0.51	0.43	0.58	0.39
WF1W	0.38	0.19	0.30	0.24
WF2W	0.70	0.71	0.56	0.96

Table 3: Squared Multiple Correlation Values (R^2)

As a further indicator of model acceptability, standardized residual covariance values between indicators are each below the critical value of 2.58 as suggested by Hair, Anderson *et al,* (1998) and are significant at the 0.05 level.

IS practitioners appear to place a low emphasis on the value of IS education with the regression weight IS Professional->IS Ed being quite low and the R^2 value indicating a very low explained variance.

Most of the R^2 values were similar for most groups, with some interesting exceptions. The work_aspects factor is of similar importance to all groups except IS Professionals. Similarly, all groups except IS Professionals place similar value on non-IS education. All groups except IS Decision Makers place a relatively low value on OAF1W, non-IS academic subjects. IS Decision Makers place a much higher value on OAF2W, outwardly focused non-IS subjects which are those most directly connected with soft skills development.

Not surprisingly, all groups place a high value on F1W, high level application IS Academic Subjects. Students and academics place a somewhat lower value on F2W, design and development IS Academic Subjects. Web related subjects, F3W, are also highly rated by all groups.

All groups place high value on work related factors, WF2W, resulting in the highest R^2 values across the table. The high value ($R^2 = 0.96$) from the IS Decision Makers group suggests that they view components such as salary, company shares, company cars, and other hygiene factors as of paramount importance to a greater degree than do the other groups of stakeholders.

5   DISCUSSION

Most research published in the area of skills is based on one view of the IS professional. A number of studies have been published on technical skills required as perceived by the various stakeholders or comparing the perceptions of stakeholders. There is also a body of work illustrating the growing importance of soft skills, again from the perspective of various stakeholders. A number of studies have also been published concerning the effects of the working environment on IS professional perceptions of their work situation. Another body of work has been presented illustrating the importance placed on business related skills acquired as part of the IS graduate's preparation.

To the authors' knowledge, no research has appeared which links these areas together in a dynamic structural model. The research reported in this paper addresses this issue. The findings suggest that there is a stable and interactive relationship between these four factors. The model shows the relative importance and strength of the factors. Development of a structural model advances our knowledge of the constellation of skills, knowledge, and values held by IS stakeholders beyond conventional factor analysis which does not allow for comparison of the significance of these factors. For the first time it is possible to show the interacting relationships of the four factors along with measures that suggest their relative importance to each of the stakeholder groups.

The model shows a good fit for all four sets stakeholder data. An important requirement for any model is that it is able to fit to independent sets of data, a requirement satisfied in this case.

The results presented here indicate that the perceptions of four stakeholder groups can be described by a second order, four latent factor model described in terms of hard IS skills, non-IS educational skills, personal attributes and soft skills and the job conditions.

It should be stressed that the model is not necessarily the only one that can fit the data. It does however show that it is possible to develop a comprehensive model to explain the various attributes of the IS professional. Ultimately it is hoped that such a model can be useful in improving the career prospects of new graduates and as providing indicators of shifting emphasis and value of these factors as individuals change stakeholder groups as their careers develop.

6   REFERENCES

ACM-AIS "IS 2002 - Model Curricula and Guidelines for Undergraduate Degree Programs in Information Systems," New York, (Accessed 7 January 2004), 2002. Available at: http://www.acm.org/education/curricula.html#IS2002.

Ashley, N.W. and Padgett, T.C. "Information Systems Graduates: Evaluation of Their IS Curricula," (Accessed 7 January 2004), 1997. Available at: http://www.westga.edu/~bquest/1998/infosys.html

Beachboard, J.C., and Parker, K.R. "How Much is Enough? Teaching Information Technology in a Business-Oriented IS Curriculum," Ninth Americas Conference on Information Systems, AIS, Tampa, FA, 2003, pp. 3026-3031.

Cappel, J.J. "Entry-Level IS Job Skills: A Survey of Employers," *Journal of Computer Information Systems* (42:2, Winter) 2001/2002, pp 76-82.

Cheney, P.H. "Information System Skill Requirements: 1980 & 1990," *ACM*:4) 1988.

Cronbach, L.J. "Coefficient Alpha and the Internal Consistency of Tests," *Psychometrika* (16), 1951, pp. 297-334.

Davis, G.B., Gorgone, J.T., Couger, J.D., Feinstein, D.L., and Longenecker, J., H.E. (Eds) "IS'97 Model Curriculum and Guidelines for Undergraduate Degree Programs in Information Systems," *The Data Base for Advances in Information Systems* (28:1) 1997.

Doke, E.R., and Williams, S.R. "Knowledge and Skill Requirements for Information Systems Professionals: An Exploratory Study," *Journal of IS Education* (10:1 (Spring)) 1999, pp 10-18.

Farwell, D., Lee, D.M., and Trauth, E.M. "Critical Skills and Knowledge Requirements of IS Professionals: A Joint Academic/Industry Investigation," *MIS Quarterly*) 1995, pp 313-337.

Farwell, D., Lee, D.M., and Trauth, E.M. "The IS expectation gap: Industry expectations versus academic preparation," *MIS Quarterly* (17) 1993, p 293.

Gorgone, J. T., D. L. Feinstein, et al. (2002). Undergraduate Information Systems Model Curriculum Update - IS 2002. Eighth Americas Conference on Information Systems.

Goles, T. "A View from the Entry Level: Student Perceptions of Critical Information Systems Job Attributes." SIGCPR 2001, San Diego CA, 2001, pp. 57-64.

Hair, J.F., Anderson, R.E., Tatham, R.L., and Black, W.C. *Multivariate Data Analysis*, (5th ed.) Prentice-Hall, Upper Saddle River, NJ, 1998.

Holmes-Smith, P. "Introduction to Structural Equation Modelling," ACSPRI 2000, 2000, p. 143.

Lee, S., Koh, S., Yen, D. and Tang, H.-L. "Perception Gaps Between IS Academics and IS Practitioners: An Exploratory Study," *Information and Management* (40(1):October), 2002, pp. 51-61.

Leitheiser, R.L. "MIS Skills for the 1990s: A Survey of MIS Managers' Perceptions," *Journal of Management Information Systems* (9:1, Summer) 1992, pp 69-91.

Leonard, L. "Survey Shows Skills Gap Still a Problem," 1999. Available on-line at <http://www.itac.ca/> Accessed 23/6/2002

Litecky, C., and Arnett, K. "An Update on Measurement of IT Job Skills for Managers and Professionals," Seventh Americas Conference on Information Systems, 2001, pp. 1922-1924.

Little, J.C., Granger, M.J., Boyle, R., Gerhardt-Powals, J., Impagliazzo, J., Janik, C., Kubilis, N.J., Lippert, S.K., McCracken, W.M., Paliwoda, G., and Soja, P. "Integrating Professionalism and Workplace Issues into the Computing and Information Technology Curriculum," *ITiCSE '99 Working Group Reports* (33:4) 1999, pp 106-112.

Orr, J., and von Hellens, L. "Skill Requirements of IT&T Professionals and Graduates: An Australian Study," ACM SIGCPR, Chicago, 2000, pp. 167-170.

Ross, J., and Ruhleder, K. "Preparing IS Professionals for a Rapidly Changing World: The Challenge for IS Educators," Special Interest Group on Computer Personnel Research Annual Conference, St Louis MO, 1993, pp. 379-384.

Schumacker, R.E., and Lomax, R.G. *A Beginners Guide to Structural Equation Modelling* Lawrence Erlbaum Associates, Mahwah, New Jersey, 2004, p. 288.

Snoke, R., and Underwood, A. "Generic Attributes of IS Graduates - a Queensland Study," Proceedings of the Ninth Australasian Conference on Information Systems, Sydney NSW, 1998a, pp. 615-623.

Snoke, R., and Underwood, A. "Generic Attributes of IS Graduates - an Australian Study," Sixth European Conference on Information Systems, Granada: Euro-Arab Management School, Aix-en-Provence, 1998b, pp. 1713-1720.

Tang, H.-L., Lee, S., and Koh, S. "Educational Gaps As Perceived By Is Educators: A Survey Of Knowledge And Skill Requirements." *Journal of Computer Information Systems* (41:2) Winter 2001, pp 76-84.

Trauth, E., Farwell, D., and Lee, D. "The IS Expectation Gap: Industry Expectations Versus Academic Preparation," *MIS Quarterly* (17:3 (September)) 1993, pp 293-307.

Turner, R., Fisher, J., and Lowry, G. (2004). Describing the IS Professional with a Structural Model. PACIS 2004 Conference, Shanghai, China.

Turner, R., and Lowry, G. "The Compleat Graduate: What Students Think Employers Want and What Employers Say They Want in New Graduates," Sixteenth Pan-Pacific Business Conference, Pan-Pacific Business Association, Nadi, Fiji, 1999, pp. 272-274.

Turner, R., and Lowry, G. "The Third Dimension of the IS Curriculum: The Importance of Soft Skills for IT Practitioners." ACIS 2001, Coffs Harbour, NSW, Australia, 2001, pp. 683-686.

Underwood, A. "The ACS Core Body of Knowledge for Information Technology Professionals," 1997. On-line at <http://www.acs.org.au/national/pospaper/bokpt1.htm> Accessed 21/7/2000

Van Slyke, C., Kittner, M., and Cheney, P. "Skill Requirements for Entry-Level IS Graduates: A Preliminary Report from Industry," 1997. Available on-line at <http://groucho.bsn.usf.edu/~vanslyke/isecon_1.htm> Accessed 26/4/2000

Williams, P.A. (1998). "Employability Skills in the Undergraduate Business. Curriculum and Job Market Preparedness: Perceptions of Faculty and Final-Year Students in Five Tertiary Institutions..." Unpublished PhD Dissertation, Andrews University.

Wong, E.Y.W. "The Education and Training of Future Information Systems Professionals," *Education + Training* (38:1) 1996, pp 37-43.

Young, D. "The Relative Importance of Technical and Interpersonal Skills for New Information Systems Personnel." *Journal of Computer Information Systems* (37:Summer) 1996, pp 66-71.

Young, J. and Keen, C. "The Emergence Importance of Broader Skills and Personal Attributes in the Recruitment of Australian IS Professionals," In *Eighth Australasian Conference on Information Systems*, D. J. Sutton (Ed.), Australian Computer Society & ACIS Executive, Adelaide, South Australia, 1997, pp. 682-692.

THE INDUSTRY AND EDUCATION NEXUS
How one School Tackled Certification

Andrew Stein, Con Nikakis, John Bentley, Rob Jovanovic
School of Information Systems, Victoria University, Melbourne, Australia
Andrew.Stein@vu.edu.au

Abstract: Over a period of 40 years, the Information Systems (IS) discipline has become an essential component in the employment of information technology personnel in business and government organisations. In recent times there have been discussions by IS professionals on how to best respond to developments in the information technology and communications industry. At the same time there has been a downturn in employment opportunities in this industry (ICT Skills Snapshot, 2004). Recent research also indicates that many of the entry-level positions that graduates traditionally entered have diminished due to the economic downturn and to companies outsourcing positions to off-shore companies. This "in-progress" paper presents the path that one Australian University school took in introducing multiple certification programs in an endeavour to better connect a university school with ICT industry requirements. The certification programs include SAP, ITIL, I-Net+ and Microsoft accredited programs. The results of this in-progress research show that flexibility in delivery mode and effective merging of curriculum and certification content is crucial to achieving successful programs.

Key words: Vendor certification, curriculum, certification implementation.

1 INDUSTRY FOCUSSED TERTIARY EDUCATION

"Mobile, flexible, highly-trained, industry-focussed, experienced ...", cries that are heard from the Information Technology industry in relation to the expertise that is expected from tertiary graduates these days. Until the recent cyclical downturn of the computer industry demand had been extremely high for graduates from tertiary institutions that could fit the chameleon-like nature of the computer industry's graduate skills deficit gap (NOIE, 2003; DES, 2001; Knight, 2001; DHFE, 2000). Much of this deficit was due to the rapidly changing nature and focus of the industry itself. It still is. The IT industry is constantly evolving with localised demand for graduates with skills in the latest technology upgrade (software and hardware). This demand exhibits much of the "here today, gone tomorrow" mentality that pervades industries that focus on new and developing but much hyped innovations. The modern marketing machine has trained many of us to "keep up with the technological Jones". Industry decision makers too, have been seduced by the hard sell. This trend is clearly manifested in the need to have employees and consequently IT graduates trained in the latest hardware and software. Industry is very quick to sound the alarm bells when there is a shortfall in the skills base (ICT Skills Snapshot, 2004).

1.1   Government Demands on Tertiary Institutions

The clamour for up-to-date, skill-focused, graduates has spilled over into the political arena. Governments through policy; and the press through emotive industry pieces; are demanding that tertiary institutions become focused on 'practical research', the delivery of 'skilled graduates' and be more 'outcome orientated'. This manifests itself in the requirement of governments to get greater value from the tertiary education dollar (SACES, 2002; ACNielson, 2000; Ahmadi & Brabston, 1997; Castleman & Coulthard, 1999). Universities, along with other tertiary institutions have in recent years gradually turned their focus to reacting to the pressures of governments and the community in general and at least have started talking about the need to increase their industry collaboration and in a number of instances have begun to action 'Collaborative Research' and 'Industry Partnerships'. A particular focus area is that of IT courses that run within Universities and TAFE institutions (SACES, 2002). A response within these courses has been to include industry-based training and industry liaison within and along side existing tertiary IT courses. It seems that IT courses and industry training are seen to be particularly conducive to using these approaches (Bartlett, 2002; Flynn, 2001; McCain, 2001; Filipczak, 2000).

1.2   Certification: An avenue for Industry Collaboration?

IT industry certification programs are seen as a respected and widely-established vehicle for attaining specific, practically based expertise – areas that many tertiary courses seem to lack or with which they have chosen not to be involved (Basu, 2002; McCain, 2001). Some tertiary institutions (mainly TAFE) have taken certification programs on board enthusiastically, to the extent that they are supplementing their own programs in a significant way (ITT, 2000). Others have ignored such programs labelling them as being too training or proprietary oriented to be considered as educative ('high-brow' response) (Flynn, 2001). In very recent times selection data (university selection popularity polls) have caught up with the significant downturn of employment experienced in the IT industry during 2001-2003. These trends place a greater burden on the University sector to react positively towards "adding value" to their offerings. For University IT/IS courses to be more industry relevant, practically focused and to add value in tune with industry and government funding pressure, IT/IS certification needs to be looked at more seriously than it has been to date (Mehaut, 2001).

1.3   Certification Program Implementation

The implementation of certification programs has been ad hoc and reactionary and little has been done to investigate the implementation of IT certification programs within tertiary IT/IS programs (Rothke, 2000; McCain, 2001). There are several distinct certification classifications:

- Industry body certification - ACS, PPP programs.
- Proprietary certification programs - MCSE, CNE, CISCO.
- Industry generalised certification programs - A+, i-Net+, Network+.
- Specific purpose certification - SAP professional, and
- Academic certification - Degree, certificate & short course programs.

Assuming the case can be made to enhance existing programs with certification programs the 'Why' is answered, the 'How' can therefore be crucial to success. A wider classification is presented in Table 1.

Table 1. Certification models with example programs.

Certification Model	Example Program
Value-Added, End-On	ACS PPP program: Employment Driven, End-On
Distance Learning	Charles Sturt University, Microsoft, CISCO, Sun
Full Fee (Tertiary)	
Full Fee (Private)	
Hybrid (Tertiary/Private),	James Cook University, ITTI Master of IT
Curriculum Inclusive	VU TAFE: Cisco Accreditation – Curriculum Inclusive in Separate Subject
Mapping to Industry Certification	PowerLan Microsoft Certification: Hybrid, Curriculum Inclusive, Mapping
Specific Subject	SAP Professional Program
Industry Employment (Co-Operative Education)	Citrix Certification: Specific purpose, Employment Driven, End-On

This paper will focus on identifying forms of certification, their relevance to tertiary education, strengths and weaknesses and models of certification implementation. The endpoint of this research is recommendations for implementation of certification within the School of Information Systems, Victoria University. The formal research questions for this paper are:

- What types of certification programs would augment learning at VU?
- What models of certification implementation would be suitable for VU?
- Which model(s) is best suited to the needs of the School of IS?

2   RESULTS AND DISCUSSION

2.1   ERP Certification at VU (Course Mapping)

Victoria University has been a member of the SAP University Alliance since 1998. It adopted a faculty approach to introduction of ERP curriculum that was seen as a tool to reinforce many of the business and information systems concepts taught. The university now has approximately twenty-five subjects at both the undergraduate and postgraduate levels that incorporate SAP and related products. These subjects form part of master degree program that is taught in Australia, Singapore, China and Thailand in 2005. Even though the university has a well-established curriculum, it was also faced with the dilemma of how it could take advantage of industry acceptance of SAP. An important question that must be asked relates to the relevance of current ERP curriculum to industry requirements. The SAP University Alliance, established in the mid-nineties, closely followed the growth in ERP usage in industry. Universities which have worked very hard to develop ERP curriculum are now faced with the dilemma of evolving their curriculum to reflect the evolution of ERP systems and industry requirements. The curriculum employed by universities could be classified into one of four different curriculum approaches or a hybrid: Training into ERP, ERP via Business Processes, Information Systems Approach, ERP concepts, and The Hybrid.

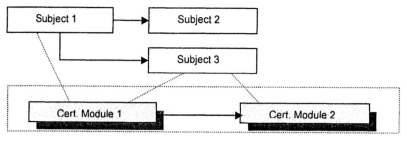

Figure 1. ERP Certification Implementation Model

The VU approach uses elements of all models and could be classified as a hybrid. Certification of ERP education came about through the linking of subject content with SAP accredited programs. Students upon completion of subjects receive SAP industry accreditation that they can use to further their career prospects. The SAP certification model is displayed in figure 1.

2.2 ITIL Certification at VU (Inclusive and End-On)

ITIL is a widely recognized computer industry certification. It has about 100,000 certified professionals mainly in Europe, Australia and Canada. Information Technology Infrastructure Library (ITIL) is a set of best practices used to deliver high quality IT services derived from over a decade of work by thousands of IT workers world-wide. Because of its depth and breadth, the ITIL has become the de-facto world standard for IT best practices. ITIL frames all activity under Service Support and Service Delivery. By focusing on the critical business processes and disciplines needed to deliver services around IT, the ITIL provides a maturity path for IT that is not based on technology (ITIL, 2004).

The School of Information Systems has established an alliance with a private provider of ITIL training. The provider supplies an e-learning course at a 50% reduced cost to VU students. The international certification exam cost is unchanged (this cannot be reduced as it is an external independent body that controls ITIL certification). A student's participation is optional and will not affect their assessment in the subject. Advantages for students to undertake the certification include: gaining an industry accreditation in IT Service Management, being well placed for work-integrated learning positions, having exposure to ITIL practices used in over 60% of large Australian IT departments, helpful for other subjects (eg BCO2044 Computing Practice), and enhanced job prospects (the number of jobs being advertised in IT that require ITIL certification is growing rapidly. There are expanding job opportunities for ITIL practitioners).

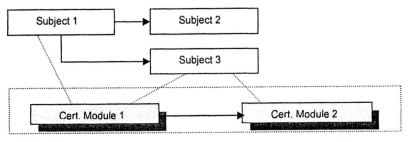

Figure 1. ERP Certification Implementation Model

2.3 i-Net+ Certification at VU (Curriculum Inclusive)

Electronic Commerce Technologies is a subject (incorporating i-Net+ certification) that is an integral part of a group of four Electronic Commerce subjects that constitute the Electronic Commerce specialisation. CompTIA i-Net+ certification is an international industry-credentialing program developed for practitioners within the e-commerce technology field. This program has been developed by expert e-commerce industry practitioners, with objectives including Internet basics, Internet clients, EC development, networking, security and business concepts. The CompTIA i-Net+ certification program establishes base-line technical knowledge of Internet, intranet and e-commerce technologies, independent of specific Internet-related career roles and proprietary implementations.

The i-Net+ certification program is undertaken during workshops so as to provide this "EC Consultant" capability. The i-Net+ workshop exercises provide the basis for putting together an EC Consultant Portfolio Document that is then used as the basis for the creation of an EC Consultant Credentialing document. The latter together with a presentation on a specific Electronic Commerce topic and a mid-semester i-Net+ Certification Test "license" the student to undertake the final stage of the major assignment – a multi-level solution of the provided case study.

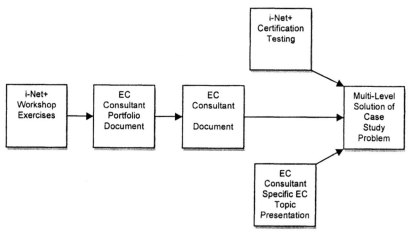

Figure 3. I-Net+ Certification Development

On completion of the course students are encouraged to sit the i-Net+ Certification Exam. To this end, the School of Information Systems has obtained educational CompTIA membership with the testing program being available to students at significantly lower rates.

3   CONCLUSION

Certification literature points to benefits and pitfalls of certification that are described in Table 2. The benefits that underpin use of certification at Victoria University all relate to the transfer of skills from industry environs to educational programs. Undertaking SAP certification, ITIL, i-Net+ and Microsoft certification at VU attempt to better prepare students as they exit university programs and make the transition to the workforce.

Table 2. Benefits and pitfalls of certification programs.

Strengths	Weaknesses
Adding Value to degree programs	Exist to support training industry
Work related experience	Proprietary nature
Practical rather than just theoretical focus	Lack of educational rigor
"Up-to-Date" nature of certification programs	Often lacks "real-world" experience
Specific targeted content very relevant to employers	Industry partnership inadequate or unstable
	Too focused
Industry liaison opportunities	Training oriented rather than education oriented
Adjunct to education programs offering verifiable testing of skills and knowledge	"Value-for-Money" ignorance of certification
Potential employment advantages for graduates	
Precursor to licensing requirements	Too market and popularity driven

Additionally IT industry certification programs are seen as a respected and widely-established vehicle for attaining specific, practically based expertise – areas that many tertiary courses seem to lack or with which they have chosen not to be involved. In very recent times selection data (university selection popularity polls) have caught up with the significant downturn of employment experienced in the IT industry during 2001-2003. These trends place a greater burden on the University sector to react positively towards "adding value" to their offerings. The School of Information Systems has therefore seen it as a necessary strategy to investigate and has commissioned this current research into certification implementation models. This research has been focusing on identifying the various forms of certification, relevance to tertiary education, strengths and weaknesses of programs and models of certification implementation. The outcome of this research project is recommendations for adoption of certification within the School. Three varieties of implementation model (Course Mapping, Curriculum Inclusive, End-On) are being currently trialled within the School and the results will be reported in a later paper.

4 REFERENCES

ACNeilson, (2000) *Employer Satisfaction with Graduate Skills*, Department of Education Training and Youth Affairs: Canberra, pp. 1-61.

Ahmadi, M. & M. Brabston (1997) *MIS Education: Differences in Academic Practice and Business Managers Expectations.* Journal of Computer Information Systems, Winter, pp. 18-25.

Basu, K.S., (2002) *Training strategies in the emerging hi-tech banking environment.* Indian Journal of Training and Development, XXXI, (4), pp. 13-22.

Bartlett, K.R. (2002) *The perceived influence of industry-sponsored credentials in the information technology industry.* National Centers for Career and Technical Education (U.S.) (NCCTE), 10: pp. 83.

Castleman, T. & D. Coulthard (1999) *Not Just a Job: Preparing Graduates for Careers in the IS Workforce.* [*Tenth Australasian Conference on Information Systems*], 1999, Wellington, NZ.

Dept for Education and Skills, (DES), (2001) *An assessment of skill needs in information and communication technology / Dept for Education and Skills.* Skills Dialogue: Listening to Employers. Vol. VII, Nottingham, U.K, Dept for Education and Skills, pp. 93.

Department of Higher and Further Education, (DHFE), (2000) *A study of the Northern Ireland labour market for IT skills: a report prepared by the Priority Skills Unit, Northern Ireland Economic Research Centre.*, in *A Northern Ireland Skills Task Force Report.*, Dept of Higher and Further Education, Training & Employment: Belfast, pp. 68.

Filipczak, B., (2000) *Certifiable!*, Training, 32(8), pp. 38-40, 42.

Flynn, W.J., (2001) *More than a matter of degree: credentialing, certification and community college,* The Catalyst, 30(3), pp. 3-12.

ICT Skills Snapshot, (2004) The State of ICT Skills in Victoria, Department of Infrastructure, [http://www.itskillshub.com.au/render/exec/render_content.asp?subgroup=courses&file=it+jobs+market+brighter%2Ehtml&title=IT+jobs+market+brighter]

ITIL, (2004) ITIL Survival, September 2004, [http://www.itilsurvival.com/]

ITT, (2000) *Industry Report, Information-Technology Training: Teaching computer skills to American workers*, Training, pp. 62-71.

Knight, K.S., (2001) *Raising the bar on certification,* The Catalyst, 30(3), p. 13-17.

McCain, M., (2001) *Business Approach to Credentialing,* Community College Journal, American Association of Community Colleges, 71(5), pp. 40-41.

Mehaut, P., (1999) *Training, skills, learning: how can new models be developed?* Vocational Training European Journal, 3, Thessaloniki, Greece, CEDEFOP, (18), pp. 3-7.

National Office Industry Education, (NOIE), (2003) *Project Overview - ICT Skill Needs.* [http://www.itskillshub.com.au/render/exec/render_content.asp?subgroup=courses&file=it+jobs+market+brighter%2Ehtml&title=IT+jobs+market+brighter]

Rothke, B.C. (2000) *The Professional Certification Predicament.* Computer Security Journal, 16, pp. 29-35.

South Australian Centre for Economic Studies, (SACES), (2002) Unmet demand for information technology and telecommunications courses / report prepared by the SA Centre for Economic Studies for the Department of Education, Training and Youth Affairs, Canberra, pp. 128.

EXPERIENCES AND CHALLENGES IN FOSTERING INDUSTRY AND UNIVERSITY COLLABORATIONS
Focus Group - 1

Mikko Ruohonen (Finland, Chair), Peter Normak, (Estonia, Rapporteur), Barrie Thompson (UK, Rapporteur), John Bentley (Australia), Till Becker (Germany), Maria Nakayama (Brazil), Rod Turner (Australia), Lu Xi Yan (China), Cindy Zhu Bin (China)

Key words: Industry, University, Higher Education, Exchange, Collaboration, Projects.

1   ORGANISATION AND PARTICIPATION

Six sessions were devoted to Focus Group activities during the conference week. These consisted of four working sessions (each of 90 minutes duration) for the nominated participants, a poster session (timetabled between the second and third working sessions) to which all conference delegates were invited, and a formal reporting session to all the delegates during the last afternoon session of the conference. The poster session provided an opportunity to get wider feedback on the Focus Group's initial proposals and an exchange of ideas. In addition to notes taken during the workshop, sound recordings were made of the majority of the sessions. Also, a photographic record was made of both the posters and white board diagrams produced during the working sessions. It is hoped that when resources allow, the recordings can be transcribed and a more detailed account of the group's discussions produced.

The remainder of this report is organised as follows. Sections 2 and 3 provide high-level summaries of the first two working sessions of the Focus

Mikko Ruohonen (Finland, Chair), Peter Normak, (Estonia, Rapporteur), Barrie Thompson (UK, Rapporteur), John Bentley (Australia), Till Becker (Germany), Maria Nakayama (Brazil), Rod Turner (Australia), Lu Xi Yan (China), Cindy Zhu Bin (China)

Group. Section 4 reports on the poster session. Section 5 provides a summary of the second two working sessions. Finally section 6 reports the groups overall findings and recommendations as presented on the final day of the conference.

2   SESSION 1: THEME, TOPICS, AND EXPERIENCES

The first of the Focus Group's working sessions took place on the first day of the conference. It began with participant introductions and the chair setting the overall theme for the Focus Group:

University and Industry Collaboration and its Effects on Education

The chair then identified and spoke briefly on three particular topic areas that he encouraged the group to consider during the remainder of their meetings. These were:

- Experiences that they had had relating to University and Industry collaboration.
- Challenges and problems that could be identified in University and Industry collaborations.
- Action plans to solving problems and addressing challenges.

The chair also provided the attendees with support material in the form of a paper by Jarvinen and Poikela (2001) which addressed learning at work. The group then had a general discussion on the issues raised by the chair. This was then followed by short participant experience reports covering particular situations in: Estonia, UK, Australia, and Germany.

3   SESSION 2: LINKS BETWEEN UNIVERSITIES AND INDUSTRY

The second working session took place during the second afternoon of the conference. It commenced with further consideration of individual experiences of University and Industry collaborations. The group then started to look at more general issues and different dimensions such as issues relating to: Undergraduate, Postgraduate/Research, National Government, and Local/Regional Government. The group also collaborated in producing models and representations on the meeting room white boards as shown in figures 1 and 2.

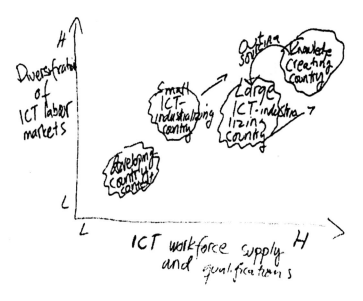

Figure 1 The diversification of ICT labour markets vs. ICT workforce
supply and qualifications

These were then converted into a set of posters that incorporated the model shown in figure 1, a list of challenges, and possible solutions relating to:

- Staff and knowledge exchange.
- Competence marketing/management.
- National development involvement.

266   *Mikko Ruohonen (Finland, Chair), Peter Normak, (Estonia, Rapporteur), Barrie Thompson (UK, Rapporteur), John Bentley (Australia), Till Becker (Germany), Maria Nakayama (Brazil), Rod Turner (Australia), Lu Xi Yan (China), Cindy Zhu Bin (China)*

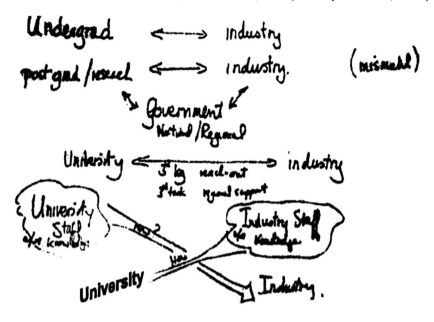

Figure 2 University and Industry Links

4   THE POSTER SESSION

This took place at the end of the second day after the formal presentation sessions. It gave the delegates the opportunity to see what the other Focus Groups had been working on, discuss the topics/issues highlighted, and provide formal comments in the form of Post-Its fixed to the posters. The comments received relating to improving University and Industry links were:

- (Academics should) get in contact with companies, offer solutions for companies problems, develop CRM.
- (Academics should) build up industry competence.
- (Academic) staff (should) work with industry on formulating criteria for the real-life problems the students are working on.
- University (should encourage) "Start-up Businesses", "Technology Transfer.
- Adopt "work" processes from each other – (with the aim of reaching) the same process in both.
- (and that both should) go for the "primary" process.

5   GROUP SESSIONS 3 AND 4: REFLECTIONS

A short session at the start of the third day of the conference was used to
reflect on the feedback and comments received at the poster session. The
longer session at the end of the fourth day was used to reflect on all that had
been covered and the models that had been developed and decide on what
would be reported in the final presentation session. When the group revisited
the model depicted in figure 1, which has as axes - the diversification of ICT
labour markets and ICT workforce supply and qualifications, another factor
became apparent. The model had been derived from consideration of the
interactions   between   Universities   and   Industry   and   the   roles   of
National/Local/Regional Government. However, what now became clear
was that in the earlier discussions the group had omitted to consider the
effects that professional and accrediting bodies could have on University and
Industry interactions. Thus a much more sophisticated model needs to be
developed (scope for a future Focus Group?).

6   GROUP PRESENTATION: OVERALL FINDINGS
AND RECOMMENDATIONS

The presentation to the assembled delegates on the last afternoon
commenced with a brief overview of the process the group had adopted and
the models that had been derived. The group's conclusions and
recommendations regarding improving University and Industry interactions
were then reported as follows:

Staff and Knowledge Exchange
- Sabbaticals in industry
- Best practice examples:
      Lessons learned
      Ways to exchange
      Industry solutions explicitly for teachers
- Student involvement with industry criteria, placements, fieldwork
- Alumni activities

Competence Marketing/Management
- Joint organization of conferences, "fireplace talks", seminars.
- Calls for company supervisors
- "Going out" for business meetings
- Professional bodies, memberships/collaborations/accreditation

Mikko Ruohonen (Finland, Chair), Peter Normak, (Estonia, Rapporteur), Barrie Thompson (UK, Rapporteur), John Bentley (Australia), Till Becker (Germany), Maria Nakayama (Brazil), Rod Turner (Australia), Lu Xi Yan (China), Cindy Zhu Bin (China)

- Incubation/start-up business promotion

National Development Involvement
- Affecting decision making (such as information society programmes)
- General publicity
- Specialized, coordinated funding applications

Proactive Policy Making
- Getting the voice to (ear of) government
- Committee working
- Participating in policy paper planning
- Legislation initiatives
- Funding bodies

However there is a problem:

Professional and Accrediting Bodies: WHERE DO THESE FIT IN?

7   SUPPORT MATERIAL

Jarvinen A. and Poikela E. (2001) Modelling reflective and contextual learning at work, Journal of Workplace Learning, Vol. 13, No. 7/8, pp282-289.

REAL LIFE LEARNING: THE DEVELOPING IMPORTANCE OF FORMAL AND INFORMAL PROFESSIONAL COMMUNITIES OF PRACTICE
Focus Group - 2

Magda Ritzen (Netherlands, Chair), Anne McDougall (Australia, Rapporteur) and Mike Kendall (UK, Rapporteur), Alexander Karapadis (Germany), Barbara Bamberger (Austria), Hannelore Dekeyser (Netherlands), Gina Reyes (Australia), Julia Walsh (Australia)

Key words: Professional, community of practice, real-life learning.

1   INTRODUCTION

The working conference has provided many examples of professional, formal and informal communities of practice that rely to a lesser or greater extent on access to and the use of ICT. The working definition we have used is based on the work of Wenger, McDermott and Snyder (2002) which states that a "Community of Practice is a group of people who share a (great) interest in a certain object, theme or knowledge domain. They *meet* [face-to-face or virtual] to exchange, to develop and to make knowledge explicit, which arises from questions and problems they have."

2   COMMUNITIES OF PRACTICE: EXAMPLES

The operation of a Community of Practice (CoP) reflects the needs of the members and their context. The members of the focus group have illustrated

Magda Ritzen (Netherlands, Chair), Anne McDougall (Australia, Rapporteur) and Mike Kendall (UK, Rapporteur), Alexander Karapadis (Germany), Barbara Bamberger (Austria), Hannelore Dekeyser (Netherlands), Gina Reyes (Australia), Julia Walsh (Australia)

different kinds of practice from their professional domains of education, government and industry.

At the HvU, the University for Professional Education and Applied Science in the Netherlands following a conference on education innovation, interest lead to four CoPs being initiated: 'Testing and Assessment', 'Student coaching and Portfolio', 'Instruments in Education' and 'ICT and project-based education'. The CoPs have approximately eight participants and meet face to face regularly (once every six weeks). Two CoPs had a relatively clear focus, i.e. a communal question, right from the start (e.g. How can a project-based approach to problems and assignments be best supported by ICT), while one CoP decided to let their agenda be composed of participants' questions. Another CoP had such a diverse set of questions that progress was severely hampered and eventually only 7 out of 15 participants remained. This CoP did manage to achieve communal results, but there is little remaining drive.

No fixed period was determined but even after a year, the participants (staff members) continue to find it worthwhile to attend CoP meetings. They meet and consult people who are working on the same things they are. In all the CoPs problems are discussed and experiences are exchanged; in some, attempts are made to generate explicit knowledge and ideas (e.g. what are the characteristics of project-based teaching) so that others may also benefit. In this way the CoPs play an important role in the professionalisation of the participants and satisfy important success criteria: demand-driven, to the point and on the job.

In Austria, teachers are using communities of practice in different ways: working together in project groups, working with students, exchanging files and discussing themes. One of the examples can be found in a consortium of teachers. In an online community they are discussing how to improve the teaching, how to integrate new media in class in learning a language. They are sharing information by exchanging files, they share news on this topic and are discussing in a forum and/or a chat. This CoP is a very agile form of cooperation in this consortium.

The British Computer Society (BCS) is the professional body for IT in the UK. It is a very large body of people who are loosely brought together having passed entrance exams and paid the necessary fees (i.e. membership is not free). In order to be effective, the members are organised into regional and special interest groups, and expert panels whose membership can overlap. For example, the Schools Expert Panel brings together educationalists to develop new understandings about ICT in education that can then be shared across the whole membership, and more widely. The BCS also works in other ways, crossing industry sectors, for example, bringing together members who live or work in an area to meet and share ideas around themes of general interest from their own experience with increased understanding. However, it seeks to support more 'informal' CoPs to bring together members around common themes, to promote learning and actions.

The growth of online tools and public policy to support 'communities' working together, whether they are CoP or even communities of interest, means it is far easier for people to start up a community, invite and advertise for new members. For example, the BBC provides a public service 'ICAN' – it is free, anyone can set up a community locally and globally – www.bbc.co.uk/ICAN

PROLEARN is an ongoing and free of charge network of excellence funded by the European Union with the aim to share knowledge in the area of professional training and qualification. The focus lies in building a European wide community of practice in professional learning and training tasks and is open for experts in research and economy who apply. The virtual competence centre www.prolearn-online.com is the central working and service platform of PROLEARN in the Internet. The centre enables experts of the service industry and research, to publish and use newest knowledge about innovative ideas, products and results from research and practice and the construction of network relationships ("research meets industry", "industry meets research"), supporting the transfer of knowledge. The community of practice offers options and services to share and receive knowledge in professional training: a knowledge pool in professional learning events, projects, partners, trends and news; an exchange platform with experts and power-user in professional learning; surveys about latest trends in the area of professional learning; a networking community in professional learning; you can post or upload your own events, publications, projects and news; find experts and information in professional learning tasks.

The target groups are: *Intermediary organisations* to spread wide the results of the competence centre; *companies as end-users* to name their requirements and find solutions or ideas to solve; *research institutes and universities* to bring their expertise in and find inspirations out of the requirements the companies bring; and *companies as providers* of services and products in professional training.

Consideration of the examples has lead to the identification of a range of attributes that can be modelled within an emerging framework.

272   *Magda Ritzen (Netherlands, Chair), Anne McDougall (Australia,*
Rapporteur) and Mike Kendall (UK, Rapporteur), Alexander
Karapadis (Germany), Barbara Bamberger (Austria), Hannelore
Dekeyser (Netherlands), Gina Reyes (Australia), Julia Walsh
(Australia)

3   QUESTIONS

A clear focus of the discussion was how Communities of Practice can operate successfully. Success should mean that can a CoP supports Real-Life Learning and learning in general. The place and the function of CoP in the learning process needs to be clarified. Three categories of questions have been identified: 1) pedagogy, 2) organisation of learning including business model, 3) implementation of tools:

1. What are the benefits in the organisational and personal dimension which can be gained from a CoP? How can collaboration and the exchange of experiences be seen as a positive element in learning and innovating? In what ways does the CoP help to support a demand-driven and problem-based learning environment?

2. How can the CoP support the organisation of a meaningful learning process? What are the mission critical factors for learning and working in a CoP? What has to be agreed before starting a CoP? What are the conditions for starting, running and ending a CoP? What are the incentives for members and organisational assumptions (consumer relation management) to join and stay in a CoP? How can we create a win-win situation for all members by a balanced exchange of knowledge and experience? How can a CoP be embedded in a general information plan of the driving organisation? What are typical business models behind a successful CoP?

3. What are the typical functions and characteristics of a CoP? What are the skills which can be presumed from the participants? What role does usability play and what specific factors of functionality and design which have to be taken into consideration?

4   EMERGING MODEL

The considerations of the group have resulted in an emerging model that provides a framework to consider the questions we have proposed. The model supports the consideration of a series of general bi-polar attributes that have emerged from the examples presented above.

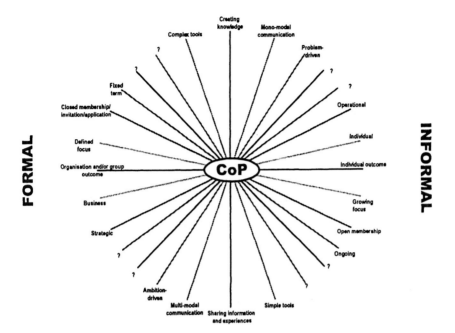

5 ATTRIBUTES OF THE MODEL

The attributes of the proposed model:

- *Formality* cannot be characterised by one attribute but a crucial characteristic is being more or less rule-based; to what extent are CoP members supposed to follow stricter rules, do they have freedom to determine the rules during CoP interaction or is everything strictly formulated in well defined working methods?
- *Orientation/* expected outcome/ targets: CoPs can be oriented towards the individual (personal?) or to the business/ to organisational benefits. Slightly related to previous aspect, the orientation can focus on operational rather than on strategic needs.
- *Driving factor*: problem or ambition? The driving factors for CoPs can be problems, but also the desire to realise something, an ambition, or aspiration.
- The *focus* of a CoP can be well defined from the start, but a lot of times focus grows or shifts during the process.

Magda Ritzen (Netherlands, Chair), Anne McDougall (Australia, Rapporteur) and Mike Kendall (UK, Rapporteur), Alexander Karapadis (Germany), Barbara Bamberger (Austria), Hannelore Dekeyser (Netherlands), Gina Reyes (Australia), Julia Walsh (Australia)

- *Information or knowledge?* CoPs vary from information sharing instruments to real knowledge creating entities.
- *Duration:* While certain CoPs have a fixed term, others are set up to be ongoing.
- The *size* can be limited or free.
- *Membership* can be open or closed (only on invitation or by application).
- *Communication* modes can be mono-modal (only one communication mode is used) or multi- modal (a variation of communication modes).
- *Tool* driven: in some CoPs the interaction is strongly steered by the tools in use, in other CoPs, the choice of tools is more free and steered by the needs of the members.

6   APPLICATIONS OF THE MODEL

The Focus Group has developed a model to represent these ideas about communities of practice and their characteristics. The model is illustrated by a set of axes. Each axis represents one of the characteristics we have listed, with opposites at each end. We include some additional axes marked with question marks to acknowledge that the model may not yet be exhaustive.

The Group is still working on deciding the most useful way of visualizing the model. The axes might be seen as all mutually orthogonal, defining a multidimensional space as is done in factor analysis; then an individual community of practice could be described by a multidimensional profile determined by its position or "score" on each of the axes. Alternatively, the diagram could be viewed as a two-dimensional one; this would allow for relationships among the characteristics to be illustrated by the relative positioning of their axes.

The Group sees three valuable ways in which this model can be used:

1. **For research.** For example, studies might assign "scores" on each of the axes for individual communities of practice and these could be related to the perceived extent and nature of their success, to improve understanding about the nature of successful communities of practice in particular contexts.
2. **In establishment of communities of practice.** Individuals or groups setting up a community of practice could use the model to structure

    planning and implementation, making decisions about positions along axes that will be most appropriate for the purpose of the community.

3. **To provide a structure for discussion** and/or improvement of the operation of existing communities of practice.

7   RECOMMENDATIONS AND FUTURE OPTIONS

    The increasing importance of Communities of Practice, whether they are formal or informal, for the development of professional and vocational education is reported in this paper. The members of the Focus Group have proposed a model to analyse the effectiveness and to support the development of CoPs. It is at an early stage in its development with many questions still to be considered and answers proposed. It appears that the proposed model can be applied in many different communities, including education, industry, government and social contexts. The proposed model should help answer the three questions of pedagogy, organisation and tools and visualising solutions.

    This paper raises issues of importance that should be matters for future research and consideration at IFIP conferences and working groups.

8   BIBLIOGRAPHY

Wenger, E. McDermott, R. and Snyder, W.M. (2002) *Cultivating Communities of Practice; a guide to managing knowledge* Harvard Business School Press, Boston, Massachusetts

REAL LIFE LEARNING: THE CHALLENGE OF CREATING AND ESTABLISHING THE ROLE OF ONLINE AND VIRTUAL LEARNING ENVIRONMENTS FOR ALL
Focus Group - 3

Anton Knierzinger (Austria, chair), Marijke Hezemans (Netherlands, rapporteur), Paul Nicholson (Australia, rapporteur), Joberto Martins (Brazil), Ricardo Azambuja Silveira (Brazil)

Key words: Virtual learning environment, online learning, real-life learning.

1   PROBLEM SITUATION

In discussing the focus question in an international group of educational professionals, we concluded that the critical element in creating and establishing the role of online and virtual learning environments is the *teacher* rather then the virtual learning environment itself. We adopted the perspective of seeing the virtual learning environment as a tool; its effectiveness in the learning process depends on the way it is *used*. **So ICT (the virtual learning environment) is like a football.** For an exciting match we need to train the football players rather then enhancing or redesigning the football that is being used.

They need to know how to play the game!

Therefore our problem definition reads:
- Teachers need a minimum level of ICT-competence, and

Anton Knierzinger (Austria, chair), Marijke Hezemans (Netherlands, rapporteur), Paul Nicholson (Australia, rapporteur), Joberto Martins (Brazil), Ricardo Azambuja Silveira (Brazil)

- Need to be exposed to a range of different kinds of multi-media, distance-learning methods and other 'ICT-tools' commonly found in educational settings, and
- Need to change their culture to become learners too.
- But first and for all: they should develop expertise in the selection and use of a range of different pedagogical models.

1.1 The Football Player

If you have a new shining football, you want to master nice tricks with it ...

The introduction of new types of media – streaming videos, hyper-videos, and video-based E-Lectures – into classrooms was addressed in a nationwide Austrian school project in which a large number of digitized audiovisual media were developed. The aim of the project was to create an Internet-based platform which allows teachers to access a large database of digitized educational movies, equip it with convenient tools for searching, ordering and downloading, and gain some empirical insights in its acceptance by teachers and students, its feasibility for classroom teaching, and its appropriate instructional scenarios.

After its components had been designed, implemented, and tested, the AVS media was made available via the World Wide Web, and all Austrian schools were given the opportunity to participate in a field trial. Overall, 89 schools decided to take part in the field trial, which lasted over one year and was free of charge. After resolving most of the technical problems during the first few months, the teachers were encouraged to try out these new possibilities in their classroom.

One of the findings in this project was that AVS media led the participants to change their teaching strategies. The majority (54%) reported an increase in their usage of audiovisual media in the classroom lessons. But media use did not only change in quantity, but also in quality, ranging from "chalk and talk" modes to learning projects and group work.

Thus, in sum, the strategy of providing such material in a digitized and easy-to-access manner seems to be a promising contribution of new media in the endeavour of introducing more enriched and varied teaching styles at school.

1.2 The Football Trainer

The use of new materials creates a faster game – players need to be trained in new tactics ...

Dutch universities of professional education are working in co-operation with institutions in the field to develop and implement programmes which are intended to give students optimum preparation for the reality and dynamics of professional practice. These new programmes aim to provide learning environments which enable students to develop into starting professionals: they develop their competence and professional expertise in learning environments of varying complexity.

This short case description shows how a tutor, supported by ICT, can realise a personal learning process in such a way as to effectively guide and supervise an analogous learning process for the student. In this case the tutor and the student are central; the professional field provides the (ICT) tools for practising this competence management. The case description is taken from the project 'Competence development & portfolio': a project which was carried out in the part-time Economics programmes at the Utrecht University of Professional Education (Hogeschool van Utrecht). The project aims to maximise the part-time students' competence development (learning) with the help of a digital learning environment (e-folio environment) developed by tutors who are coached by two educational staff members attached to the project.

In this learning environment part-time students learn among other things to reflect on their work experience by means of a personal development plan and the competence profile of the programme. As well as self-reflection, which on the student's initiative is coached by the tutor, reflection also takes place in peer groups. The project aims to produce an instrument, a digital learning environment including portfolio functions, which supports and/or makes visible competence development on the basis of a personal development plan. Accompanying assignments, and a tutoring and assessment protocol are also developed, so that coaching and assessment are related to the competence profile of the programme.

Analogous to the part-time students' learning process, a programme was set up within the project in co-operation with the Virtual Learning Centre (VLC) of the Utrecht University of Professional Education to support the tutors' competence development in the e-folio environment. The aim of the course is two-fold:

- To train competent e-folio tutors, both in relation to guiding the students' development as well as ICT-skills; and

Anton Knierzinger (Austria, chair), Marijke Hezemans (Netherlands, rapporteur), Paul Nicholson (Australia, rapporteur), Joberto Martins (Brazil), Ricardo Azambuja Silveira (Brazil)

- To act as an example to students and colleagues.

Starting from their personal learning needs (personal competence profile), the e-folio tutors each made a personal development plan. The development plan shows the way in which the above competencies will be developed (learning activities) and which forms of support (e.g. training or peer assisted learning) are needed. The tutors collect their evidence in their digital portfolio (e-folio) by means of which they can demonstrate that they have completed learning activities and thus have developed the above competencies. The course is rounded off with a portfolio assessment. In the portfolio assessment two assessors independently assess the evidence presented in relation to the competence profile of an 'e-folio tutor'.

The preceding has shown how tutors as professionals can give form to their own learning process supported by ICT: they create a portfolio and make a personal development plan. In the process of tutoring, students use the same tools; they too after all are being trained as starting professionals. Through guiding students by means of the same sort of learning assignments as they themselves are carrying out, tutors can act as role models; they show students how they themselves learn as professionals and use ICT-tools.

2   CONCLUSIONS

The 'real-life focus for creating and establishing the role of online and virtual learning environments 'for all' is strongly dependant on people. This means that:

- The people involved, in particular, teachers, should have (or be supplied with) a minimum set of 'pedagogical abilities' in order to promote a successful project/learning initiative.
- In overall strategic terms it is also agreed that people and resources (technology, services, platforms etc.) should be coupled and integrated in an effective case-by-case basis.

3   REMAINING QUESTIONS: TOPICS FOR FURTHER RESEARCH

- How can ICT support 'real-life' learning? (How many teachers were exposed to a virtual learning environment as students? If not, are teachers disadvantaged?)

- Who's 'real-life' is it?
- What is so good about real-life learning? ('real-life' learning vs. 'school'-learning)
- What are the attributes of real-life learning?
- When is 'virtual' real? (When is it perceived as real by stake holders?)

3.1 The Football

Enhancing the quality of the ball enables smooth playing.

In our focus group discussions we wondered about what the attributes are of a good (virtual) learning environment. We asked the conference attendants for suggestions. They came up with the following ones:

- adaptable, multi functional
- personalized
- flexible
- find a customer who pays for it! + return of invest
- acknowledges and utilises earlier research + development work on screen design and educational computing, doesn't re-invent bad wheels
- supporting collaboration and joint knowledge creation (within)
- minimize technical problems
- reliable (works all the time!)
- functionality that is really needed / helpful to user
- friendly interface
- good useability
- easy to use
- portfolios
- virtual lab prototype
- receptive mind
- contextualised
- authenticity
- authentic complex challenging

Although most of us try to address the suggestions mentioned above in our ongoing projects, we think that here also questions remain. So further research in more technical aspects is needed as well.

KEY WORD INDEX

Printed in the United States
71227LV00002B/209

9 780387 259963